TERRA INCOGNITA

Sara Wheeler is the author of five previous books, including *Cherry: A Life of Apsley Cherry-Garrard*, *Too Close to the Sun: The Life and Times of Denys Finch Hatton* and most recently, *The Magnetic North: Travels in the Arctic Circle*

SARA WHEELER

Terra Incognita

Travels in Antarctica

VINTAGE BOOKS
London

Published by Vintage 1997

14 16 18 20 19 17 15

First published in Great Britain in 1996 by
Jonathan Cape

Vintage
Random House, 20 Vauxhall Bridge Road,
London SW1V 2SA

www.vintage-books.co.uk

Addresses for companies within The Random House Group Limited
can be found at: www.randomhouse.co.uk/offices.htm

The Random House Group Limited Reg. No. 954009

A CIP catalogue record for this book
is available from the British Library

ISBN 9780099731818

The Random House Group Limited supports The Forest Stewardship
Council® (FSC®), the leading international forest certification organisation.
Our books carrying the FSC label are printed on FSC® certified paper.
FSC is the only forest certification scheme endorsed by the leading
environmental organisations, including Greenpeace. Our
paper procurement policy can be found at
www.randomhouse.co.uk/environment

MIX
Paper from
responsible sources
FSC® C016897

Printed and bound in Great Britain by Clays Ltd, St Ives PLC

To Mark Collins, finally

CONTENTS

CONTENTS

ACKNOWLEDGEMENTS

I owe everything to two people: Guy Guthridge at the National Science Foundation in Virginia and Frank Curry at the British Antarctic Survey in Cambridge. Without them, there would have been no journey – just a dream.

Mario Zuccelli, who heads up the Italian Antarctic Programme, also contributed hugely by getting me to Terra Nova Bay against what looked liked insuperable odds. Malcolm Macfarlane (in summer) and Warren Herrick (in winter) made me more than welcome among the New Zealanders at Scott Base and in the field. The Chilean Antarcticans started it all by taking me to Marsh, their station on King George Island.

Many people helped me on the ice, and I want to thank them all. I can only mention a few here; the others know who they are. The scientists who took me along when they didn't have to at all include Hermann Englehardt at the Dragon on Ice Stream B, Imre Friedmann in the Convoy Range, Ross Powell at the Mackay Glacier, Brian Howes and Dale Goehringer at Lake Fryxell and John Priscu at Lake Bonney. Tony Stark helped me get to grips with astrophysics at the Pole. My thanks go to the South Pole summer crew 1994/5, with whom I celebrated Christmas, and to Gaetano Rizzi and the Italians with whom I travelled around Victoria Land. At McMurdo innumerable people helped, especially Kristin Larson and Lisa Mastro in the Crary Lab; Robin Abbott, the Helicopter Queen; Kirk Salveson, and everyone at the Berg Field Center. I especially want to thank Lucia deLeiris. She and I had our own camp on the ice for many weeks. At

Acknowledgements

Rothera and elsewhere on the peninsula Ben Hodges, Al Wearden and Steve Rumble generously extended the hand of friendship at a difficult time.

In warmer climes, my editor in London, Tony Colwell at Jonathan Cape, taught me so much. 'Thanks' seem inadequate for what he has done for me – but I give them anyway. Joe Fox at Random House in New York took the book on and encouraged me greatly, and, tragically, he died while I was finishing it. Lawrence Larose gallantly took up the baton and made me feel part of the team. I owe a debt to my agent, Gillon Aitken; to Oliver Garnett, who created my polar library almost single-handedly; to Robin Gauldie, who ransacked his encyclopedic mind; to the endlessly obliging Shirley Sawtell and her colleagues at the Scott Polar Research Institute; and to Mike Richardson at the Foreign Office, who sanctioned *Terra Incognita* from the beginning, and told me funny stories. John Hall, Richard Hanson, Mary Sutton and Bruce Tate at the British Antarctic Survey headquarters in Cambridge were always helpful, and it was a pleasure to work with them. Many people sat through interviews: they all appear in the text, named or unnamed, and I thank them all.

Some people read *Terra Incognita* in its early versions. On the ice Lisa Williams and Bob deZafra read an entire draft and made many helpful suggestions. Bruno Nardi commented on almost every line of the first chapters in between despatching balloons into the stratosphere. On solid ground, Bob Headland, archivist at the Scott Polar Research Institute, read the typescript carefully and gave me the benefit of his imagination, insight and vast polar knowledge. The SPRI librarian, William Mills, generously helped with bibliographical queries. Professor Robin Humphreys provided a cogent reading, and so, as always, did Phil Kolvin. Cindy Riches once again proved an incomparable reader. She picked over many drafts, and her contribution was incalculable – I can see her hand on every page. More than anyone else, she has shared this journey, and that, surely, is what friendship means.

*

The lines from T. S. Eliot's *The Waste Land* and 'Little Gidding', both included in *Collected Poems 1902–1962*, are quoted with the kind permission of the publishers Faber & Faber. I am also grateful to Faber for permission to reprint the lines from W. H. Auden's

Acknowledgements

Atlantic which appears in *Collected Poems*; to Edwin Mickleburgh and the Bodley Head for permission to quote from *Beyond the Frozen Sea*; to A. P. Watt Ltd. on behalf of Michael Yeats for the extract from *The Cold Heaven* by W. B. Yeats which appears in *The Collected Poems of W.B. Yeats*; and to Mrs Angela Mathias for her generous permission to use many lines from *The Worst Journey in the World* by Apsley Cherry-Garrard.

I am indebted to STA Travel in London for organising all my commercial flights, as they always have, and to Damart for thermal gear, G. B. Britton for Goretex and Thinsulate boots, Moomba Marketing for survival aids, Taunton Leisure and Pentax Ltd for discounted goods, Sunshine Ellis in New Zealand for emergency gear repair, my local Marriott at Swiss Cottage for training facilities, and Johnson & Johnson for condoms to protect microphones against moisture.

The New Zealand Operational Support team of Roger Sutton and Jo Malcolm in Christchurch, and of course Camilla Sutton (Wellington Branch), saw me come and go four times over the course of a year, always with smiles and an open house. They made New Zealand a home for me.

Finally, the Patron of my expedition, Jeremy Lewis, did nothing Patrons are supposed to do (though neither of us was ever clear what this might have involved), and I in turn did not hang a framed photograph of him in my tent. But he did so much; so much that I cannot convey my thanks on a page. He had a clearer idea of what I wanted to write than anyone else, and talked or wrote to me about it almost daily, from the heady era of the synopsis to the crucifixion of the last months. I am miraculously fortunate to have benefited from his wisdom, and I shall never be able to repay it.

S.W.
March 1996

'You wait. Everyone has an Antarctic.'

Thomas Pynchon, *V*

INTRODUCTION

'IT IS THE LAST GREAT journey left to man,' Shackleton said. He didn't mean that we all had to pack our crampons and set off, ice axes in hand. For Shackleton, Antarctica was a metaphor as well as an explorer's dream, and he added, 'We all have our own White South.' It is true that for me Antarctica was always a space of the imagination – before, during and after my own journey. No cities, no bank managers, no pram in the hall. Some people think that before the ice came Antarctica was the site of Atlantis, the ancient civilisation which disappeared in a cosmic gulp, but when I went there I learnt that Atlantis is within us.

As I struggled out of stiff sleeping bags over waterbottles, VHF radios, batteries and stray items of scientific paraphernalia stowed alongside me in the epic battle with the big freeze, I didn't think about Atlantis or Shackleton or metaphorical allusions. I thought about how cold I was.

Until I was thirty, my relationship with Antarctica was confined to the biannual reinflation of the globe hanging above my desk, its air valve located in the middle of the mis-shapen white pancake at the bottom. As far as I was aware, the continent was a testing-ground for men with frozen beards to see how dead they could get. Then, in 1991, I travelled several thousand miles through Chile for a book I was writing. As I prodded around in the hinterland of the national psyche I discovered that the country did not come to a stop in Tierra del Fuego. A small triangle, was suspended at the bottom of every map. They called it *Antartida chilena* and behaved as if it were their fifty-first state. I had to go

1

down there if I wanted to paint a complete portrait of contemporary Chile, so one day in February I hitched a lift from a blustery Punta Arenas to King George Island, off the tip of the spindly Antarctic peninsula, on an antediluvian Hercules belonging to the Chilean Air Force.

With nothing but Chile on my mind and a carpetbag on my shoulder I climbed down the steps of the plane into the rasping air and shook the bearpaw extended by the hapless wing-commander who had been appointed as my minder. I looked out over the icefields vanishing into the aspirin-white horizon. Above them, a single snow petrel wheeled against the Hockney blue. Much later I climbed a snowhill with a Uruguayan vulcanologist, already feeling that I had found a blank piece of paper. There was no sound on the top of the hill except the occasional tap-tap as the vulcanologist scraped snow into a specimen tin, and as the shadows lengthened on the rippling Southern Ocean I looked beyond the small base in the foreground and thought – that's an ice-desert bigger than Australia. Antarctica is the highest continent, as well as the driest, the coldest and the windiest, and nobody owns it. Seven countries might have 'claimed' a slice for themselves, and there might be almost two hundred little research camps, but the continent is not owned by anyone.

Standing on the edge of the icefield in a wind strong enough to lean on, squinting in the buttery light, it was as if I were seeing the earth for the very first time. I felt less homeless than I have ever felt anywhere, and I knew immediately that I had to return. I sensed that the icefields had something to teach me.

After consorting with Russians, Chinese, Uruguayans and Poles on King George Island and observing how the continent blunts the edges of nationality, I realised that I had found the perfect *tabula rasa*. When I left, wedged into position on the same decrepit Hercules, I wrote *Terra Incognita* on the cover of a virgin notebook.

*

I discovered that the ancient Greeks had sensed it was there because something had to balance the white bit at the top of the globe. Medieval cartographers had a stab at mapping it and called it *Terra Australis Incognita*, the Unknown Southern Land. For centuries, it seemed, everyone thought it was rich, fertile and populous and that finding it would be like winning the National

Lottery. It was Captain Cook, the greatest explorer of all time, who sent the message back to the naval hydrographers fidgeting through the long reign of George III to say no, down here there are no golden fields or burgeoning trees or tall people with flaxen hair. Down here there is only cold hell.

After that most people forgot about it for a while, and when all the other white spaces on the map had been coloured in, they came back to it. The British were especially keen on Antarctica, as they had done Africa and spent much of the nineteenth century fretting over the Arctic. By the time the twentieth century rolled around they were fully engaged in the great quest for the south. For these British people the quest culminated in the central Antarctic myth, that of Captain Scott, a man woven into the fabric of our national culture as tightly as the pattern in a carpet.

Once I had glimpsed it, the Antarctic lodged in my mind's eye and rose unbidden on every horizon. I forced my friends to sit in empty cinemas whenever Charles Frend's 1948 film *Scott of the Antarctic* resurfaced, and we watched John Mills striding across a psychedelic backdrop which made the continent look like a seventies album cover. Shaw had used Antarctica as a metaphor, T. S. Eliot recycled Antarctic material in *The Waste Land*, and I found it in Saul Bellow, Thomas Pynchon, Vaclav Havel, Doris Lessing and Thomas Keneally. When I went to the National Theatre to get away from its blinding light I found that Tony Kushner had set a whole scene of his epic *Angels in America* down there. All places are more than the sum of their physical components, and I saw that Antarctica existed most vividly in the mind. It was a metaphorical landscape, and in an increasingly grubby world it had been romanticised to fulfil a human need for sanctuary. Mythical for centuries, so it remained.

It took two years to organise the journey. During that period I was accepted as the first foreigner on the American National Science Foundation's Antarctic Artists' and Writers' Program. The two years unravelled in a seamless roll of letters, interviews, meetings, conferences on two continents, endless hand-to-mouth freelance work, exhaustive medicals and long walks through the bowels of the Foreign Office in London to get to Polar Regions, which was a long way from anywhere else in the building and the temperature dropped as I approached it. Nobody knows what my dentist and I went through to satisfy the punitive requirements of the U.S. Navy. My tattoo was logged in the Disabilities and Disfigurements section of the British Antarctic Survey's medical records. Three weeks before departure I had to undergo various unpleasant tests to produce documentation that my heart murmur was not one of the uncommon kind likely to stage a rebellion on the ice. The cardiologist in Harley Street who applied himself to this task was Brazilian, and I had made an appointment to collect the results at eight o'clock on the morning after Brazil won the World Cup. I sat taut with tension on the steps outside his elegant practice, clinging helplessly to my dream until he fell at my feet out of the back of a taxi, his tie unknotted, shouting, 'You have the best heart I have ever seen.'

At the British Antarctic Survey pre-deployment conference in Cambridge I was woken each morning by the padding footsteps of a dog-handler in the chilly corridors of Girton College, and the padder and I went running along the river Cam together. On the last night I sat in candlelight under dour oil portraits of tweed-skirted Victorian scholars in the Great Hall, listening to Barry Heywood, the head of BAS, telling us in hushed tones that we were about to experience the time of our lives.

The very next day I picked up the telephone in an institutional room in the vast Xerox Document University in Leesburg, Virginia, at the American Antarctic Program's pre-deployment conference, and a computer-generated voice said, 'Good morning, this is your wake-up call'. Through it all, my dream sustained me.

I sat in Scott's cabin aboard *Discovery* in Dundee and stood in pouring rain on the Eastern Commercial Docks in Grimsby among excitable relatives waiting for the *James Clark Ross* to arrive at the end of its long journey from Antarctica. Week after week Shirley, the obliging information assistant at the Scott Polar Research Institute in Cambridge, unlocked the dust-encrusted basement so I could get at the fiction section, which was hidden behind dented tins of film spools and cardboard boxes of redundant dogfood. At the same institute I worked my way through blubber-splashed pages of leather notebooks inscribed by the men who gave Antarctica a history: reading them all was like looking at an object through the different angles of a glass prism. On assignment in India, I escaped to find the headquarters of the Indian Antarctic Programme in the asphyxiating concrete heartland of New Delhi, and when I walked up to its ramshackle eighth-floor offices, the air-conditioning had just sighed to a stop and a tall secretary in an orange sari was fanning herself in front of a photograph of a pristine snowscape. I drank warm beer outside railway stations in the south of England, waiting to be collected by veteran explorers, long since retired, and later, in their neat homes, liver-spotted hands turned the stiff black pages of cracked photograph albums. In Hampshire I was entertained by Zaz Bergel, granddaughter of Sir Ernest Shackleton, the Antarctic explorer's Antarctic explorer, and when I put on my coat to leave she said, 'Grandfather was much happier there than anywhere else.'

As for the profound appeal of ice on the imagination, I had only to think of the chilly opening line of Garcia Marquez's novel *One Hundred Years of Solitude*: 'Many years later, as he faced the firing squad, Colonel Aureliano Buendia was to remember that distant afternoon when his father took him to discover ice.'

There were psychological preparations too, though these were more difficult. In the Foreword to a seminal book about the opening up of the continent I read: 'Some of the most prominent challenges of polar living fall into the provinces of mind and emotion, rather than muscle and matter.' A man with many years experience on the ice wrote in the same book: 'The Antarctic generally wields a profound effect on personality and character and few men are the same after a stay there.' I wasn't afraid of loneliness; I had learnt that it doesn't arrive on the coat-tails of isolation. All the same, I was apprehensive about where Antarctica would take me, and about seeing my life *sub specie*. Robert Swan, who walked to both Poles, told me that going to either is like watching a child's magic slate wipe away your life as you knew it.

In an academic book on Antarctic psychology I read, 'It is intuitive that life in a confined environment is an adverse experience and may lead to human dysfunction.' A scientist who went south with both Scott and Shackleton coined the phrase 'polar madness', and Admiral Byrd packed two coffins and twelve straitjackets when he led one of the earliest U.S. Antarctic expeditions. Soon I was familiar with the folklore: the base commander who torched all the buildings in camp, the man who started talking with a lisp, the chef who set to with a meat-cleaver, the Soviet who killed a colleague with an ice axe during a game of chess (to ensure it didn't happen again, the authorities banned chess). One of the earliest behavioural findings in Antarctica was Mullin's discovery of spontaneous trance states, and papers had been written on alterations in consciousness induced by exposure to Antarctic isolation. At the same time it had melted frozen hearts. 'At the bottom of this planet', wrote Admiral Byrd, the first man to fly over the South Pole, 'is an enchanted continent in the sky, pale like a sleeping princess. Sinister and beautiful, she lies in frozen slumber.' 'There, if anywhere,' said another explorer, 'is life worthwhile.'

The people lighting my way had one thing in common. They were all men. It was male territory all right – it was like a gentleman's club, an extension of boarding school and the army. Only the U.S. programme even approaches normality in its ratio of men to women. Alastair Fothergill, who produced the *Life in the Freezer* television series and wrote the accompanying book, told me that for British men, going south was still like going to the pub. I had tea with Sir Edmund Hillary in New Zealand. 'My experience has been', he said between mouthfuls of chocolate cake, 'that the scientific community in the Antarctic regard it as their property and bitterly resent any outsiders venturing there.' Men had been quarrelling over Antarctica since it emerged from the southern mists, perceiving it as another trophy, a particularly meaty beast to be clubbed to death outside the cave. Mike Stroud, who played a Boswellian role to Ranulph Fiennes's Johnson when the pair of them attempted an ambitious trek across the continent, was more honest with me than most of the Frozen Beards. 'Sometimes I think I didn't have time to stop and appreciate it,' he said. 'I walked across, but most of the time I was miserable.'

*

The Antarctic continent is shaped roughly like a cross-section of the human brain, with a grossly misplaced finger tapering towards South America (this is usually shown coming out on the left at the top, depending which way round the map is drawn). More than ninety-nine per cent[1] of this landmass is permanently covered with ice formed by thousands of years of tightly compacted snowfalls. The other 0.4 per cent consists of exposed rock. Like glutinous white icing flowing off a wedding cake, the layer of ice on

---

[1] 99.6 per cent is the latest figure from the BAS/SPRI satellite map.

the surface of Antarctica is slowly but persistently rolling towards the coast, forcing its way between mountains, turning itself into glaciers split by crevasses and inching its way into a floating ice shelf or collapsing into the Southern Ocean. As a result, ice shelves surround the jagged Antarctic coastline. One of them, the Ross Ice Shelf, is larger than France.

The continent consists, broadly speaking, of two geological zones divided by the Transantarctic mountain chain. Greater Antarctica (also known as East Antarctica) is generally thought to be one stable plate. Lesser Antarctica (or West), on the other hand, consists of a lot of smaller, unstable plates – that's why all the volcanoes are in it. Besides the Transantarctics slicing down the middle, mountains form a ring around much of the continent. Beyond these coastal heights, in the interior, topography tends to disappear into thousands of miles of apparently flat ice – the enormous polar plateau. Mountain ranges as high as the Appalachians are hiding under this flat ice. The South Pole, the axis of the earth's rotation, is located in Greater Antarctica, on the polar plateau.

For much of the year, Antarctica enjoys total darkness or total daylight. The cusps between the two are short and exciting: it might be eight weeks from the moment the sun makes it first appearance over the horizon to the day it never sets. The summer season, broadly speaking, runs from mid-October to late February.

One of Antarctica's most salient characteristics is that of scale. The continent, one tenth of the earth's land surface, is considerably larger than Europe and one-and-a-half times the size of the United States. It has ninety per cent of the world's ice, and at its deepest, the ice layer is over 15,000 feet thick, pushing the land under it far below sea level. Thousands of cubic miles of ice break off the Antarctic coast each year. It is, on average, three times higher than any other continent. It never rains and rarely snows on most of it, so Antarctica is the driest desert in the world.

Into this land of superlatives I plunged. My plan was to fly in from New Zealand with the Americans in November, just as the austral summer was under way. Their main base is on one of the many hundreds of islands scattered around the Antarctic coast, and from there I could travel to a variety of field camps on the continent itself, perhaps make the Pole for Christmas, and later hook up with the New Zealanders, who were based nearby, and the Italians in Victoria Land only a couple of hundred miles away.

At the end of January I was going to make my way over to the British Antarcticans, all working on the peninsula, the finger tapering off towards South America. As this was on the other side of the continent, I was obliged to travel back to New Zealand on an American military plane and take a fiendishly roundabout route to the Falklands (so diabolical was it that I ended up back in my own flat in London in the middle) in order to catch a lift on the British Antarctic Survey Dash-7 plane down to the Antarctic Peninsula. I was going to travel with my compatriots for two months, by which time night would have begun its swift descent, and then sail up the peninsula in an ice-strengthened ship and arrive in the Falklands in early April.

In my grandmother's youth a restless spirit would probably have got her as far as Spain, then as exotic as Xanadu. The world has shrunk, and I was able, now, to go to its uttermost part.

By the end of the beginning I understood something, at least. I understood that Scott was right when he endorsed Nansen's exhausted remark, 'The worst part of a polar expedition is over when the preparation has ended and the journey begun.'

When someone asked Jonathan Raban why he was making his journey down the Mississippi, he said he was having a love affair with it. Antarctica was my love affair, and in the south I learnt another way of looking at the world. What I want to do now is take you there. As Shackleton said, 'We all have our own White South,' and I believe that the reach of the imagination extends far beyond the snowfields.

PART ONE

Antarctica left a restless longing in my heart beckoning towards an incomprehensible perfection for ever beyond the reach of mortal man. Its overwhelming beauty touches one so deeply that it is like a wound.

Edwin Mickleburgh, *Beyond the Frozen Sea*

THE ANTARCTIC CONTINENT

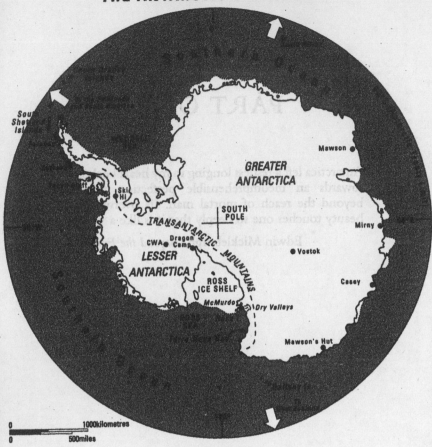

Temperature

To convert the Celsius Scale (that which we used to call Centigrade) to Fahrenheit, multiply the temperature by nine fifths and add 32. In reverse, take 32 from the Fahrenheit temperature and multiply by five ninths. Taking 0°C as equivalent of 32°F, thus we obtain:

−50°C = −58°F	5°C = 41°F
−30°C = −22°F	10°C = 50°F
−20°C = −4°F	20°C = 68°F
−10°C = 14°F	30°C = 86°F
− 5°C = 23°F	50°C = 122°F

The absolute zero temperature (the lowest possible) is −273.15°C. A temperature of −40°C = −40°F.

10

CHAPTER ONE

The Big White

Come, my friends,
'Tis not too late to seek a newer world.
Push off, and sitting well in order smite
The sounding furrows; for my purpose holds
To sail beyond the sunset, and the baths
Of all the western stars, until I die.

Alfred, Lord Tennyson, from *Ulysses*

EACH DAY was hotter than the last, and I soaked up the November sunshine like a lizard. Two Sundays after landing in New Zealand I had to present myself at nine in the morning at the headquarters of the U.S. Antarctic Program in Christchurch in order to be issued my Extreme Cold Weather clothing. I borrowed a mountain bike and cycled along deserted roads tasselled with silent shopping malls to the snoozing outskirts of the city where the sun had already burnt the blue from the sky. The bike had a matching helmet with a tiny rear-view mirror protruding from the side. I swung up to the entrance of the institutional snow-white building where a sprinkling of fellow travellers had settled on the low walls and warm grass. I couldn't unstrap the helmet and was obliged to solicit the help of a vulpine Russian glaciologist.

At nine sharp we were ushered inside to take our places in a windowless room festooned with posters of icescapes, and there we waited for the last arrivals in the silence of strangers while a man ticked off our names on a clipboard and scowled like Beethoven. I felt very alone at that moment, in a strange country bound for a stranger continent. I had come right up to the pane of the looking-glass, after so long.

The safety video began, optimistically, with Scott's 'Great God, this is an awful place' delivered in a sonorous thespian voice and accompanying footage of well-clad individuals crashing into crevasses. When it was over we trooped through to the changing rooms. There were three other women, and our room was bare except for four pairs of tagged, overstuffed orange fabric bags the size of medium suitcases.

The bags yielded a bewildering array of footwear, underwear, headwear, handwear, eyewear and unidentifiable items which didn't look as if they would fit comfortably over any part of my body. At the bottom of one of my bags, underneath an enormous vermilion parka, lay a coiled chain and a pair of metal dog tags engraved with my name and a long number. I arranged my clothes in neat piles on the carpet and eyed the others. They were beginning to try things on, so I tackled a pair of thermal longjohns with a willy-slit at the front. At one end of the room a curtain shielded us from a long counter to which we returned ill-fitting items to a blue-overalled clothing assistant who would scuttle away to pluck a different size pair of windpants or polypropylene glove liners from unseen mountain ranges of gear lurking in the hinterland.

As we pulled, zipped, laced and unrolled, my companions began to talk. One was a cook, another a senior ice-corer and the third a NASA technician. The ice-corer had six seasons of 'ice time', and she showed me how to switch on the white rubber bunny boots. They were insulated by air, and had a valve on the side which you had to open and close on aircraft.

When we had satisfied ourselves that no part of our extensive new wardrobe would chafe or pinch or expose our soft flesh to the rigours of frostbite, we packed up our bags and the scowler despatched us into the sunshine, ticking a clipboard and issuing threats about the consequences of arriving late for the plane.

The sun made me squint as I cycled back along the straight artery into town. The malls had opened, and I stopped to have a roll of film developed, drifting around the shops for the waiting hour, consumed by a desire to buy almost everything I saw, given that it was my last chance — as if anything could help me now. I groped around in my addled mind for the dream that had brought me here to the other side of the planet, but it seemed to have evaporated in the heat.

I was a guest in Christchurch of Roger Sutton and Jo Malcolm, who lived in a ramshackle house on the outskirts of the city. Roger's sister Camilla was an old friend of mine from her wild London days. The entire clan had embraced me as one of their own, and I enjoyed their company enormously. Jo was a news reporter on New Zealand television and Roger bought energy for SouthPower. He was obsessively committed to the outdoor life, and flung off his suit to go running or bicycling or climbing at the first opportunity. That evening they drove me to Lyttelton, a potent toponym in the history of Antarctic exploration and the last stop for most voyages early in the century. We went, on the way, to Kinsey Terrace and the clifftop house where Scott stayed with his New Zealand agent, signing his name above the fireplace, and emerged from the high passes overlooking Quail Island where he grazed his second-rate mules. In Lyttelton I saw hollow-eyed Russian seamen and tired brothels with shreds of grass struggling through cracks in the front step. It was quiet, and old-fashioned even by New Zealand standards. It seemed to dwell in another age. In one bar, the table soccer was equipped with small wooden teams of Jews and Nazis.

The crews of the first ships to drop anchor off the unknown southern continent reported pleasing success with the women of Lyttelton, noting in their journals that mention of imminent departure for Antarctic exploration constituted the most effective chat-up line they had ever deployed. 'No mere ship's officer had a chance against a polar explorer, even if only in the making,' one of them wrote. Roger suggested keenly that I should test the contemporary application of this theory, and stopped the car outside several bars, urging me inside and saying that he would pick me up later. Apparently it still worked, at least for men. I read in a textbook on Antarctic psychology published recently by Victoria University of Wellington that when two men placed a personal ad in a magazine asking for 'active female companionship for a week for fit men about to go to the Antarctic', they were inundated with offers.

When we got home I called my friend Cindy in London; I needed to speak to her before I left. She said she was glad I'd rung as she wanted the recipe for pisco sour, which they were planning to have before lunch. I was furious that they were going to drink pisco sour without me, as I had discovered it in Chile and introduced it to my friends. Still, I told her how to make it, and at the end of the conversation, as we said goodbye, she said she felt as if I were disappearing into a black hole.

*

The taxi arrived at four and Roger struggled out of bed to say goodbye. It had rained in the night and the tarmac glistened in the deserted roads, the only trace of life a cat rubbing its ear in a pool of light from a sodium streetlamp. At the airport I found my orange bags in the changing room, layered up in my new cold-weather garments and slipped the dog tags round my neck so that in the event of a crash my charred remains could be airmailed to my parents. Then I joined thirty other dim-eyed people in the lobby, and we all shifted from foot to foot while the pilot of our LC-130 turbo-prop, a ski-equipped Hercules, barked out the drill for the eight-hour flight.

'The toilet facilities on board', he said, 'are primitive at best. They consist of a urinal and a honey-bucket. I advise y'all to go for the major purge before departure, to avoid the honey-bucket.'

So that was another American achievement. They could turn their bowels on and off.

As the first creeping glow of dawn hesitated above the eastern skyline we carried our gear through to the customs building observed by a handful of saturnine U.S. Navy personnel. Then we eddied around a machine which dispensed plastic cups and squirted out an inch or two of weak Nescafe until we were marshalled into line in front of our baggage by short-haired men in combat fatigues while a sniffer dog idled among us.

At this point we were despatched into the watery dawn light and across the grass to have breakfast in the mess canteen. I was desperate for real coffee, but the shadowy form of a honey-bucket loomed between me and the pot. In the strip-lit dining room, an American football game screaming from the television, we sweated in our thermals and ate eggs and hash browns while a biochemistry graduate from North Dakota who had recently learnt the rules of cricket discoursed upon them at length. It took the rest of the table some time to grasp the basic principles involved. I dealt confidently with all appeals to me as custodian of this British

14

secret; it didn't matter that I too had never understood the rules. Those elysian Sunday afternoons on the edge of sunlit village pitches never seemed to have anything to do with cricket.

Two hours later we boarded the plane, a crocodile of bulky vermilion parkas differentiated only by velcro strips on the breast pocket emblazoned with our names. As I stepped inside the belly of the plane someone handed me a brown paper lunch bag and pointed to the end of a row. I strapped myself into a red webbing seat, wedged up against a stack of cargo crates, and looked around, like Jonah.

The man next to me was an astrophysicist involved in the study of supernova explosions. He planned to send a balloon up over Antarctica to record the spectral properties of gamma rays. We pushed in our earplugs and the plane rushed down the runway and into the morning sky, and then it was too noisy to hear any more about his balloon. I couldn't see a window either, so I hurtled towards Antarctica in my own private capsule. I slept fitfully, squashed between the astrophysicist and the cargo. None of us could find space for our enormous feet, and our legs crossed in the aisles at our ankles like upside-down guards of honour.

After an hour the temperature rose swiftly from glacial depths to tropical heights, and we struggled out of our parkas and balaclavas and neck gaiters just in time to feel it plummet again. The Russian glaciologist sat with his head in his hands for most of the journey, staring at the floor, while the astrophysicist gazed benignly into the middle distance, serene and untroubled, floating along like one of his balloons. He was so eminent that he knew exactly where we were at any given time. At one point he smiled beatifically and shouted in my ear that we had passed the PSR. Months later I found out that this stood for Point of Safe Return, which means over half the fuel has gone. It used to be called Point of No Return, but it frightened people, so they changed it.

We picked at our sandwiches and muffins and long-life chocolate puddings in plastic pots. Over the next months I was to become very familiar with the contents of these brown paper lunch bags.

When we landed and a crewman opened the door, it was as if he had lifted the lid of a deep freeze. Bloodless icefields stretched away to mountains below softly furred cumulus clouds, and ice crystals came skittering towards us through the blistering air. The

Hercules had landed on the frozen sea between Ross Island and the Antarctic continent, and along the wiggly island coast land met solid sea in a tangle of blue-shadowed pressure ridges or the pleated cliffs of a glacier. I began to readjust my perception of 'land' and 'sea'. Not far off, a tabular iceberg was clamped into the ice, its steep and crinkled walls reflecting the creamy saffron sun. The sky was a rich royal blue, marbled up ahead by the volcanic plumes of Mount Erebus, and a paler blue sheen lay over the wrinkled sea ice like a filmy opalescent blanket. A spur reached from the island towards the continent, and on a hump at the end I saw a wooden cross, man's tiny mark. It was Vince's cross, erected in 1904 by Scott's men in memory of a seaman who fell down an ice cliff during a blizzard. When I looked, it gave me an almost Proustian rush: I had been here so often in my dreams.

Tucked into a hollow between the spur and an arc of hills, and at first obscured, a hundred buildings huddled on the ice-streaked volcanic rock of Ross Island.

I was prepared for McMurdo, the largest of the three American bases in Antarctica. It did not shock me to find what looked like a small Alaskan mining town with roads, three-storey buildings, the ill-matched architecture of a utilitarian institution and a summer population of more than a thousand people. The lower echelons of other Antarctic communities, none of whom had been anywhere near the place, are fond of parroting diatribes against McMurdo because of its size and sophistication, by implication asserting the superiority of their experience of 'the real Antarctica'. I liked Mactown from the beginning, as one is drawn to certain anomalous characters in films, and my affection for it never faltered.

After a hundred introductions I was allotted a bedroom in a chocolate brown dormitory block. It was a pleasant room with two beds, two wardrobes, two desks and several sets of drawers, and it shared a shower and toilet with the room next door. I obviously had a roommate, but she was nowhere in evidence.

I duly layered up in my multiplicity of cold-weather garments, but when the wind dropped, the ambient temperature on Ross Island was no colder than a particularly bitter winter's day in London. Although the mean annual temperature at McMurdo is minus 17.7 degrees Celsius, in summer it can rocket to plus eight (it plunges as low as minus fifty in the winter). In those balmy

16

days of summer when I first arrived the temperature hovered around minus five. It is true that if the mercury touches minus five in London the weather is headline news and the trains grind to a standstill – and it feels worse at home because one doesn't stroll around swaddled in three layers of polypropylene, two layers of fleece and an industrial-strength parka. For many of the Americans on station, winters at home are a good deal colder than summers on the edge of Antarctica.

What no one ever quite gets used to, however, is the brutalising effect of the wind. The average windspeed at McMurdo is ten miles per hour (twelve knots). Extremely high winds, common all over Antarctica and terrifyingly swift to arrive, can freeze exposed flesh in seconds. That, effectively, is what constitutes frostbite, not initially a highly dangerous injury but one that can soon become fatal if untreated. A wind racing along at thirty-five miles per hour (56 knots), for example, which is fairly usual, reduces an ambient temperature of minus six degrees Celsius to a windchill factor of minus twenty-eight.

The Crary Lab was a long, wet-cement-coloured building on stilts, the showpiece of American science in Antarctica. It consisted of mysterious enclaves of petri-dishes and microcentrifuge tubes, well-heated offices, antiseptic conference rooms and a lounge presided over by a scrofulous penguin in a glass case. Each lab door bore a number corresponding to the project number of its occupants. These Science or S numbers were the key to many things in McMurdo. The small and unfunded Artists' and Writers' Program, in which I was a participant, dispensed W-numbers (for Writer), and my number was W-002; a textbook writer from the Midwest had got W-001. On some doors, a metal sign had been stuck under the project numbers. Most of these signs were self-explanatory, such as Penguin Cowboys or Sealheads, but some were more gnomic: The Bottom Pickers, I found out later, were investigating the seabed.

The best thing about the Crary was the view from the picture window which ran the length of the lounge. It looked directly over McMurdo Sound at the Transantarctic Mountains. They stuck up like the bones of the planet.

I had been given an office, and its door sign said, *W-002: Wheeler.* It was a windowless room about eight feet square with two modern desks, a set of bookshelves and a blackboard. Around the corner, in the wide corridor, a collection of startlingly ugly Antarctic fish leered out from glass cases under belljars labelled with Latin names. Among them a bright blue plastic fish with yellow protrusions and goggle eyes glared out of its own jar of formaldehyde.

Later that day I was inducted into the intricacies of the Waste Management Program. I learnt that there were eighteen different kinds of waste ranging from Light Metal to Cooking Oil, though for complicated reasons a broken glass did not belong in 'Glass' nor should a cereal box be thrown in 'Cardboard'. This explained the behaviour of people I had seen standing in front of a row of bins clutching a small item in one hand and scratching their head with the other. Hazardous Waste constituted an entirely separate department of even more Byzantine complexity. The sprawling piles of rubbish once photographed by Greenpeace were a distant memory. Only veterans could remember the barrel which had been roped off between McMurdo and Scott Base after it allegedly fell off the end of the Geiger counter. The 413-ton nuclear reactor brought to the station in 1961 was a distant memory, as were the noxious brown clouds which used to billow from the high-temperature incinerator every Saturday. Two decades ago, waste was simply left on the frozen sea until the ice melted. This practice was outlawed by the U.S. Antarctic Program in 1980, however, before Greenpeace had entered the fray. Burning too had subsequently been outlawed, and waste was retrograded to the United States to be burnt there, or used as landfill, or recycled. The reactor was removed in 1972.

The American presence in Antarctica, financed and managed by the National Science Foundation, a government agency, and maintained by a private contractor based in Colorado, has outgrown its naval origins. With a budget hovering just below $200 million, the Antarctic programme represents six per cent of the NSF budget. As the U.S. Department of Defense has contracted, so the Navy (more properly, a joint military force) has been withdrawing from Antarctic operations, a process which looks set to continue.

At breakfast one day I sat next to a man with a chipped tooth and a ponytail who was fortifying himself with boiled eggs before setting off to collect meteors from the polar plateau. He had already discovered meteors from the moon, and he reckoned he

18

had some from Mars too. He told me this quietly over his yolky toast, explaining how he could identify whence the rocks came as someone else might recount the story of a film they had watched on television the previous night.

'By the way,' he said when I got up to leave. 'Where do you live in the *real* world?'

*

It happened that the elderly Oscar Pinochet de la Barra, the distinguished head of the Chilean Antarctic Institute, was at the end of a short honorary visit to McMurdo. He had published widely on Antarctica and, like any self-respecting Chilean, had written poetry about his experiences. I sought him out, and we sat in a hut overlooking the frozen Sound, talking about Chile. He was an enthusiastic character who seemed terribly grateful to speak Spanish. The more famous Pinochet was his cousin, and he muttered uncomfortably 'we are not friends'. In the midst of my grand passion for Antarctica I occasionally looked over my shoulder at Chile, guiltily, as if at a lover I had betrayed. Oscar facilitated a reconciliation, and as I got up to go he touched my arm, and with his fingers resting in the crook of my elbow he said gently, 'Chile is Chile, my dear. But Antarctica is about much more than ice.'

*

Many images of the Heroic Age of Antarctic exploration have burnt themselves into the imagination, but the wind-blasted huts constitute the most potent symbol, frozen set-pieces of old socks and tins of Fry's cocoa. I was longing to see the huts. I wanted to pay homage, and I hoped it would help me to understand the most highly charged chapter of the continent's history.

The Heroic Age began at the Sixth International Geographical Congress at London's Imperial Institute in 1895. On 3 August those present passed a resolution 'that this Congress record its opinion that the exploration of the Antarctic regions is the greatest piece of geographical exploration still to be undertaken', and went on to urge scientific societies throughout the world to start planning. Six years later, on a balmy summer's day in 1901 in the middle of a glittering high society yacht week off the south coast of England, a smiling King Edward VII stepped aboard *Discovery* and pinned the insignia of Member of the Victorian Order on the chest of her barely known young captain, Robert Falcon Scott, wishing him Godspeed on his journey to the ice. The period drew to a close little more than two decades later, on 5 January 1922, when Sir Ernest Shackleton clutched his heart and died in the cramped cabin of his last ship, *Quest*, off the lonely island of South Georgia.

Robert Falcon Scott, Ernest Shackleton, Roald Amundsen and Douglas Mawson: the Big Four. These were the heroes of a generation of children who pored over images of bergs towering above wooden ships and men and dogs straining in front of sledges. Queen Victoria had only been dead six months when *Discovery* steamed away from the Isle of Wight, and the twentieth century hadn't yet gathered momentum; when it did, it would steamroller these and many other dreams.

Scott, as English as overcooked cabbage, led two expeditions, setting out first in 1901 in the specially commissioned *Discovery* and ten years later in the spartan converted whaler *Terra Nova*. During the second expedition he reached the South Pole a month after Amundsen. When he saw the Norwegian flag flapping in the distance Scott wrote in his journal, 'The worst has happened.' Two men died during the march home, and Scott and his two remaining companions perished in their tent, holed up in a blizzard eleven miles from a supply depot.

Shackleton was an Anglo-Irishman, and he first went south aboard *Discovery*, under Scott's command. On that expedition he sledged to the 81st parallel with Scott, but was eventually invalided home with scurvy. In 1907 Shackleton set out aboard *Nimrod* as leader, at last, of his own expedition, and on that journey he got to within 97 nautical miles of the Pole. It was, at the time, the furthest south ever reached. In 1914 he went again, leading an ambitious expedition in which two ships, the *Endurance* and the *Aurora*, deposited parties of men on opposite sides of the continent. The plan was that one party, led by Shackleton, was to sledge across Antarctica while the other laid depots on the opposite side. It didn't work out like that. *Endurance* was crushed by pack ice in the Weddell Sea and Shackleton was obliged to embark on an epic struggle to save himself and his men. It was an exceptionally difficult ice year, and on the other side the Ross Sea party also got into severe difficulties. After the First World War, Shackleton left Britain again, this time aboard *Quest*, with the aim of mapping an unknown sector of Antarctic coastline. On the journey out, he died.

Together with Ibsen and Grieg, Roald Amundsen brought his young country out of the shadowy realm of northern mists. He had extensive experience in the north, made the first transit in one vessel of the Northwest Passage, and travelled with Fridtjof Nansen, the greatest polar explorer of all. Amundsen was planning to reach the North Pole, but when he heard that Frederick Cook claimed to have got there, he decided to go south, and set out in 1910 aboard *Fram* – though he didn't tell the crew or the rest of the world his true destination until he reached Madeira, off the north African coast. Until then, only his brother knew. Amundsen and four companions reached ninety degrees south on 14 December 1911 and raised a Norwegian flag on the brick-hard ice at the South Pole.

Mawson was a scientist. A British-born Australian, he first went south with Shackleton, aboard *Nimrod*. Mawson was one of three men to reach the South Magnetic Pole, the south pole of the earth's magnetic field (as opposed to the geographic South Pole, which is the southern point of the earth's rotation). In 1911 he led the Australasian Antarctic Expedition, also aboard *Aurora*, and made a legendary one-man journey by walking hundreds of miles back to base after his two companions had died, one of them disappearing down a crevasse with almost all the food and the other going mad from food poisoning. Sixteen years later Mawson led a joint British, Australian and New Zealand expedition, and he ended his career as Professor of Geology and Mineralogy at Adelaide University.

On the *Discovery* expedition Scott's men built a hut on the spur protruding into McMurdo Sound. The spur became known as Hut Point and the hut was primarily used for storage, though they also performed plays in it – larky rituals being *de rigueur*. It was subsequently used as an advance base by other sledging parties.

McMurdo had risen up less than a mile from the Point. The wind was blowing steadily at about 25 miles an hour when I first walked down to the hut, and the exposed flesh between my goggles and balaclava immediately began to feel as if it were burning. I quickly covered every square inch. I was already quite used to sub-zero temperatures, but I only had to take off my gloves and glove liners for five or ten seconds to feel what would happen to me in a high wind if I failed to dress properly. If I tried to take a photograph without my glove liners when the wind was blowing hard, however speedily I went about setting up the shot I almost invariably lost sensation in one or two fingers. I couldn't begin to imagine what the old explorers had suffered when they pushed further south, month after crucifying month. I saw them with fresh eyes then.

When I entered the hut, the stillness came upon me like a benediction. There was a mummified seal, a frozen mutton carcass and stacked tins of Huntley and Palmer biscuits. It was colder than a sepulchre. They used to light a blubber stove, but the heating was always inadequate, according to the diaries. Shackleton wrote later that 'The discomfort of the hut was a byword of the expedition,' and when he was back there in 1908 he reported that some men preferred to sleep outside in their tents, as it was warmer. In the sixties a New Zealander stepped on a mousetrap that had been brought down by Scott's men to protect the food stores. I wouldn't have fancied a mouse's chances in those temperatures.

Of course, the Heroic Age didn't suddenly appear on the global landscape like a meteor. It grew organically out of what had gone before. Nineteenth-century explorers had been gobbled up by Victorians hungry for role models embodying the aspirations of the age. Peter Fleming wrote in *Bayonets to Lhasa*, his book about the 1904 British invasion of Tibet, 'By the end of the nineteenth century there were few major enigmas left on the African continent. Save for Antarctica, whose austere secrets were already arousing the competitive instincts of explorers, Tibet was the only region of the world to which access was all but impossible for white men . . .' But Tibet was small beer. Press attention shifted from the Dark Continent to the Arctic and thence to Antarctica, and the conquest of the last white spaces became a metaphor for the triumph of imperialism. The cultural vacuum of Antarctica provided the perfect *tabula rasa* on which to play out a vision. At Scott's farewell dinner Leonard Darwin, President of the Royal Geographical Society, said in his speech: 'Scott is going to prove once again that the manhood of our nation is not dead and that the characteristics of our ancestors who won the Empire still flourish among us.'

*

22

Twenty-four-hour daylight proved irredeemably desynchronising, and watching Mount Discovery glittering away busily in the small hours was like stealing a march on time.

Although McMurdo had two bars, as well as a Coffee Shop where temperate people sipped cappuccino, the best place to go drinking was an unofficial nightspot on the gloomy top floor of a dorm. It was known as the Corner Bar, and any reprobate who arrived on the ice was ineluctably drawn towards it like an iron filing to a magnet. It was not advertised, it was not even spoken of very often, and some people spent whole seasons on base without knowing of its existence. Yet anyone with lowlife inclinations appeared at the Corner Bar within forty-eight hours of arrival.

The Corner Bar was the creation of four enterprising support staff who had turned their two-bedroom-plus-connecting-shared-bathroom configuration of rooms into a communal lounge bar and four-bed bedroom. No money ever changed hands there. The bar, presided over by a hyperactive carpenter called Mike, ran on goodwill, and customers contributed bottles, or cash, or sent care parcels from New Zealand at the end of their tour. As the curtains were never drawn back the room was as Stygian and smoky as a shooting gallery. The Corner Bar kept erratic hours, but its schedule was simple: if the door was shut, then so was the bar. It was equipped with a large, low, smoked-plexiglass table and bar paraphernalia ranging from a huge Budweiser clock to a lifesized model penguin with the concentric circles of a shooting target painted on its chest. There was constant through-traffic, and new faces would loom out of the smoke among the hard-core movers and shakers. It was a great place.

I met a seismic geologist from Texas in the Corner Bar. He had blond hair, come-to-bed eyes and been-to-bed clothes, and one night he said to me, 'Being in McMurdo, I feel I've come halfway round the world to find the outskirts of Austin.' I often heard people expressing disappointment at finding modern conveniences on Antarctic stations. I never felt sorry or guilty or upset about it; I perceived bases as the tiniest fragments of human life on a vast, unspoiled white continent. It would be like getting upset about a couple of specks of dust on the Bayeux tapestry or one inharmonious note in a Mozart sonata.

Before moving out of McMurdo and into a field camp I was required to attend Survival School, a training course which would equip me to handle tents, stoves and radios, and enable me to swing nimbly out of a crevasse or come to a halt should I slide uncontrollably down an ice hill. 'Survival School' sounded more like a group therapy class you might come across on the Upper East Side or in Islington. People called it Happy Camper School, and as Americans are not strong on irony I thought the nickname was promising.

First, I was obliged to attend a snowcraft lecture. It took place in the Crary lounge, and the teacher, a field leader called Bill with eyes the colour of cornflower hearts, produced a fistful of frozen sausages from a glove to illustrate the danger of frostbitten fingers.

The Berg Field Center managed the practical aspects of life off base, and in it tents languished in various states of undress, stoves lay dismantled and sleeping bags were stacked in neat rows and categorised according to temperature requirements, the ones at the bottom marked '*Snowy Owl. Minus Fifty.*' Ice axes stood menacingly in close-ranked battalions between small armies of harnesses, ropes, thermarests, neoprene waterbottles and first aid kits. A large poster hijacked from colleagues in the Arctic warned of the dangers of polar bears. It was at the Berg Field Center one mild, sunny morning, the ambient temperature minus twelve degrees Celsius, that fourteen of us loaded up a tracked vehicle in preparation for Survival School. There were two instructors, one of whom was Frozen-Sausage Bill, and eleven pupils besides me – three navy personnel and eight scientists. Everyone was in high spirits.

We headed out a few miles, on to the ice shelf. By the time we embarked on the first session, at the foot of a snowhill, a band of cloud had descended and visibility had shrunk to thirty feet. The morning culminated in techniques for self-arrest while sliding down a snowhill supine and upside down. To do this, you plunge your ice axe into the snow at your side with the adze pointing towards the sky, twist your legs over, roll and pivot yourself round the axe until you are lying face down, head at the top, with the weight of your body over the axe, knees in and bum up.

Afterwards, we trooped off for lunch. They had put a small hut on the ice to facilitate happy campers, and in it Bill discoursed on the niceties of stoves as the rest of us concentrated on trail-mix, expedition cheese, crackers and chocolate and sucked on cartons of cranberry juice. Between bouts of eating we mastered pumping and priming and nodded gravely about the dangers of carbon monoxide poisoning. When we had finished, we walked across the ice shelf towards Mount Erebus to learn how to build igloos.

Erebus is an active volcano, and to those who love the south it is more perfect than Fuji, even Hockney's Fuji. The most recent measurement of its height, generally agreed to be the most accurate, is 3793 metres. It is the Eiffel Tower of the continent. Named after the ship in which James Clark Ross fought through the pack ice to almost 79 degrees south in the sea now named after him, on one side Erebus overlooks the Ross Ice Shelf. Called the Barrier by the early explorers and formed by ice flowing off the continent, this shelf consists of a roughly triangular slab of floating ice the size of France which is glued to the continent on two sides. The third side meets the ocean. During the summer months, when the thinner sea ice breaks up, the edge of the ice shelf crumbles off as bergs. This is what Edwin Mickleburgh wrote about the ice shelf in *Beyond the Frozen Sea*. 'The ice shelf is a region of unearthly desolation, a place of strange forebodings stirred by the loss of horizons into an endless encirclement of the ice invading the explorer's mind.' The helicopter pilots called it 'The Big White'.

During the course of the afternoon we engaged ourselves enthusiastically in building a snow mound, sawing ice bricks, constructing a wall and digging a trench. Frozen Sausage showed us how to spiral bricks into an igloo; this was very difficult. After we had accomplished these tasks we put up the tents and the instructors handed us a radio and went off to stay in the hut half a mile away. I shared a Scott tent with a scientist sporting a beard like Trotsky's (it seemed dangerous, with so many ice axes about), and we ate our dehydrated dinners sitting on our snow-brick wall. It was Thanksgiving Day, and, gathered chummily around the two stoves, we toasted it with more cranberry juice, though not being American I felt like an imposter at a Masonic ceremony. One of the navy men, a chief petty officer, was about to embark upon a mission to recover a radioisotope thermoelectric generator powering an automatic weather station at a remote spot on the polar plateau. A number of small RTGs had been working nicely in Antarctica before anyone began to worry about the environmental impact of radioactivity. All the others had been removed, but the last one was so inaccessible that no one had got round to going to find it. The RTG hadn't been seen for ten years, and whether this man and his team would ever find it was clearly a matter of conjecture. He didn't seem to be worried, anyway.

We had an English accent competition, easily won by an amiable Norwegian-American graduate student called Lars who was subsequently disqualified when he revealed that he had lived in Britain for five years. Lars had opted to sleep in the covered snow trench we had built – a terrible mistake, as it turned out, because it rained ice on him all night. He planted a Norwegian flag outside and called the trench Framheim after Amundsen's base camp. Late in the night Lars and I strapped on cross-country skis and headed out over the ice shelf. He reminded me of a big shaggy dog.

When we awoke next morning, great snowdrifts had formed around the tents. I had forgotten to stow my waterbottle in my sleeping bag, and the water had frozen. Everything had frozen. But it didn't matter. Trotsky was labouring over some feeble joke while rehydrating sachets of oatmeal when Frozen Sausage and Mike reappeared. They were talking about 'scenario training', so after despatching the oatmeal we struck camp and headed off.

A handful of new recruits were waiting in the hut. 'Right,' said Mike as we arranged crates in a circle and sat on them. 'Go round the circle, introduce yourself and say something personal, like whether you prefer blondes.'

This was a difficult question. I began compiling a mental list of ex-boyfriends to see if it revealed a predilection for a particular hair colour. Once I got back to 1990 I became muddled as to who came where, so I had to fish out a pen and straighten the wrapper of a granola bar, and write a column of names next to a column of dates, with a third column for hair colour. In some instances I seemed to have an extremely hazy recollection of hair, and of course there was the boxer in 1989 who was totally bald, so he had to be struck off the list altogether. I was engrossed in this important task when Mike called my name.

'Um,' I stammered, 'can't seem to find any evidence of a preference for blonds . . .' I pulled myself together. 'No beards though.' Everyone looked at me, hatchet-faced.

Scenario training involved responding to a simulated plane crash outside the hut. We were asked to list our skills, so that roles could be allocated. Between them, the navy men had almost every known skill covered, and they suggested helpfully that my role could be to write the bestselling book of the disaster after the event. In the end I was consigned to communications. Having rigged up the HF antenna from bamboo poles in the snow and headed off a short burst of machine-gun fire, I found the Field Operations Communications Center on the airwaves and checked in our party, disguising my English accent in case I said the wrong thing. 'Reading you loud and clear, Sara', came the crackling reply. Trotsky and the others were busy stretchering a supine Bill into the hut, so I strolled about – no doubt in gross dereliction of duty – and enjoyed the scenery. It was a clear morning and I could pick out Mount Discovery and Mount Morning as well as White Island, Black Island and Minna Bluff. It was all starting to look familiar.

*

Back at base, a series of urgent messages were waiting. I had been invited to the Italian station at Terra Nova Bay a couple of hundred miles away, and a helicopter would be leaving the next day. Although I had liaised with the head of the Italian Antarctic pro-gramme, Mario Zuccelli, from London, and he had invited me to Terra Nova Bay, I hadn't been expecting the visit to materialise yet; I had scarcely expected it to materialise at all. It was embarrass-ing to run away from my American hosts the minute I was quali-fied to do so and before I had been anywhere with them.

For the rest of the day I occupied myself by climbing Obser-vation Hill overlooking McMurdo. The team Scott left behind at the hut had put a jarrah wood cross on top as a memorial to the five men who died on the trek back from the Pole. Just before the *Terra Nova* left Antarctica they had inscribed it with the last line of Tennyson's *Ulysses*: 'To strive, to seek, to find, and not to yield.' They got the idea for the quotation from Nansen, who had used it to pay homage to Amundsen's voyage through the North-west Passage. Tennyson was their poet, though Browning came a close second, and once they even held a competition to decide between them. It was difficult to imagine members of a contem-porary expedition sitting round arguing over the merits of Auden and Yeats.

The disparate buildings of the station were spread out in the hollow below Observation Hill, adding a pattern of dull colour to the icescape around it. My eye followed the coastline of Ross

Island. In places, especially where it had been engulfed by a glacier, it was difficult to distinguish where the island ended and the frozen sea began. The topography of the island was powerful and muscular, bulging with volcanic unrest, and it was a relief to turn away to hundreds of miles of flat, frozen sea. Beyond the sea, the mountains on the fringe of the continent were too distant, and too perfect, to seem threatening. They were frosty sentinels, unassailable and infinitely desirable; a tease. Although I hadn't yet experienced anything of 'the real Antarctica', already I had a profound sense that I was in the right place. To start with, the relief of actually getting there was incalculable after the interminable preparations. But it was more than that. In some bizarre way I had an atavistic sense that I had come home. I couldn't imagine what this meant; but I didn't seek to understand it then. I had only just arrived.

The next morning I carried a packed bag and a set of cold-weather clothes to my office and attempted to locate my helicopter by means of the station telephone network. The machine, it emerged, had already flown to Scott Base, the New Zealand station two miles from McMurdo. As these bases are linked by telephone I was able to track down an Italian climatologist called Claudio who announced that they were delighted I was joining them on the journey to Terra Nova Bay. He would call me, he said cheerfully, when departure was imminent. We hung up.

Trapped in my office for four hours, waiting for a call, I had my first lesson in the logistics of Antarctic travel. Part of the journey was about learning to keep still.

When the telephone rang, a Kiwi pilot introduced himself. He was very sorry but he couldn't possibly take me as the helicopter was already overloaded. He had no idea when there would be another trip, if ever.

Ten minutes later, as I was still sprawled miserably in my swivel chair, the telephone rang again. Another Italian was gabbling. Mario, I established, had ordered Claudio off the flight so that I could take his place. 'You come to Scott Base immediately!' I heard this unknown voice demanding, and I began pulling on my cold-weather clothes.

Scott Base has been called a suburb of McMurdo, so close that a shuttle bus runs between the two stations and Americans make daily raids on the tiny shop run by the New Zealanders. It was usually possible to catch a lift, and this I did. Scott Base was probably about one twenty-fifth of the size of its neighbour, at first sight a neat collection of pale green buildings overlooking the frozen shore and a bank of pressure ridges strewn with Weddell seals. I found the entrance and stood redundantly in the lobby, waiting for whatever was going to happen next.

A tall, athletic figure burst through a door.

'Are you our passenger?' he asked brightly, and as I nodded he stretched out his hand. 'I'm Ben, the co-pilot. Pleased to meet you. You must be a very important person.'

I wondered, as I shook his gloved hand, how such erroneous information had made its way into the system, and what the consequences might be when everyone found out that I wasn't important at all, but this was no time for petty worries. Within ten minutes I was reaping the fruits of the misconception, wedged into the back of a smart orange-and-white Squirrel helicopter emblazoned with the ItaliAntartide logo next to several bulging cardboard boxes and three ice axes. On the other side, a mechanic was fixing me a headset.

With only a very shaky idea about where I was going and with whom I was travelling, and no idea about when I might return, if ever, we took off over the frozen Sound towards the Transantarctics, the sky a brilliant blue and sunlight flashing off distant glaciers. I caught a glimpse, in those first few moments, of what I might learn in Antarctica. The world seemed freshly made, and the future cast all its terrors away on to the timeless snowfields. First, however, I had to learn about Antarctic weather systems.

The Italian Antarctic programme leased three Squirrels, four pilots and an air mechanic from a New Zealand company, and the five non-Italian-speaking Kiwis spent the austral summer at Terra Nova Bay supporting the science programme. Two of them were already there. The other three, my companions, were looking worried. After we had travelled about fifty miles a low bank of cloud appeared on the horizon ahead. Over the headset I heard them weighing up our options. The weather reports sounded gloomy, and we hadn't even reached the refuelling depot yet. The pilot decided to return to Scott Base.

Back we trooped into the pale green buildings, disrobing in the boot room and settling in the galley to drink tea until the weather changed. As far as I knew, they might have been talking about minutes or months. The Squirrel team used Scott as their base on that part of the continent, and they had metaphorically put their feet up. Embarrassed about walking into a base and drinking tea without having the smallest idea who lived in it, I introduced myself to a very nice man in a Batman t-shirt who immediately invited me to stay for dinner. During our meal I was horrified to meet the displaced Claudio, but he was beaming like the Cheshire Cat. I began to think that perhaps I had done him a favour.

At seven o'clock in the evening the pilot proclaimed that the flight was off for the day. The Squirrel had to be flown back to McMurdo, there being no tiedown facilities for overnight parking at Scott Base, so I hitched a lift home in it. All three of the crew came on the five-minute flight, so I offered them a drink before they headed back, leaving my bag strapped deep in the net on the side of the helicopter as I hadn't the heart to ask them to retrieve it. The plan was that, after our drink, they would return to Scott Base and telephone me in the morning, when they had weather information, with a revised departure time.

The Southern Exposure was a regular American bar with a shuffleboard, a popcorn machine, a video screen and no windows, so it was dark all the time, neatly reversing the environment outside the door. Knots of scientists sat around marking frustrated time while they waited to get into the field and start work, delayed by weather, or a broken plane, or both. When dancing broke out, I noticed Trotsky wobbling around on the floor. Everyone said he was one of the most brilliant scientists of his generation, and in line for a Nobel Prize. When I ran into him at the popcorn machine, he was yawning.

'I keep waking up at five o'clock,' he complained. 'I've got this new alarm clock, and I can't work out how to use it.'

At midnight we were still in the Southern Exposure. I hadn't even changed out of my cold-weather clothes, though several layers had been peeled off, and I was traipsing about in my huge boots like Gulliver. One drink had slid seamlessly into another, and to make matters worse, or better, the blond Texan seismic geologist had appeared halfway through the evening. Most New Zealanders are game for a party at any given moment, and these three were no exception, not least because there was no bar at Terra Nova Bay and so this might be the last one they'd see for a couple of months. They obviously felt that it operated on the principle of the camel's hump. As for Seismic Man, I had never met a more natural party animal.

We left at twelve-thirty, but only because the bar closed, and staggered off to consume several vats of coffee and numerous slices of toast in the galley. After this the Kiwis were finally induced to walk back to Scott Base, leaving Seismic Man and me to fritter away what was left of the evening.

*

The telephone rang at some brutally early hour. We were leaving in ten minutes. I slammed down the handset, used my absent roommate's toothbrush (mine was strapped to the side of the helicopter) and layered up hastily once again. As I careered over to the helipad I saw Seismic Man running down the hill.

'I heard them starting the helo,' he said. 'I came to say goodbye.'

As I climbed into the back of the Squirrel it occurred to me that I probably ought to tell someone that I was leaving. I wriggled out and ran up the steps to the National Science Foundation Chalet, the administrative centre of the base. It had a sign on the door saying it was closed for Thanksgiving, so I took a pencil out of my pocket and scribbled a note on the sign. It said, 'Gone to Terra Nova Bay in a Squirrel. W-002.'

CHAPTER TWO

Terra Nova Bay

Suddenly I saw the cold and rook-delighting heaven
That seemed as though ice burned and was but more ice,
And thereupon imagination and heart were driven
So wild that every casual thought of this and that
Vanished.

W. B. Yeats, from *The Cold Heaven*

I PULLED OUT THE MAP from my pocket and unfolded it as we flew along McMurdo Sound. The Pole was at the top, so on paper we were going down in order to travel north. Scott and Shackleton had obviously sent science teams out all over this area, as the names they had bestowed clung to the landscape like flies to flypaper. It made it all seem so English.

We landed on a cape first sledged during Shackleton's *Nimrod* expedition. The party named it Cape Roberts after William C. Roberts, their cook. The large-grained surface snow was glittering like millions of tiny mirrors, and two bearded and grizzled figures emerged from a Scott tent among clusters of black volcanic rocks. This modest camp was the embryonic heart of one of the most ambitious cooperative projects ever conceived in Antarctica. To investigate the late Cretaceous to mid-Cenozoic history of the Ross Sea region, geologists from five countries were proposing to drill offshore rock cores which would yield information on millions of years of tectonic and climatic change. We went into the hut for a cup of tea.

The others chatted; the two beards couldn't stop talking.

William Roberts kept coming into my mind. I wondered what had brought him to the bottom of the world. As a cook, it could hardly have been a career move. At the turn of the century a great number of men had signed up to go south. Many did it for money. Carsten Borchgrevinck, who stood on the cusp of the Heroic Age and whose expedition was the first to winter on the continent, wrote in 1900, 'The Antarctic may be another Klondike . . . there are fish – fisheries might be established . . . here is quartz in which metals are to be seen.' Some British explorers claimed to be motivated by national rivalry, and an entrenched belief that it was Britain's right to be first. Others had demons to escape; but they probably found them waiting on the ice. Scott's geologist on the *Terra Nova*, Frank Debenham, wrote, 'Man strives for complete knowledge of his world just as a small boy climbs an apple tree even if there is no apple at the top.'

In addition, after all those long, hard centuries, it was widely believed that man had attained the most alluring geographical goal on earth. He had reached the North Pole. Just as people tired of the moon after 1969, in 1909 eyes sated on the north turned in another direction. They looked south.

As Scott noted in his diary, the bloated body of Arctic literature contrasted sharply with the skeletal material on its southern counterpart. At the beginning of the Heroic Age an editorial in the *Daily Express* commented, 'The South Pole has never caught the popular imagination as its northern fellow has done . . . it is inconveniently distant from any European base, so its environment remains a kind of silence and mist and vague terrors.' Arctic discovery dated as far back as the late Norsemen who performed epic feats of discovery in Greenland and beyond, and by the nineteenth century the far north constituted another space on a map to be painted with the queasy colours of British imperialism. The loss of Sir John Franklin's fleet as it searched for the elusive Northwest Passage in 1847 had ignited the imagination of the nation and stoked the ideal represented by glorious death in remote spots in the service of the motherland. It spawned a whole colony of art, too, notably Edwin Landseer's famous 'Man Proposes, God Disposes', depicting a pair of polar bears gnawing at the remains of a sailing ship, and Frederick Church's 'Icebergs'.

Until Captain James Cook set out on his second voyage in 1772, Antarctica had been little more than a shadow crouching on the white horizon of the European imagination. Seafarers had charted sub-Antarctic islands which they surmised were the great southern land, but nobody really had the first practical idea what, if anything, was down there. Before Cook, it was a myth. It had always been a myth. The ancient Greeks looked at the winds and the oceans and *sensed* that it was there. Conceiving as they did of a balance in nature, they decided that the *arktos*, the bear in the north, must therefore be balanced by an *anti arktos* in the south. Simple!

In AD 150 Ptolemy drew a continent on his map called *Terra Australis Incognita*, the Unknown Southern Land, and the existence of an Antarctica became fixed in the collective geographic mind. The fires Magellan saw burning on Tierra del Fuego in 1520 fuelled the notion of a great land still further to the south. If people lived that far down, why not further? When Drake got round Cape Horn in 1578 he declared there was nothing beyond it, because he could see the union of the Pacific and the Atlantic. None the less, Plancius's Planisphere, published in 1592, shows both the continent and *circulus antarcticus*. Plancius, Mercator and the other medieval cartographers struggling to make sense of it all interpreted medieval theory in the light of Spanish and Portuguese voyages. They decided, on at best flimsy evidence, that this land must be very big, mightily hard of access – and populated.

From the sixteenth century on, at least until Cook's second voyage, cartographers were kept busy lopping off bits of Antarctica which didn't exist, like pruning an unruly tree. One cartographer, Oronce Fine, gave the continent the snappy name *Terra australis nuper inventa sed non plene examinata* (the lately discovered but not completely explored southern land). This failed to catch on. The ghostly image of a fertile, wealthy Shangri-La was finally laid to rest by Cook in the latter part of the eighteenth century. His second voyage made all the Antarctic exploration which had gone before him look insignificant. He discovered that there could be no people there after all; it was too cold. The myth died. They were hoping for fertility and riches, the land of their dreams, and all they got was an interminable icescape.

*

We landed again shortly after leaving the two beards. The Kiwis refuelled the Squirrel from a drum line, eyed beadily by a line of skuas, the ugly brown migratory gulls ubiquitous around the coast of Antarctica in summer. The fuel cache was located on the edge of the continent itself, a hundred miles along the Sound from McMurdo. In the background the faces of the Transantarctic mountains zigzagged downwards in gradations of creamy blue. The sky was mottled with cirro-stratus like fishscales, and shafts of sunlight fell on the creased surface of an ice tongue, a massive projection fed by two glaciers. Beyond it ink-dark seals lay around their holes. On one side mountains sank into glacier snouts, and on the other the sea ice had melted into a berg-studded ocean which rippled lightly, like a wheatfield touched by the wind.

'Look,' said Ben, disengaging the fuel pump and pointing at a field of crevasses on the side of a mountain. Each rift was miles long, and no doubt miles deep. So often it is the landscapes most inimical to life that are the most seductive. In this respect they are like boyfriends. It doesn't seem fair.

Before the *Resolution* sailed out of Sheerness on 21 June 1772 under Captain Cook, more than half the crew deserted. Cook was under Admiralty instructions to find the great southern land. He had always suspected that there was no such thing, despite the fact that the weight of the scientific establishment at home pressed upon its existence. Joseph Banks, the brilliant naturalist who sailed with Cook, recounts in his logbook that on the *Endeavour*, Cook's other ship on the 1772 voyage, the men were divided into two camps according to their opinion on the existence of Antarctica. They called themselves 'we Continents' and 'no Continents'. In 1770 the 'no's thought they had sailed around what constituted definitive proof – but they were still footling about off New Zealand.

Cook was a Yorkshireman without formal education, and he worked on the Whitby coal-carriers before signing up with the Navy and applying himself to the cutting edge of eighteenth-century science. He was measured and, like Shackleton, always had his finger on the pulse of his men, who were frequently drunk. Cook took care to learn from those who had gone before him, and unlike the crews battling around Antarctica over a century later, Cook's men never got scurvy.

In the end the pack ice stopped him. He wrote that the sea was so 'pestered' with ice that land was inaccessible. In the *Resolution* he crossed the Antarctic Circle, the first man to do so, and discovered the circumpolarity of the Southern Ocean. In January 1775 he claimed South Georgia, though he wasn't impressed with the island, writing in his journal that the land he had seen was 'a country doomed by nature never once to feel the warmth of the sun's rays, but to lie buried under everlasting snow and ice, whose horrible and savage aspect I have not words to describe'. As he sailed away he concluded, 'There is not the least room for the possibility of there being a continent, unless near the Pole and out of reach of navigation.' Four years later this great man, only fifty years old, was stabbed to death with an iron dagger by natives in the clear blue waters of Kealakekua Bay in Hawaii.

After Captain Cook, sealers and whalers ushered in the next phase of discovery as they eddied around southern waters in the 1820s. The continent probably wasn't sighted before 1820, and it was almost certainly the Estonian Fabien Bellingshausen who saw it first. Born the year Cook died, and despatched south by Tsar Alexander I, Bellingshausen turned out to be a great explorer, and took up Cook's baton. The British Edward Bransfield and the American sealer Nathaniel Palmer also made early sightings. Palmer was twenty-one when, in 1820, he rang the bell of the *Hero* in thick fog off the coast of the South Shetland Islands. He thought he was hundreds of miles from another ship, and then he heard a bell clanging in reply. It was from Bellingshausen's ship, and the Admiral quickly put on his regalia and formally invited Palmer aboard the *Vostok*.

James Clark Ross crossed the Antarctic Circle and penetrated the sea which now bears his name during a Royal Navy voyage he led between 1839 and 1843. He discovered great swathes of the ice edge. Ross joined up when he was eleven, went off to the Arctic with his uncle to look for the Northwest Passage, the geographical grail of its day, became a scientist and located the North Magnetic Pole. He was said to be the most handsome man in the Navy. When he reached home, after more than four years in the south, he was knighted. He was also married, but only after his father-in-law had extracted a contract from him that there would be no more polar voyages. He settled in a small village near Aylesbury in Buckinghamshire, where he now lies in the churchyard.

In 1898 the *Belgica* expedition became the first to winter in the pack ice. Amundsen was on it, so was Frederick Cook, the man who later claimed to be the first to reach the North Pole. Seven nationalities were represented: as T. H. Baughman put it in his book *Before the Heroes Came*, 'The *Belgica* expedition was a fugue in seven voices.' The ship was not properly equipped for an Antarctic winter. Many of the crew showed signs of scurvy, and each man made his own private journey into despair during the long, dark months of the polar night. When a lieutenant died, it almost broke their spirit.

Carsten Borchgrevinck went south aboard the *Southern Cross* at the turn of the century. Although it was a British expedition, Borchgrevinck was a naturalised Australian whose father was Norwegian, and to the British geographical establishment of the day this was tantamount to playing football for a non-league side. He got along so badly with physicist Louis Bernacchi that the latter refers to Borchgrevinck in his diary as *l'enfant*. Still, the dogs they had brought south proved remarkably successful when harnessed to the sledges, with ground-breaking results for the expedition. Another unsung hero, William Spiers Bruce, led the Scottish National Antarctic Expedition in 1902–4. The artist of the voyage, W. G. Burn Murdoch, wrote a book called *From Edinburgh to the Antarctic*, and he ended it with an expression of malaise about the land they left unexplored. 'And so we returned from the mysteries of the Antarctic, with all its white-bound secrets still unread, as if we had stood before ancient volumes that told of the past and the beginning of all things, and had not opened them to read. Now we go home to the world that is worn down with the feet of many people, to gnaw in our discontent the memory of what we could have done, but did not do.'

We flew over the ice-locked Inexpressible Island, and the cockpit dials showed that 50-knot katabatic[1] winds were flying down from the Reeves Neve.[2] It was the island where Victor Campbell was stranded for eight months with five men in their summer clothes and two months' rations during the Antarctic winter of 1912. They suffered from a painful condition they called 'igloo

---

[1] Winds that cool, grow denser and therefore rush downwards.
[2] A neve is a snowfield at the head of a glacier which has yet to become compacted into glacier ice. A typical configuration of ice from the inland plateau passes from neve to glacier, thereupon to ice sheet, ice shelf, sea ice and then, eventually, to liquid sea. Neve snow squeaks when you plunge in your ice axe.

back', their lives so troglodytic and their faces so caked with blubber that they were recognisable only by their voices. Yet they enjoyed concerts on Saturday nights, and issued copies of a newspaper called *The Adelie Mail*.

Victor Campbell was an Old Etonian, a scientist and first officer on the *Terra Nova* on Scott's second expedition. He went to Antarctica partly because his marriage was rocky. Having been conveyed to the edge of the Ross Ice Shelf by the *Terra Nova* in January 1911, the intention of the Eastern Party, which consisted of Campbell, three seamen and two officers, was to carry out extensive surveying work, but they failed to find an eastern landing. Initiative being the key to Antarctic science then as now, they went north to Cape Adare instead.

On the way, much to the surprise of both groups, they met Amundsen and the other Norwegians in the Bay of Whales. When the watchman of the *Fram* – clearly a man who liked to hedge his bets – saw the *Terra Nova* sailing past, he brought out his Jarman gun, which he loaded with six bullets, and an English phrasebook from which he quickly learnt to say 'Hello, how are you this morning?' The encounter was cordial, and they inspected each other's quarters. The British were astonished at the efficiency with which the Norwegians handled their dogs, and Amundsen recorded in his diary that after the visitors left all the Norwegians caught colds.

At Cape Adare, Campbell and his five men waved the ship goodbye and renamed themselves the Northern Party. After a fruitful season the *Terra Nova* picked them up again and dropped them at what became Inexpressible Island, supposedly for six weeks. But when it came to fetch them that time, it failed to get through the pack ice and returned to New Zealand, leaving Campbell and his men marooned in an ice hole for eight months.

Then men got used to a meat and fat diet, though its high acid content meant that some frequently wet themselves. After eight months on the edge of endurance they had to trek 230 miles back to the hut on Ross Island, and when they got there, they learnt that Scott and the others had perished.

Beyond the island, a flash of colour caught my eye. I realised it must be the Italian station, crouched on the edge of Terra Nova Bay. In five minutes the rotor was shuddering to a stop on the helipad in front of the base.

The main building was on stilts, with Prussian blue corrugated metal walls, a Siena orange roof and Beaubourgesque chimneys. From it emerged Mario. He was a dark-haired and olive-skinned man in his late forties, wearing glasses and a permanently hunted expression. He welcomed me, looking anxiously over my shoulder at the helicopter cargo, of which there was very little. We walked in, but he was distracted, so I tried to keep a low profile, not an easy task when thrust among forty Italians eager for new blood. I was introduced to almost everyone at once, and propelled into the Operations Room – *la sala comando*. It was a long narrow room with one continuous window overlooking the helipad and a great sweeping panorama encompassing the whole bay, frozen as far as the Campbell Ice Tongue and metamorphosing beyond that into the beckoning turquoise of open water. Presiding over it all was Mount Melbourne, the 2900-metre volcanic cone named by Ross after the British prime minister. It dominated the Italian presence as completely as Mount Erebus dominated the Americans and the New Zealanders. The operations room was run like a wartime bunker by Gaetano, a wiry lieutenant-colonel aged around thirty who flew about the room, spluttering like a grenade, and gave the impression of constant and almost fatal overwork. He thrust a VHF radio into my hand and barked a few sentences of unintelligibly acronym-laden Italian.

Shortly before supper Mario asked sheepishly if I minded sleeping on the floor of a *laboratorio*. The dorms were full, and the alternative was an isolated outbuilding. I was perfectly happy. The laboratory was a narrow room with a sink, shelves lined with bottles of lurid substances, a smell of formaldehyde and a camp bed. When I opened a cupboard door a deluge of syringes rained down. I tried to disconnect the long rubber tube from the tap, so that I could clean my teeth *in situ*, but the project failed amid geysers of very cold water. At the end of the room there was a window, which was fortunate, as the lab grew unaccountably hot at night.

*

The accommodation, the kitchen, the *sala comando* and most of the labs and offices were located in the main building, which meant that you didn't have to face whiteouts to get to breakfast. In the evening *cena* was eaten at the civilised time of 8.30 and in this department the Italian nation excelled itself. Not only were wine boxes provided at both lunch and dinner, but the chef, an endlessly cheerful Neapolitan called Ciro who was like a small rubber ball, created unbelievably delicious meals. His kitchen was not resupplied regularly with fresh foods and I never understood how he managed to perform his culinary feats. When I asked him, he said the important thing was to cook *con amore*.

On top of this, an industrial-sized espresso machine in one of the two lounges was permanently connected to the water supply. To me, this was akin to attaining Nirvana. The lounges were furnished with brown Dralon sofas, a fridge containing soft drinks and mineral water (the Italians drink bottled water on the ice, a habit held up by veterans of the British Antarctic Survey as an example of wanton profligacy and the moral turpitude of Foreigners) and a video screen. In a small room next door there was a table football game, hunched over which people regularly worked themselves into a frenzy. After dinner, the Italians enjoyed lounging around in the corridor outside the dining room and jabbering over tiny cups of espresso. Mario often used this period to inform the team of his latest project.

'I have decided', he said one night, throwing his head back and gulping down a mouthful of espresso, 'to bring the Pope out to the ice.' He paused to allow for digestion of this information. 'What do we all think of that?'

'Well,' said Gaetano, spluttering quietly, 'I cannot really see His Holiness on a snowmobile.'

There were three women on station, and they used to gather for a cigarette outside the metal shower cubicles in the bathroom.

'How are you finding our base?' the eldest one asked me during one of these fag breaks. She was a woman of feisty spirits and Chaucerian ribaldry whose role at Terra Nova Bay I was never able to ascertain.

'Fine!' I said.

'Look, don't panic if the men seem desperate – you know, for women. They are just talk – ' she finished the sentence by imitating the working of a jaw with her fingers and thumb. 'In this very cold,' she continued, whereupon the other two began laughing, as if they knew what she was going to say, 'their little *cazzi* become this tiny,' and she held her thumb and forefinger half an inch apart. With that, she slapped me on the back with one hand, stubbed a cigarette out in the sink with the other, burst through the swing door and sailed into the corridor.

During the day the base exuded a permanent sense of urgency. It was a summer-only station,[1] which put everyone under pressure, and besides this, the Italians were a long way from their nearest neighbours. It all contributed to a kind of frontier spirit, as did the fact that the history of the Italian presence in Antarctica was shorter than a decade. They still referred to their presence as *una spedizione* – an expedition. Perhaps Terra Nova Bay recaptured the excitement and energy of American and British bases operating thirty years before the Italians headed south.

*

I had just divested myself of my cold-weather clothes after a bracing walk around the bay when Gaetano's voice boomed over the tannoy announcing that an *elicottero* was waiting for me, his tone indicating that each minute that elapsed precipitated the base further towards nuclear fission. I rushed to pull on my cold-weather clothes again, jamming the zip of the vermilion parka.

Ben was resupplying a pair of biologists working on a penguin project at Edmondson Point on the other side of Mount Melbourne. It was not a beautiful spot. Only partially snow-covered, it was heavily invested with skuas on the lookout for penguin eggs. The huge Adelie colony dominated the landscape, and as the Squirrel began its descent we could see individual birds waddling about with stones in their beaks. When we opened the doors, a sulphurous gust of wind blew in a blizzard of ice and rock particles. Edmondson Point reminded me of a curled old photograph I had seen of an early British base on the Antarctic Peninsula with the words *'semper in excreta'* above the door of the hut. A permanent low murmur hung on the air. Edward Wilson, Scott's confidant, said that walking up to a penguin rookery was like approaching a football ground during a match.

The two women came to meet us. They had been living at this bleak spot with thousands of penguins for three months, and later I watched them capturing nesting birds with what looked like a large black butterfly net, stowing the egg lying under each one in

---

[1] Approximately thirty of the 200 research camps in Antarctica are operational all the year round.

a skua-proof box, tying the bird up by its feet, weighing it on a weighbridge, opening its cloaca to determine its sex, measuring its beak, passing an infrared wand over it and painting a number on its back. The penguins kept quite still throughout this ordeal, and afterwards settled back on their stone nests with a quick wing-flap as if little more than a minor inconvenience had occurred.

One of the women, Francesca, was about twenty-five, and she had never lived in the field before; when they weren't working she seldom strayed far from the tent. Raffaella, the other one, probably wasn't older than thirty, but she had years of field experience behind her and seemed much more at ease in the landscape. I imagined that the penguins felt safer with her.

'Don't you get bored?' I asked in my sketchy Italian.

'No,' she said, pushing her hair behind her ears. 'I bring a skipping rope. The penguins are good company – though I like some better than others. Take that one over there – the one poking his nose into someone else's nest. Miserable *diavolo*!'

'How do you tell which is which?'

'How you tell which man is which?'

'Er, well, they sort of look different.'

'Yes, so penguins look to me.'

And that, it seemed, was that.

Then we headed south along the coast to pick up a pair of scientists at Dunlop Island. Below us, suffused in a primrose light, seal pups were slithering over the ice sheet, and in the distance the last remnants of sea ice lay on the bright blue water like a membrane.

A geomorphologist and his *alpinista* – the Italian version of the field leader – had already struck camp when we arrived, and they were waiting next to a mound of rucksacks and boxes. We milled around for a few minutes, then loaded up. The geomorphologist wanted to take samples at Depot Island some way to the south, and he and I were dropped there while Ben and the *alpinista* went off to refuel. The small, snowy island was discovered by Mawson and the South Magnetic Pole party at the end of October 1908 and named after a cache of rock specimens. The geomorphologist grew increasingly excited about the soil he was digging, and gabbled away happily in Italian.

Later that day we landed at the snout of the Mawson Glacier

for a picnic. The *alpinista* was a sturdy little marine commando called Nino. After despatching several wedges of bread and salami the geomorphologist strode off to repeat his earlier success while Nino, Ben and I sprawled in the sun. I struggled to translate for them. That morning, we had heard over the radio that a coalition of opposition parties in Rome was on the verge of bringing down the government. Swallowing the last mouthful of chocolate, Ben asked Nino what he thought about it.

'Not much,' said Nino.

'You must think something! It's your bloody country!'

'Look, politics in Italy has no surprises since Caligula proposed a horse for senator,' said Nino, who came from a village in the high Alps. 'Besides, all that seems so trivial here.' Yes, I thought. Antarctica represents everything beyond man's little world. Most of time and space is like Antarctica, untouched and unowned.

Sometimes, in the evening, a group of us would repair to the *pinguinatolo*, a wooden hut among the outbuildings. The walls were graffitoed with the imprimata of a generation of Italian Antarcticans, and half-consumed bottles of grappa from seasons past loitered on the shelves. The Italians never got drunk. They enjoyed wine with their meals but never took more than two glasses. It was the Kiwis and I who had a winebox *fest* when the spirit moved us. There were many cultural differences between the New Zealand air unit and their Italian employers. While the New Zealanders were frequently frustrated by Italian emotional outbursts, they recognised their hosts' technical abilities; if a helicopter part needed fixing, once they handed it over to the electronics engineers it would come back not only mended but *improved*. Everything the Italians did, they did stylishly. They had the best gear, and far outclassed any other nationality on the ice with their red *tute* bodysuits and red-and-white rucksacks. They made the British look as if they hadn't left the continent since 1912.

'It's Giuseppe's birthday today,' someone told me one evening in the *pinguinatolo*.

'Which one is Giuseppe?' I asked.

'You know, the fellow from Umbria.'

They talked often about where they came from – it constituted a vital part of their identity. 'You see, Sara, I'm from Spezzio . . .', someone would say, and in the dining room they took every opportunity to deliver a paean to some special dish from their region. If ever one of these dishes made an appearance a huge portion would be set before me while arguments raged about variations on the recipe. It was very endearing, particularly as it was obvious that none of them ever went anywhere near a kitchen at home.

On Sunday evening I offered to cook a traditional English dish. I decided on bread-and-butter pudding, and spent half the morning in the kitchen. Ciro bounced around, searching out a starched white chef's hat for me and changing the cassettes of Neapolitan music which blared out of the sticky kitchen. I made two big trays, and just as I had taken them out of the oven, five minutes before lunch, I was called over the loudspeaker to the ops room – McMurdo wanted me on the radio. When I came back down I saw that they had piled their plates with *antipasti* and bread-and-butter pudding and were enthusiastically seasoning it all with salt, pepper and olive oil.

*

One day, they took me up to the polar plateau on a survey to plot sites using hand-held Global Positioning System units. By transmitting to a series of satellites, they were able to receive accurate latitude and longitude readings – invaluable navigational information if a scientist needed to return to the scene of an experiment. Before we left base, Nino made me a thermos of tea, and Franco the doctor stuck a label on it saying '*te di Sara*'. They treated me like a doll, and would wander around looking for me, singing some Italian song involving *Sara* and the *primavera*. I was referred to as *la principessa* and schemes were devised to induce me to stay for the whole season. I felt vaguely guilty as I smiled vacuously and failed to deliver a feminist Gettysburg address. But not guilty enough, obviously.

I took off in a helicopter with Ben, a geophysicist and Nino. The air was full of diamond dust that day. We chatted over the headsets, interrupted by Gaetano who kept breaking in from base. 'Don't touch Sara,' he said. Then Ben put on a Strauss tape. The snow at the bottom of the Priestley Glacier was beaten into wide dunes, like a bleached Sahara, and as we wheeled upwards the

44

pitted pale blue glacier rushed beneath us, reflecting the violet streaks of the limpid sky. We crested the ridge, momentarily buffeted by a gust of wind, and then, ahead, we saw the polar plateau.

Life felt very sweet, at that moment.

We landed at flagged points, to take observations. It was minus 25 degrees Celsius, and very windy. I learnt about the 30-Knot Club, entry into which involved pissing into a 30-knot wind without splashback. It was quite a sophisticated club, with a President and a Secretary. I trailed around behind Nino, and we found a small meteorite. Nino seemed impervious to the cold. When I watched him working I thought of Birdie Bowers who died in the tent with Scott. He was so resilient to cold that people have written medical papers about him in learned journals. When he undertook the Winter Journey to Cape Crozier with Bill Wilson and Apsley Cherry-Garrard it was seventy-seven below zero Fahrenheit and he didn't need the outer layer of his bag.

*

One more Hercules was scheduled before the runway on the sea ice melted. After that, they had to wait for the ship. I was obliged to hitch a ride on this last plane as far as McMurdo, and woke on the day feeling unutterably depressed. Life had been very easy at Terra Nova Bay. The rest of the journey wasn't going to be as straightforward.

I made a little speech of thanks in Italian over the loudspeaker, and they presented me with a satellite map, signed by everyone, with the places I had visited marked with yellow asterisks. Instead of Victoria Land they had printed Sara Land.

Almost everyone came over to the ice runway to see me off. The LC-130 eventually hove into view above the furthest mountain, and the Italians started jabbering, as if they hadn't really believed it was going to come at all. The plane was flown by a crew from a Pisa-based squadron of the air force. It made the round trip from Italy via Christchurch, and shut down for one night at McMurdo on the way from Terra Nova Bay back to New Zealand. After a batch of scientists had emerged from the hold, and much armwaving and kissing and a slew of mouthed imprecations to write, I walked up the ramp and into the back of the plane.

45

A pair of Italian fire engines chased us up the runway as we left so that our departure resembled a scene from *Dad's Army*. Even then I hadn't left them, as Gaetano had radioed the captain, a friend of his, and told him to let me sit next to him, so I was ushered straight up to the flight deck.

CHAPTER THREE

Landscapes of the Mind

... people are trying to fathom themselves in this antarctic context, to imagine their coordinates, how they are fixed in time and space.

Barry Lopez, Crary Lab dedication talk, McMurdo, 1991

A FRENCHMAN appeared in my office shortly after I returned to McMurdo: someone had told him I spoke French. He was an ice-corer en route to Vostok, the Russian base in the empty heart of East Antarctica. Vostok was a potent name in the history of the continent. There they had recorded the coldest temperature in the world, minus 129.3 degrees Fahrenheit, which is minus 89.2 Celsius. The annual mean temperature at Vostok was minus 55 Celsius – five degrees colder than at the South Pole. They had also drilled deeper than anyone else, so they had the world's oldest ice. The harsh conditions at the base had earned it a reputation as a gulag of the south. The French corer knew it well.

'It's not unusual to wake up to fist fights outside the bedroom door,' he said airily. And to think that in the sixties, at the height of the Cold War, the Soviets used Vostok as a behavioural testbed for the Salyut space programme,

I had read a book by the geophysicist who was station chief at Vostok in 1959. Despite dabs of Russian colour, such as frequent references to cabbage pie and the October Revolution, the text was painfully guarded. Besides the temperature, they had to cope with the problems of living at an altitude of 4000 metres, and Viktor Ignatov, the author of the book, reports grimly that

47

potatoes boiled at 88 degrees Celsius and took three hours to cook. Being so high and so remote, Vostok cannot be adequately supplied by air, and therefore each summer a convoy of Kherkov-chenka tractors heavily laden with food, fuel and other essential goods sets out from Mirny, the Russian station on the east coast. I once saw a film of this traverse, shot in the late sixties. The Amsterdam Film Museum found the spools languishing in their dungeons, restored them, put them on video and sent me a copy. It told a story of polished Ilyushins, white huskies, a solitary grave (well-tended), grubby calendars with days crossed-off and men sunbathing in pneumatic bathing trunks on the deck of a vast icebreaker and polishing stiff lace-up shoes when they saw land. It ended with a little girl's face, eyes tightly closed and thin arms clutching her weeping father's neck. The sombre military music played over the footage of the traverse itself made it seem as if they were marching across the steppe into the Siberian permafrost to defend the motherland against a marauding barbarian horde. When the tractors arrived at Vostok it was to bearhugs and a tray of vodka. The fact that I couldn't understand a word of the nar-ration only made the film seem more exotic.

The Frenchman eventually left for Vostok, and on the same day Seismic Man and his group finally took off for their deep-field destination. They had been delayed by both weather and planes for two weeks, and some of them had checked in for their flight fifteen times. Most of them hadn't known each other before they came south, and during the fraught waiting period they had knitted together as a team. I was terribly jealous of that, especially as I had got to know them as they lounged over the sofas on the top floor of the Crary and wandered the corridors like nomads. I was sorry to see them go, though they had invited me out to their camp, an invitation which wouldn't, in theory, be difficult to take up as their project was being supported with a large num-ber of fixed-wing resupply flights. They called me Woo after my W-002 label, and as we waved goodbye they shouted that when I arrived they would have a Welcome Woo party on the West Antarctic ice sheet.

It was seven o'clock on Saturday night, and I felt depressed. I sat in my office, listening to people next door arguing about fish bait. When this group were out of their office, which was most of the time, they put a sign on their door saying 'Gone fishin''.

Going fishing involved drilling holes in the sea ice and hauling up primeval creatures which survived the depths of the Southern Ocean by producing their own anti-freeze. The project leader was an Antarctic soldier who first came to the ice the year I was born. His name was Art DeVries, and he appeared in my doorway brandishing a small, dead fish.

'Come fishing tonight!' he said imperiously. I kept a set of cold-weather clothes under my desk, so I put them all on and walked out of the door. A tracked vehicle with DR COOL stencilled on the fender was warming up outside, and various members of the team were fiddling with equipment in the back. Art had a knack of assembling a disparate bunch of research scientists and graduate students, from ex-janitors to an antifreeze specialist he had met at an airport. They were all good fun, and they all smelt of fish.

We drove to a small wooden fish hut on the sea ice in which a battery-operated winch positioned over a hole in the floor was lowering bait 1,500 feet into the spectral depths of the Sound. The bait consisted of fish brought in from New Zealand. Much winching later, the fish which emerged weighed 125 pounds and looked as ancient as the slime from which we all crawled.

'*Dissostichus mawsoni* – Antarctic cod to you,' said Art as he heaved it off the scales. 'Phenomenally small brain.'

'Can you eat them?' I asked.

'Sure you can. Sashimi cut from the cheeks is kind of nice. But it's the antifreeze everyone's after. Aircraft manufacturers want it to develop a product to prevent airplane wings from freezing.'

When a row of specimens were lying on the floor, the biologists started arguing again, this time about which to keep, talking about 'nice shaped throats' as if they were judging a beauty contest. Most of their fish were named after explorers: *mawsoni, bernacchii, borchgrevinki*. Art had his own – a deep-water bottom dweller called *Paraliparis devriesi*. The Channichthyidae 'ice fish' which live in slightly warmer Antarctic waters have no haemoglobin at all, and their blood is white.

★

The Chapel of the Snows was a pink and confectionary-blue Alpine chalet with a stained-glass penguin at the end looking out over the Transantarctic mountains. It was serviced by a Catholic priest and a protestant minister, and on Sunday morning I went to mass. The priest called us the Frozen Chosen. It was after this service that I met Ann Hawthorne, a photographer in her early forties who was over six feet tall with salt-and-pepper hair down to her waist. She came from North Carolina and spoke in a beguiling southern drawl. Ann was also on the Artists' and Writers' Program, and we saw a good deal of one another while we were at McMurdo. She had first come south to take pictures ten years previously, and on that trip she had fallen in love with a pilot and subsequently married him. It hadn't worked out as planned, and I got the feeling that she was back laying ghosts to rest. Ann had an eye for a party, and if we had spent any more time together than we did, we would have got into trouble.

'Hey, I've borrowed a tracked vehicle,' she said to me triumphantly one morning. 'I figured we could go to Cape Evans for the day and hang out in Scott's hut. It's about twelve miles along the coast. What d'you say, babe?'

'Can we drive over the sea ice, then?'

'Sure we can.'

'What happens if it gets thin?'

'We fall in. But that won't happen, because every so often we get out of the vehicle and drill the ice to test its thickness. If it's thinner than thirty inches, we turn back. Trust me.'

Cape Evans was the site of Scott's main hut on the *Terra Nova* expedition. It had almost pushed the smaller one I had visited on Hut Point out of the history books. Hut Point was not intended as a permanent 'home' and was never used as such. The Cape Evans hut, on the other hand, erected in January 1911, was occupied continuously for two years. In 1915 one of Shackleton's sledge parties from the ill-fated *Aurora* arrived, and they also lived in it intermittently for a couple of years. Preserved by the cold, and recently by the efforts of the New Zealand Antarctic Heritage Trust, it stands on its lonely cape, intact, like some icy Valhalla of the south.

Scott named the cape after Lieutenant Teddy Evans, later Admiral Sir Edward, who went on four Antarctic expeditions. He returned home sick in 1911 after almost dying of scurvy and exhaustion on the 750-mile march back to the hut from the top of the Beardmore Glacier. Two years later he went back to Antarctica in command of the *Terra Nova* to pick up Scott and the other men who had remained on the ice. As the ship sailed up to the hut, the officers' dining table was laid for a banquet. Evans, pacing the deck, was worried about the Northern Party. Then he spotted Campbell on shore. They had made it!

'Is everyone all right?' he yelled across the pack ice.

Campbell hesitated. 'The polar party have perished,' he shouted back.

Every death is the first death, and so it seemed, at that moment, to Teddy Evans.

*

For generations, the myth that had been created obscured the fact that Scott was a human being. Just as the image of the band on the *Titanic* playing 'Nearer My God to Thee' is cemented on to the British national consciousness, along with tuxedoed gentlemen standing to attention as water rises over the razor creases of their trousers, so Scott has been institutionalised as a national icon, and for many years criticising him was a heretical act. Yet he wasn't universally popular in Antarctica. Among the four he took on the last haul to the Pole, Titus Oates wrote home to his mother 'I dislike Scott intensely.' At times, Scott's leadership was questionable. When everything – food, tents, fuel and depots – was arranged for four-man units, at the eleventh hour he decided that five were to go to the Pole. The perfect hero of the great English myth never existed, just as our national emblems, the lion and the unicorn, never roamed the South Downs.

All the same, there is much that is heroic about Scott. His expeditions still constitute landmarks in polar travel. As a man, rather than a Navy captain, Scott was much more than a wooden product of his background. Like all the best people, he was beset by doubt. 'I shall never fit in my round hole,' he wrote to his wife Kathleen, and on another occasion, 'I'm obsessed with the view of life as a struggle for existence.' He was a good writer, especially towards the end of his journey. 'Will you grow to think me only fitted for the outer courtyard of your heart?' he asked Kathleen. The Antarctic possessed a virginity in his mind that provided an alternative to the spoiled and messy world, and he wrote in his diary about 'the terrible vulgarizing which Shackleton has introduced to the Southern field of enterprise, hitherto so clean and wholesome'.

Through his writings, Scott elevated the status of the struggle.

It was no longer man against nature, it was man against himself. The diaries reveal a sense of apotheosis: the terrible journey back from the Pole was a moral drama about the attainment of self-knowledge. Scott went to the mountaintop, there on the blanched wasteland. He failed to return from the last journey, but in that failure he found a far more precious success. Defeat on this earthly plane was transfigured. The journey becomes a quest for self-fulfilment, and Scott's triumph is presented as the conquering of the self.

Similarly, after George Mallory and Sandy Irvine disappeared into the mists of Everest twelve years after Scott perished, everyone quickly forgot what had actually happened and glorified the climbers' transcendental achievements. At their memorial service in St Paul's Cathedral, the Bishop of Chester used a quotation from the Psalms to establish a connection between Mallory and Irvine's climb and the spiritual journey upwards, referring to it 'as the ascent by which the kingly spirit goes up to the house of the Lord'. So it was, too, that out of the tent on the polar plateau rose the myth of the saintly hero.

By nimble sleight of hand in their portrayal of Scott, the mythmakers reversed the David and Goliath roles of Norway and Britain. Scott was the gentlemanly amateur who played the game and didn't rely on dogs. Amundsen, on the other hand, was a technological professional who cheated by using dogs. Frank Debenham, Scott's geologist on the *Terra Nova* expedition, wrote in his book *Antarctica: the Story of a Continent*, published in 1959, that both Scott and Shackleton deployed techniques which were slower, more laborious, and failed, but that to criticise them for doing it their way instead of Amundsen's 'is rather like comparing the man who prefers to row a boat across a bay with the man who hoists up a sail to help himself'. Scott's advocates made a virtue of the fact that he had hauled to the Pole without dogs or ponies, and they still do, but this is disingenuous. He had been perfectly prepared to use caterpillar motor-sledges and took three south on the *Terra Nova* (these were a failure). Furthermore, as Debenham himself wrote, 'The fact of the matter is that neither Scott nor Shackleton, the two great exponents of manhauling, understood the management of sledge dogs.'

As he lay dying, Scott somehow found the rhetorical language to invest the whole ghastly business with the currency of nobility.

This is his greatest achievement, and with it he paved the way for the making of the legend. 'Had we lived,' he wrote famously, 'I should have had a tale to tell of the hardihood, endurance, and courage of my companions which would have stirred the heart of every Englishman.' He even had the presence of mind to recognise the emotive value of altering 'To My Wife' on Kathleen's envelope to 'To My Widow'. In a few pages he scorched himself into the national consciousness. By the time the letters and diary reached home the spiritual and the national coalesced perfectly. *The Times* said of Scott's last venture, 'The real value of the expedition was spiritual, and therefore in the truest sense national . . . proof that we are capable of maintaining an Empire.' King George expressed the hope that every British boy could see photographs of the expedition, 'for it will help promote the spirit of adventure that made the empire'. On the wilder shores of journalism Scott actually became the nation: 'Like Captain Scott,' proclaimed *World's Work*, 'we are journeying in a cold world towards nothing that we know.' True enough.

Scott touched the imagination of the country and exemplified not just England but a strain of Edwardian manhood. Later, Apsley Cherry-Garrard, who was there, wrote of Scott and his dead men, 'What they did has become part of the history of England, perhaps of the human race, as much as Columbus or the Elizabethans, David, Hector or Ulysses. They are an epic.' In the Great War, Scott became a handy placebo for the soldiers floundering in muddy trenches. Over 100,000 officers and men in France alone saw expedition photographer Herbert Ponting's moving-picture film, and in his book *The Great White South*, Ponting quotes from the following letter despatched by a Forces chaplain ministering to the frontline troops.

I cannot tell you what a tremendous delight your films are to thousands of our troops. The splendid story of Captain Scott is just the thing to cheer and encourage them out here . . . The thrilling story of Oates' self-sacrifice, to try and give his friends a chance of 'getting through', is one that appeals to so many at the present time. The intensity of its appeal is realised by the subdued hush and quiet that pervades the massed audience of troops while it is being told. We all feel we have inherited from Oates and his comrades a legacy and heritage of inestimable value in seeing through our present work. We all thank you with very grateful hearts.

When Kathleen Scott died scores of crumpled letters from the front lines were found among her papers, the senders all telling her they could never have faced the dangers and hardships of the war had they not learned to do so from her dead husband's teaching. With Scott, they believed they could rise above it.

Would Scott have become the myth that he is had he lived? I doubt it. The most powerful hero is the dead hero, the one who never loses his teeth. Like Peter Pan, he must never grow old. It is central to the myth of Mallory and Irvine that they died on Everest. Lytton Strachey, who was passionate about Mallory and his Dionysian good looks, perceptively noted before the 1924 expedition even sailed from Birkenhead that the legend of Mallory would only survive if the climber died young. 'If he were to live,' Strachey wrote, 'he'll be an unrecognisable middle-aged mediocrity, probably wearing glasses and a timber toe.' Instead, Mallory became Sir Galahad, like Scott before him.

Though it is tempting to indulge the cliché that a national preference for dead heroes is peculiarly British, an examination of, say, Russian polar literature also reveals a large cast of heroic dead. Like most clichés, however, this one is woven with a thread of truth, and Scott would probably have had to stagger back to the hut to cut much ice with North Americans.

When Tryggve Gran, one of Scott's men, emerged from the tent on the plateau after he had seen the three frozen bodies which had lain there through the long polar night, he said that he envied them. 'They died having done something great,' he wrote. 'How hard death must be having done nothing.'[1]

*

The ice was more than four feet thick wherever we drilled it, and

---

[1] The importance of Scott's death was brilliantly illustrated in a seven-part Central Television series, *The Last Place on Earth* (screened on PBS in the States), based on Roland Huntford's book. Amundsen, back in Norway after his great triumph, is soaping himself in the bath. His brother and confidant appears in the doorway to tell him that Scott died on the journey back from the Pole. 'So he has won,' says the actor playing Amundsen quietly.

an hour after we set out for Cape Evans, around Big Razorback island, we lay down among the Weddell seals.

'Listen to that,' said Ann. It was a faint scraping sound, like hard cheese on a grater.

'The pups are weaned,' she announced. 'It's their teeth raking against the edge of the ice holes.'

Adult Weddells weigh up to 1,000 pounds and are able to live further south than any other seals because they can maintain an open hole in the ice with their teeth. Ann went off to photograph them doing it, and I pressed my ear to the ice and heard the adults underneath calling their ancient song, ululant and ineffably sad.

Later, I recognised the gabled ridged roof and weatherboard cladding of the hut in the distance. It was a prefabricated hut, made in England and shipped south in pieces. I once saw a picture of it taken when it was first erected, not at the foot of a smoking Mount Erebus but in a grimy urban street in Poplar in London's East End. The men had stitched quilts with pockets of seaweed to use as insulation between the walls.

When I pushed open the wooden door I smelt my grandmother's house when I was a child – coal dust and burnt coal – and it was chilly, as it used to be at six o'clock in the morning when I followed my grandfather downstairs to scrape out the grate. The Belmont Stearine candles Scott's men had brought were neatly stacked near the door, and the boxes said, 'made expressly for hot climates', which some people would say summed up their preparations. The wrappers bore the picture of a West Indian preparing something delicious on a fire under a palm tree. It was the familiarity of the surroundings which struck my English sensibility – blue-and-orange Huntley and Palmer biscuit boxes, green-and-gold tins of Lyle's golden syrup, blue Cerberos salt tubes and the shape of the label on Heinz tomato ketchup bottles. Atora, Lea and Perrins, Fry's, Rising Sun Yeast ('certain to rise'), Gillards *Real* Turtle Soup – the brand names cemented in our social history. I still lived with many of these products, and the continuum they provided intensified the hut experience. I remembered a very long novel by an American woman called Elizabeth Arthur who had spent some time on the ice. Describing the profoundly moving experience of visiting the hut, she talked about a 'Hunter' and Palmer biscuit box. To an English sensibility this sounds as odd as 'Heinzer' baked beans.

A single beam of sunlight fell on the bunk in Scott's quarters, the small space immortalised by Ponting and described by Teddy Evans as the 'Holy of Holies'. On the desk, someone – a good artist – had drawn a tiny bird in violet ink on the crisp ivory page of a pocket notebook. Unlike Shackleton, Scott separated the quarters of men and officers, and the difference is often deployed to illustrate their contrasting styles of leadership. Wayland Young, Baron Kennet of the Dene and Kathleen Scott's son by her second marriage, has set out a convincing defence of Scott's decision. As far as the state of class divisions in the Navy was concerned, Young wrote that it was 'unchanged for 1,000 years, so to complain about it now is no more interesting or original than to complain about it in the army of Wellington, Marlborough, Henry V or Alfred the Great'.

They were extremely resourceful. Clissold, the cook, rigged up a device whereby a small metal disc was placed on top of rising dough, and when it reached the right height it came into contact with another piece of metal, and an electrical circuit rang a bell next to his bunk. The battered books included Kipling (of course), and a tiny edition of *The Merry Wives of Windsor* held together with string, in the fly of which a spidery hand had inscribed Milton's 'When will the ship be here/Come sing to me.' There is something disingenuous about Scott's hut, however, just as there is about the myth. The mummified penguin lying open-beaked and akimbo next to a copy of the *Illustrated London News* had been placed there by the New Zealand Antarctic Heritage people, and Ponting's photographs show that Scott's desk is not the original (the replacement was brought over from the Cape Royds hut). The historic huts were often plundered in the early days. Richard Pape visited Cape Evans in 1959 with one of the American Operation Deep Freezes under Admiral Dufek. In his very bad book, *Poles Apart*, he records quite candidly that he pocketed 'a glass inkwell on which "R.F. Scott" had been painted, also a bottle of Indian ink marked "Wilson" '.

Still, I saw them everywhere. A gap in a row of cuphooks, the dented rubber of a Wellington boot tossed aside, a carefully re-rolled bandage, the whiff of Ponting's developing fluid in his tiny darkroom, a half-spent candle in a chipped candlestick – perhaps it was the whistling of the wind, but I swear I could have turned round and seen them tramping back, spent dogs at their heels.

Later, the public manipulated the myth according to its own needs and ends. A crackpot society called the Alliance of Honour, founded in 1903 and devoted to purity, had spawned flourishing branches in 67 countries by the 1930s. The Alliance was vigorously opposed to masturbation, and the following quotation is culled from its voluminous literature: 'We may safely assert that among the heroes of that dreadful journey from the South Pole there were no victims of the vice which the Alliance seeks to combat.'

Secondhand bookshops are rife with musty first editions of the diaries inscribed in a Sunday School teacher's best copperplate, rewarding a child for good attendance. I found a 1941 bus ticket pressed inside one of them. It was a tough time to be living in London, and perhaps the diaries helped. During the Second World War the calls of the legend were legion, and they were often voiced by cranks. In 1941 Kathleen received a letter from a woman in New York who said she had borne Scott's illegitimate child when she was fifteen. A handwritten note on the envelope said, 'The lady is now dead.'

A few years after the war crocodiles of schoolchildren marched through provincial towns and into cavernous cinemas to watch *Scott of the Antarctic*. John Mills had already played countless war heroes, so he was a prepacked role model. By the mid-fifties, however, liberals at least were suspicious of the myth and had lost faith in the concept of England. In Peter Vansittart's recent book of social and cultural commentary, *In the Fifties*, he recalls a game he devised during that period to test the objectivity of his intellectual chums. He would read out a passage from Scott's diaries, including 'We are showing that Englishmen can still die with a bold spirit, fighting it out to the end . . .' Assuming that Vansittart was being ironic, the audience tittered. Later he amended the reading to make it sound as if it had come from the Warsaw Ghetto in 1944, or from Mao Tsetung, and on those occasions his friends applauded respectfully.

Shibboleths were mocked. Scott became a cliche. In the Monty Python television sketch 'Scott of the Sahara', the captain fights a 25-foot electric penguin. Similarly, Scott appears as an astronaut in Tom Stoppard's play *Jumpers*, written in 1972. The first Englishman to reach the moon, Scott's triumph is overshadowed by the plight of his only colleague Astronaut Oates. Scott kicks Oates to the ground at the foot of the spacecraft ladder and pulls it in behind him with the words, 'I am going up now, I may be some time.'

Historical revisionism is as unavoidable as the grave: it pursues leading figures of any age long after their work on earth is done. In the 1970s, when imperialism was widely reviled, Roland Huntford published his joint biography *Scott and Amundsen* (called *The Last Place on Earth* in the States), a passionate book which sought to demolish the Scott myth, suggesting not only that Scott was mortal, but that he was an unpleasant character and a poor leader. According to Huntford, he used science only as an excuse to participate in the race, unlike Amundsen 'who did not stoop to use science as an agent of prestige'. Nobody had criticised Scott before, and Huntford did so comprehensively. Many felt inclined to agree with him, while the keepers of the flame would have had him sent to the Tower. The book whipped up a blizzard of angry protests, vitriolic reviews and a furious exchange of correspondence and 'statements' in national newspapers, including lengthy debate provoked by Huntford's assertion that Kathleen Scott had sex with Nansen while her husband was slogging up a glacier and was worried about becoming pregnant. The central argument was over how she recorded the arrival of her periods in her diary. How disappointing it had to come to that.

Wayland Young wrote an article refuting Huntford's criticism of Scott for *Encounter* magazine in May 1980. He demonstrates the weakness of portions of Huntford's scholarship. Others had pressed Huntford on the same points raised by Young, and in October 1979 the biographer was obliged to admit on national television that his description of Scott staring at Oates in the tent at the end to try to force him to his death was based on *intuition*. In short, he got carried away by his own argument. Prejudice is not necessarily fatal in a biography, however, and Huntford's book is intelligent, gripping, full of insight and elegantly written. I enjoyed it as much as any polar book I have read, and a good deal more than most of them. It is a pity that Huntford was quite so obsessed with the destruction of the legend, for if he had reined in his prejudices he could have produced a masterpiece.

A similar controversy raged in the Norwegian press after a book was published portraying Amundsen as a bounder and Scott a man worthy of beatification. Kåre Holt's *The Race*, published in English in 1974, was admittedly a novel; it was nonetheless a useful counterweight to Huntford's book. Bob Headland, archivist at the Scott Polar Research Institute, told me that he likes to keep the two volumes next to one another on the shelf, 'preferably with a layer of asbestos between them'.

'The Scandinavians', Huntford told me when I met him at Wolfson College in Cambridge for lunch in a dining hall smelling of boiled cauliflower, 'by and large set out from a country at ease with itself. They have no need for an ego boost. They are not play-acting. The Norwegian will always look for a glimpse of the sun, because he actually wants to be happy.' Self-delusion, he said, was the besetting sin of the British. 'Scott and Amundsen inhabited totally different mental words,' he added, leaning across the table conspiratorially. 'You mustn't be deluded by the fact that they were contemporaries. The Scandinavians live in a landscape which has enormous natural power, so that when they go to the polar regions it's sort of an extension of what they are.'

Huntford lived in Scandinavia for many years ('mainly because I like skiing'). He writes exceptionally well about polar scenery; so well that it is hard to imagine him not hankering to go south himself. When I put this to him, he prevaricated.

'No,' he said eventually. 'These are landscapes of the mind, you see.'

He had referred obliquely to a note written by Bowers on the back of one of Wilson's last letters; it apparently indicated that Bowers died last, but Huntford said the envelope had been suppressed by the people at Scott Polar Research Institute in order to maintain Scott's preeminence. When I asked them, they denied it. Who cares? I wanted to know about the power of the human spirit to transcend mortality, and what one human heart can learn from another, not whose aorta packed up first.

*

At McMurdo the project leaders were giving a series of weekly science lectures. An eminent geologist among them had developed theories on the prehistoric supercontinents in which Antarctica was attached to South America. His name was Ian Dalziel, and I found him nursing a whiskey in the Corner Bar.

'I used to be a respected geologist,' he said, 'but now I move continents around like armchairs.' His wife called it playing God. He was Scottish, had defected, but still displayed the characteristic dry wit of the Scots. He had an easy manner which was self-assured without being confident, and he was a repository of stories. He could remember the geologist who used live baby penguins as toilet paper and reported that it was important to keep the beaks out of the way.

As nature's satire on humanity, it was part of the penguin job description to provide mirth for the colonising hordes. Stories from the days before anyone had heard of environmental awareness were legion. Officers would paint bowties on penguin breasts and set the birds loose in the messroom, navy construction workers flung them down seal holes 'to watch them shoot up', and the 1956 Personnel Manual for Williams Field Air Operating Facility on Ross Island laid out procedures for obtaining a stuffed penguin. Now, abusing a penguin carried a stiffer fine than molesting a person.

*

I found myself reading a good deal about deserts while I was in the south, and at that time I was engrossed in Thesiger's *Arabian Sands*. Like Antarctica, the heart of the desert was a blank in time, devoid of human history. Both places could be perceived as a gigantic reflection of all you had known of emptiness and loss, if you were minded to internalise the landscape in that way. I felt the reverse. Even sitting in a base which resembled a small Alaskan mining town, I had similar intimations about the cold southern desert to those which Thesiger had in the hot sands of Arabia. 'Here in the desert', he wrote, 'I had found all that I had asked; I knew that I should never find it again.'

I finished the book in my office late one night, and the light from the Anglepoise lamp spilled into the dark corridor. Hans, a Danish fish biologist on Art's project, came in and installed himself on the spare chair. We must have been the only people in the building, and it was as silent as a mausoleum. He made small talk for a few minutes, but he was fidgeting, as if he were trying to release an object that had got stuck between the layers of his garments. When he started saying what he had come to say all along, it spewed out like a torrent of coins from a slot machine.

He had fallen in love five weeks before coming south.

'Britta is fifteen years younger than I, but one day after I met her, I was in love,' he said in his musical Danish accent. 'The next five weeks were like rushing towards a waterfall, becoming faster all the time. I find a branch to cling to and everything would be OK for a while, but then I would be swept away again. Then comes the day when no branches are left.'

He wrote every day, and once a week he sent a present, too, a commitment which must have tested his imagination as there weren't any shops except the navy store, and that offered a limited range of out-of-date film, tampax and Y-fronts.

'I am an all or nothing man,' he said seriously, zipping himself into his vermilion parka and setting off to write another instalment.

CHAPTER FOUR

The Other Side of Silence

... A thousand visages
Then mark'd I, which the keen and eager cold
Had shaped into a doggish grin; whence creeps
A shivering horror o'er me, at the thought
Of those frore shallows. While we journey'd on
Toward the middle, at whose point unites
All heavy substance, and I trembling went
Through that eternal chillness ...

Dante, from *The Divine Comedy*

A SERIES of arid valleys run off the Antarctic continent opposite
Ross Island, created by the advances and retreats of glaciers
through the Transantarctic mountains. These dry valleys, free of
ice for about four million years, are dotted with partially frozen
saltwater basins and form one of the most extreme deserts in the
world. NASA wanted to test robotic probes there before sending
them on interplanetary missions.
   'It's as close to Mars as we can get,' one of the engineers said.
   At the orientation conference in Virginia I had met Brian
Howes and Dale Goehringer, coastal ecologists working at Lake
Fryxell, the first of the three frozen lakes in the Taylor Valley.
They had invited me to stay at their camp, so three weeks after I
arrived in Antarctica I checked out a set of equipment at the Berg
Field Center, sorting through tents, thermarests and crampons and
painting my initials on a shiny blue ice axe, and one morning I
hitched a lift in a helicopter resupplying a camp farther up the
valley.

Less than an hour after leaving McMurdo, the pilot put down on a rocky strip of land between a parched mountain and a large frozen lake. He signalled for me to get out. It had not rained here for two million years.

A hundred yards from the edge of the lake a figure darted out of an arched rigid-frame tent known as a Jamesway. I had heard a good deal about Jamesways. They were ubiquitous in long-term American field camps and constituted the heart of camp, too, like the kitchen in a farmhouse. An invention of the military, Jamesways are portable insulated tents of standard width and height but variable length – to make them longer, you add more arches. They have board floors and a proper door, and in Antarctica are heated by drip-oil Preway burners.

The figure trotting towards me from the Fryxell Jamesway had long straight hair the colour of cinnamon sticks, and she was waving. It was Dale. At home she ran a lab at the Woods Hole Oceanographic Institute in Massachusetts.

'Welcome to Fryxell!' she said. 'We've been looking forward to seeing you. I washed my hair specially.' Taking my arm, she propelled me towards the Jamesway.

Inside, a man was slumped over a mug at a long table next to an inflated plastic palm tree. He was short, with a cloud of tangled black hair and a hat like a thermal doughnut.

'This is LD,' said Dale. 'It stands for Little Dave, and he's a grad student in marine biology. He's been up for thirty hours.' LD raised his head to flash me a Mephistophelean smile before resuming the slumped position. On the back of the door they had hung an Annoy-o-meter with an arrow which could be swivelled from Vaguely Irritating through to Murderously Provocative.

'Who's the baby?' I asked, pointing at a large chubby face smiling down from the canvas wall of the Jamesway.

'That's Mary,' said Dale. 'She's one year old. I planned the birth so that I only missed one field season – this is my eighth. Season, I mean.' She put two insulated mugs of coffee on the table. 'Before I forget – all waste from the dry valleys is retrograded to McMurdo, and that includes grey water and human waste.'

'What's grey water?' I asked.

'Dishwashing water,' she said. 'We empty it into a drum out the back. As far as going to the bathroom is concerned, there's an outhouse we use behind here' – she gestured to the back of the

Jamesway – 'and in it a funnel connects to a drum. There's a shit can for solids. And you need to take a pee bottle with you when you go for a walk, too.'

'So you can't just pee on the ground?' I asked. 'Even when you're miles from camp?'

'Nope. We're trying to maintain a pristine environment.' There was a pause. 'Listen,' she said in a low voice, as if she were about to breach the Official Secrets Act. 'Take my advice. When you want to go to the bathroom in camp, use a pee bottle and decant the contents, rather than struggling to pee into the funnel. A tall man fixed the funnel in position to suit his own aim.' She sat back in her chair. 'God,' she said, 'it's good to have another woman here.'

Going to the bathroom: I wondered if there was any lavatorial situation Americans deemed too primitive for this dignified term. I had even seen a translation of the Bible in which King Saul entered a cave 'to go to the bathroom'.

Later, I put up my tent among a sprinkling of others behind four small laboratory huts (it was typical of their attitude to their work that the labs were more luxurious than the accommodation). At the far end of the lake the Canada Glacier, grubby with dust, blocked the northern horizon. Much of Antarctica is officially classified as a desert, and nothing proved it more effectively than the salt efflorescences on the shoreline of Lake Fryxell, thin white crusts like the salt pans of northern Chile. Some ponds in the Dry Valleys are so saline that they won't freeze at minus sixty degrees Celsius, and the water is like molasses. On others the ice crusts, like lenses, concentrate so much solar energy that the bottom layers can reach temperatures of twenty-five degrees Celsius (or 77 degrees Fahrenheit).

In the afternoon I strapped on my crampons and walked out over the ice with LD and a hydrologist called Roland (LD said, 'I do mud, he does water'). The lake was surrounded by a thin layer of 'moat ice' which, as it was still early December, was frozen solid. By late January the moat ice would be gone. The fifteen-foot ice lid which covered the rest of the lake never melted. It was filled with tiny white bubbles and twisted into apocalyptic configurations – a fall might land you face down on a sword reminiscent of Excalibur. We did fall, though not on our faces. A wrong foot would not send us crashing into the glacial water, just down a foot or so through a pocket of blue neon air and on to the next layer of ice.

In the small hut in the middle of the lake, LD and Roland fiddled with their instruments.

'The lake was formed about 1,200 years ago by meltwater from the Canada Glacier,' LD explained. 'It's the forty-eight feet of water underneath the ice which interests us. The permanent ice lid facilitates a uniquely stable water column.' When they shut the door of the hut, natural fluorescent light shone up through the hole in the board floor. They had eighteen instruments in the lake at that time, and when they brought water up from the bottom it was so full of sulphides that it smelt of rotten eggs. While they pumped, they stowed the tubes inside their shirts. Like a lot of Antarctic scientists, they were engaged in a constant battle against the big freeze. LD showed me his mud; he called it 'very young rock'.

'What I'm into', he drawled, 'is phytoplankton on their long journey to oil and rock.'

As the light never changed, they were tied to the clock only by their daily radio schedule with McMurdo. Although they always ate dinner together, it had to be convened well in advance by radio and might be at four in the morning.[1] After a day and a half without sleep their eyes grew dull, like old mirrors. Brian, the team leader, said that his body clock had died years ago.

It was an easy rhythm to follow. If I wasn't out on the lake with one of them I sat outside the Jamesway listening to the moat ice crackling and watching the tobacco-yellow plumes of Mount Erebus in the distance staining the cobalt sky. I took my turn to make water, dragging a cart over to the frozen moat and chipping ice into pans. The salts had been frozen out, and the water tasted delicious.

I spent a whole day out on the lake with Steve, an oceanographic consultant, and George, a benthic biologist in his fifties. 'I'm happiest in the first ten inches of sediment,' said George. The pair dived together off Nantucket, and they both enjoyed *getting away* to Antarctica.

'It's like stepping out of your life for a few months,' said Steve.

---

[1] They free cycled, to use the standard physiological term.

The seventh member of the team was Craig, a bacteriologist studying photosynthesis cycles.

'Looking under these lakes is literally like going back in time,' he said, 'It's a microbial wonderland.'

Brian was a marsh and coastal ecologist and a bio-geochemist. He was much revered by the team, but I only ever saw him exerting authority when he stood outside the back door of the Jamesway beating a large frying pan against an even larger saucepan in order to wake up LD and Roland. Brian had his finger on the pulse of camp dynamics, and if he got tired, the whole camp began to deteriorate. The fact that it was a harmonious, well-oiled camp with its own distinct culture was in large measure a tribute to him.

One afternoon I crouched next to Brian in the hut in the middle of the lake.

'Nitrates are the single biggest cause of coastal erosion and pollution,' he said. 'That's why we're here, finding out more about them. Oceans do have an assimilative capacity for nitrates, but they shouldn't be introduced beyond that capacity. Many areas of the world are already way beyond their limit, and they're in big trouble.'

Brian believed that science in Antarctica meant adapting to the environment, not foisting techniques on to it. He had worked out that using paper plates was ecologically more sensible than burning fuel to melt water to wash plastic plates, so he had installed a trash compactor in the Jamesway. He and Dale had fought not to have snowmobiles at their camp. Like all passionate ecologists, they had made themselves unpopular. But they knew they were right.

'No amount of money', he told me as he pulled a lurid intestinal tube from the soupy water, 'could create an environment like this.'

The VXE-6 helicopter crews – the airborne squadron of the U.S. Navy – called in almost every day. VXE-6 did most of the flying for the U.S. programme. They called themselves the Ice Pirates. I called them Testosterone Airways. Sometimes they brought fresh food and they always brought news from McMurdo, which was known as Porcelain Land. If they couldn't call by they would buzz us, swooping low over camp, and they kept up a running competition to see who could drop a roll of newspapers nearest the doormat, a gesture only rendered more touching by the fact that the papers were weeks old and never read.

One day I climbed the lowest peak of the Asgaard range behind camp, and from the summit I could see the top of the glaciers at either end of the lake. I could see Roland, too, squatting outside the hut in the middle of the lake and spooling out cable. This was known as being the 'mule'. The cable ran into the hut, where it was winched into the water by LD. I switched on my radio so I could listen to them. Roland was the only team member who hadn't been south before, and he had taken over from LD as general factotum, a role he accepted with equanimity, even when Brian staked the use of him for two days in a bet with a project leader from a neighbouring camp. LD's speciality was self-deprecatory humour accompanied by facial contortions. One of his typical anecdotes featured an old man out walking with his small grandson. The man had spotted LD squatting on the steps of the Woods Hole lab where he worked, smoking a cigarette, and as if delivering a moral lesson of some import the old man told the child, 'See him? He's a bum.'

'That's enough cable now,' LD was saying to Roland. 'Stop! For Christ's sake, stop! What's your problem?'

'I have stopped,' whined Roland.

'Why didn't you stop when I first asked? Got a wedgie or something?'

'What's a wedgie?' I interrupted, keen to learn a new scientific term.

'It's when your underwear rides up,' said LD.

Later, I hiked over to the face of the Canada. When I sat on the ground and ran a handful of soil through my fingers, I half expected to find a flint arrowhead – some small sign of a human past. What I heard there went beyond quietness. It was George Eliot's 'roar which lies on the other side of silence'. In a famous passage in *Middlemarch* she wrote that it was like hearing the grass grow or the squirrel's heart beat, but that our ears didn't pick it up because we walked about 'well-wadded with stupidity'. She had never been south, of course. She didn't need to go.

The scorched Atacama Desert of northern Chile kept flashing into my mind. Two years before, I had travelled through it for weeks, much of it in a jeep with a peripatetic Australian man I had tripped over in the corridor of a doss-house. It was as hostile as Antarctica. Nothing lived there, and just as it did now, the cone of a volcano always hovered on the periphery of our vision.

Despite the candent heat and throbbing air and the dust that settled on us and our possessions like fur, it was a curiously agreeable trip, as if our minds had flattened out like the baked plain. Sometimes, after hundreds of miles of caramel pampa, we came across geoglyphs on the desiccated hillsides, crude drawings by an unknown and long-gone tribe. Although they had been crushed like a seashell under the hoof of a *conquistador's* horse, the tribe had left their imprint, and it was as if the desert still belonged to them. Here in Antarctica there was no concept of ownership. I was travelling to the sound of a different drumbeat. If Antarctica had something to teach me that was more important than nitrate data, it was not about humanity. The landscape drew my thoughts away from worldly things, away from the thousand mechanical details of my outward life. I had found the place where, loosed from my cultural moorings, I could find the space to look for the higher power, whatever it was, that loomed over the snowfields.

*

I had a secret plan not to return to McMurdo immediately, but instead to hop up the Taylor Valley from camp to camp. With some help from Dale and a few conversations over the radio, I arranged to hitch a ride up to Lake Hoare. LD and Roland had been asking me for something English, so the night before I left I whipped up a bread-and-butter pudding. The seditious effects of a heavy meal resulted in three of them falling asleep at the table.

'Wake up!' shouted Brian at two o'clock in the morning. 'Time for the after-dinner entertainment.'

They had to retrieve a cassette sampler which had been lying under the ice all winter, its eighty hydraulically-fired syringes busily collecting water samples. It was the big event of the season and the only time that I saw all seven of them on the ice at the same time. At four o'clock, after a short burst of intensive activity, most of it under a space blanket, the instrument emerged like a newborn baby. It was a prototype instrument which cost in the region of $18,000.

'What happens if I slip?' drawled LD as he grasped one end of the instrument and negotiated a sharp overhang of ice.

'Well,' said Brian, 'it would be like tossing your BMW off a bridge. Oh – and you wouldn't have a job any more.'

The camp at Lake Hoare was at the near end of the lake itself, in the lee of the Canada Glacier. When I arrived, the residents were hovering around outside the outhouse, as the toilet had just exploded. It was a propane-fuelled piece of equipment known in the valleys as a rocket shitter, and on this occasion it had backfired, causing a loud explosion which it was feared could interfere with seismic data.

An early model of the rocket shitter once caused the Heavy Shop at McMurdo to burn to the ground. There were no fatalities, but the new fire engine, which was inside the Shop at the time, was lost. Even the rocket convenience, however, had not acquired the notoriety of a high-tech eco-toilet introduced, and swiftly phased out, in the eighties. It was known as the Stealth Bomber.

The camp at Lake Hoare was the most sophisticated in the Taylor Valley, with a smart new hut fitted with a kitchen, and, predictably enough, it was devoid of character. It did have solar panels, however, which powered the laptops, and it meant that a generator rarely blighted the silence. The eight residents of the Hoare House (as they themselves inevitably called it) were graduate students working with the Long Term Ecological Research programme, a National Science Foundation global project.

I put up my tent near the others and walked out on to the lake. It was named after Ray Hoare, a member of a team from Victoria University of Wellington who had worked in the Dry Valleys in the 1960s. There were some photographs of them in the hut, and even bundled up in all their gear they looked like Hermann's Hermits. Some of the pictures showed them pulling each other stark naked over the lake in sledges. It was frontier territory then, the days of mapless land and nameless places.

The hut was divided down the middle, one half containing the kitchen and a long table, and the other a set of bunks and a couple of desks. The kitchen window looked straight at the cliff of the glacier, fissured with slits like the walls of a medieval castle. Although chunks of ice (which they called glacier berries) regularly fell off the ice cliff and were used to make water, everyone was never the less acutely aware that water was a precious commodity. When I began washing the dishes after dinner someone piped up, 'Hey, how come you get to wash your hands?'

In the evening, people drifted off to their tents or lay in the bunks in the hut. The camp was more a collection of individuals than a team; you could feel it straight away. I went to bed early, and when I opened my bag I found a cloth ration pouch inscribed with my name and the words 'from all your friends at Lake Fryxell'. Inside they had put a sweatshirt from their institution, a sew-on patch, bars of chocolate and other treats.

Everyone seemed to be feeling better in the morning; they talked to each other in polysyllables, anyway. A helicopter arrived with the post, and it took away the charred rocket toilet. One of the students received an advent calendar in the post. It was already 9 December and most of the windows had popped open in transit, causing the chocolate animals lurking underneath to slip to the bottom, disintegrate and turn magnolia white on their passage through multitudinous temperature changes.

Two scientists appeared with the helicopter, and one, a snow and ice physicist and mountaineer called Ed, was planning to hike up the valley to his camp at Lake Bonney later that afternoon. When he asked me if I wanted to go with him, I leapt at the chance as I was longing to travel overland. It turned out to be one of the best walks of my life – and of his.

I left my tent and sleeping gear behind, and someone agreed to put it on the next helicopter to McMurdo. We strode off up Lake Hoare, the sky smeared with cloud like a lazily cleaned pane of glass and Ed delivering diatribes on ice formation. At the far end Hoare blended imperceptibly into Lake Chad. One of the early explorers got diarrhoea there, and the story goes that the lake was named after the brand of toilet paper favoured by the expedition. Chad in turn petered out into moraine. The bank of black debris, pushed along by the Suess Glacier, blocked our way up the valley. Ed, who had climbed Denali and in the Himalaya and had spent half his life in the wilderness, told stories about falling into crevasses. His words bounced back at us from the wall of the Suess, like voices calling in a dream. We passed a mummified young seal on the moraine, its adolescent form coated with a mossy green fur.

'You are now', said Ed slowly and dramatically, 'in a place which knows no degradation.'

I know a good metaphor when it leaps out at me and this was the perfect illustration of the timelessness so often associated with Antarctica. As an American journalist who came south with the U.S. programme in the fifties wrote, 'Antarctica knows no dying.'

Propped up in my sleeping bag the previous night, I had written a letter to Jeremy Lewis, the Patron of my expedition. We had often talked about the symbolic properties of Antarctica. 'Can't help thinking I'm in Never-Never Land,' I wrote. The absence of decay, such a salient characteristic of my surroundings, reinforced my perception of the continent as a kind of Shangri-La (the residents of which enjoyed perpetual youth – also a key element in the legend of the dead Antarctic explorers), or an Eden shorn, by its absence of an indigenous population, of the pain of the human condition. Jeremy had steadfastly refused to accept that the notion of Antarctica as Arcadia was anything but bizarre, definitive proof (as if further evidence were required) that I was 'an odd fish'.

'An Eden has to be lush,' he would protest as we downed glasses of wine at crowded literary parties to which we may or may not have been invited. 'Comfort and the abundance of nature and warmth are its intrinsic properties. Think of the centuries of visual representations – all verdant and pastoral. Have you ever seen an Arcadia strewn with blocks of ice and peopled by indistinguishable characters with iced-up beards and swaddled in thermals?' Then he would extend his glass-holding hand in the direction of a passing waiter.

When I got there, I knew I was right. Everything was a symbol, in the context of Eden, and it made no difference whether the setting consisted of rolling green fields or thousands of miles of ice. The discomfort inevitably caused by a hostile environment like Antarctica was irrelevant. I did see it as paradise. When he received my letter, Jeremy wrote back with the grudging concession, 'I suppose James Hilton's original Shangri-La was reached via near-Antarctic extremities of cold.' It seemed like a small victory.

Ed led the way up an ice slope to the defile on one side of the Suess and we hiked along a narrow path next to walls of beaten ice which led to a rocky escarpment and down to Mummy Pond. Ed wanted to 'get a feel for the ice', and he knelt down on the pond as if he were bowing to Mecca. He had told me earlier that for anyone who studies ice, coming to Antarctica was like making the hajj. 'The history of the planet is calibrated in the ice,' he said.

He had been an English graduate before turning to science, and tried to persuade me that mathematics was a language like any other language, even stopping, when it got complicated, to draw equations in the sugar snow with his ice axe.

The skyline of the Transantarctics was now straight ahead of us, and over to the right loomed the Matterhorn, marked on Ed's map in pencil as the Doesn't Matterhorn. As we continued over rippling plateaux of coarse alluvial sand between vast sculpted, triangular, wind-formed rocks Ed said, 'Not many people have seen this.' He turned to me with a broad smile, hand extended. 'Here's to it!'

Then we began the approach to Lake Bonney, the twin peaks ahead the only thing between us and the polar plateau. These triumphal gateways of promise were backlit against a pearly blue sky, and the dimpled Taylor Glacier at the end of the lake was lit up above the dark, brooding opacity of the moraine. In front of this scene shimmered the lake, sheets of cracked and rippled frosted blue, and ribboned crystals imprisoned in the ice glimmered like glowworms. It was swathed in light pale as an unripe lemon. The scene said to me, 'Do not be afraid.' It was like the moment when I pass back the chalice after holy communion.

It had taken five-and-a-quarter hours, though we had stopped regularly for ice-inspections, and by 9.30 we were picking our way along the soft mud on the edge of the lake towards the camp, diminutive in the distance.

When we arrived, a tall figure carrying a case of beer stopped and leant against the door frame of the Jamesway. 'Here come the explorers!' he shouted, and Ed called back, 'I found a writer!' The man was the project leader at Lake Bonney, and his name was John Priscu. I had met him at the conference in Virginia, and he had immediately invited me up to see his camp. It was his eleventh season at Bonney, and he said that when he got out of the helicopter, it was like coming home. He had officially named a number of the topographical features after colleagues who had worked with him there, 'so they're still here'.

We all shook hands, and he ushered us inside. Four people were sitting around a large table, and the sound of taped jazz and peals of laughter filled the Jamesway. If it had been in an advertisement, a log fire would have been roaring in a grate and a large sheepdog snoozing on a rug.

John was a veteran Antarctic microbiologist, and he was studying the plankton in the lakes.

'These lakes are unique all the way from the ice on the top to the plankton at the bottom,' he said, handing me a beer. 'I can't figure out what's going on down there. Some of these lakes are frozen all the way to the bottom, for God's sake, and we don't know why. I'm going to keep coming back until I understand it.' He paused, and slurped at his own beer. 'We probably never will understand it – but we're learning.'

He was forty-two, had gone to school at Our Lady of Las Vegas, and played guitar in a rock band. I found out later that he also plied a trade as an Antarctic tattoo artist and ear piercer. He had tattooed three people at Bonney using a needle for repairing Scott tents, and pierced four ears.

'So, what's it like being a Fingee?' he asked me when I sat down.

'What's a fingee?' I asked suspiciously.

'Fucking New Guy!' said John. 'Like Ed here.'

'I'm not a guy, to start with,' I said.

'Everyone's a guy here!'

He had chosen the site for the camp himself, in 1989. His Jamesway had been used in the Korean War, and he claimed that the holes in the canvas at one end had been made by bullets. A notice over the door said, 'Good morning scientists! It's a good day for science!', and next to a dartboard beneath it someone had duct-taped the label from a tin of California Girl peaches. All over Antarctica people stuck up images of heat, sunshine and tropical landscapes. They reminded me of the call of whales for a lost world. The debris of human occupation had spread all over the Jamesway like creepers in a greenhouse – postcards with curling edges, bits of rope on old hooks, broken mobiles, Larson cartoons (indigenous to the American academic community), baseball caps, foot powder containers filled with plastic flowers, an inflatable sheep called a Lov Ewe and Christmas cards strung along the arched ceiling, their messages long since forgotten. The gas fridge was full of water samples and food was stored on the floor.

Two Kiwi scientists had arrived that day from Lake Vanda in the Wright Valley, which was next along from the Taylor. Clive ran a quasi-governmental environmental hydrology institute in Christchurch. He was acute and articulate with very clear eyes, and his colleague Mark was amiable and quiet. The pair of them had known John for more than a decade, and it was a great reunion.

'I wish I still had my old hut,' Clive said, looking round the Jamesway. The original Lake Vanda hut had been pulled down, and in its place Clive had been given a freezer-box style modern version from which any trace of personality was erased like a palimpsest at the beginning of each new season.

We ate a pot of bean stew, drank a case of beer, and then a bottle of bourbon appeared. Two women graduate students were working at Bonney at that time. One of them, a tall, feline individual called Cristina, was the target of a good deal of teasing, to which she retaliated in kind. John's favourite story was that on her regular trips down to base Cristina had begun stockpiling free condoms from the McMurdo medical centre. It wasn't that she needed them in Antarctica, she said, but that she never knew when they might come in handy at home, and as they were free – hey, she was a grad student. Arriving back at Bonney one day she had stepped out of the helicopter, dug her hand in her pocket to retrieve a glove and inadvertently brought out a handful of condoms which sprayed all over the helipad, whipped into the air by the blades and settling gently over her shoulders like confetti.

Clive had disappeared outside for ten minutes. 'Look,' he said when he came back in. 'We should drink this whiskey with glacier ice,' and he deposited an extremely large and alarmingly blue ice cube on the table. John took to it with an ice axe.

'What do you think?' asked Clive, after we had added chunks of glacier ice to our mugs.

'Delicious,' I said.

'Lake ice is more delicious,' said Ed, who referred to water as 'liquid ice'. With that, lake ice was fetched, and a treatise on the relative merits and properties of each type of ice hastened the disappearance of the whiskey.

The conversation moved on to drilling into the lake. Penetrating ice, yards thick, to get at the water below it posed interminable problems in those temperatures, and scientific minds were much occupied with it. The stories and their permutations were endless – about copper coils carrying heated glycol, about instruments freezing, about the advantages of hand drills. The four men shared a deep sense of the absurdity of their situation, floundering around on frozen lakes at seventy-seven degrees south. It was obvious that they all could have gone on yarning for ever.

John suddenly turned to me.

'What's your impression, then? Of Antarctica?'

'Well,' I said slowly, 'I have a million impressions.'

'Don't you have one overwhelming impression?'

I thought about that.

'I feel as if I'm getting to know a person. It's like having a love affair – I'm finding out more and more and more, it's all different and overwhelming and intoxicating, and I don't know where it's going to end.'

'Ha!' he said. 'I used to feel like that.'

*

I slept in a Scott tent overlooking the lake, and woke to a perfect spring day. Clive and Mark were already out on the ice, struggling with their instruments. We sat outside drinking coffee, and watched them. John was stretched out on the rocky shore.

'Did you notice,' he said, 'that when I got up to go to bed at five o'clock this morning Clive said, "Oh, can't take the pace, eh?" After fourteen years, it's still a pissing contest.' He laughed loudly.

I was gratified that anyone could live so patently at ease in an Antarctic environment. It seemed to like people, up there. It liked him, anyway. Even Ed, on his first trip, commented that he 'didn't feel like a foreigner'.

Later, when everyone went out to take samples, I walked up the valley. The 1:250,000 map I carried in my pocket was bisected by a jagged line marked '*Limit of compilation*', and the half to the left of the Taylor Glacier was blank. I had reached the end of the map.

I hitched a lift out on a helicopter three days later, at five o'clock in the afternoon. I had just taken a bread-and-butter pudding out of the oven. The helicopter crew were revving up for Saturday night, and as I waved to a diminishing Ed and John I heard the pilots discussing a girl over the headsets.

'Is she pretty?' one asked.

'I've been here so long I've forgotten what pretty is,' replied the other.

CHAPTER FIVE

The Naked Soul of Man

On passing our winter quarters at Cape Royds we all turned out to give three cheers, and to take a last look at the place where, in spite of discomforts and hardships, we had spent so many happy days. We watched the little hut, which had been our home for a year that must always live in our memories, fade away in the distance with feelings almost of sadness, and there were few men aboard who did not cherish a hope that some day they might again live strenuous days under the shadow of mighty Erebus.

Shackleton, from *The Heart of the Antarctic*

AT TEN O'CLOCK on Easter Monday morning, 1916, a diminutive wooden boat lurched off a rock shelf on one of the islands to the north of the Antarctic Peninsula and into the angry Southern Ocean, immediately tossing two of the men on board into the broth. Within minutes the freezing waters of a roller were pouring through the plughole. Standing on the sandless and wind-whipped beach behind, a tall Anglo-Irishman was calmly making final preparations before himself climbing into the boat. His name was Ernest Shackleton.

The two sodden men were pushed ashore with an oar, the anchor was dropped, the hole was plugged with a filthy handkerchief until the real plug was found, stores and over a ton of ballast were stowed, and at half-past twelve Shackleton gave the order to set sail. For 137 days the twenty-two men left behind grew blubbery on seal and penguin underneath a pair of upturned boats, watching themselves grow old as the chance of rescue, slim at the outset, shrank to an almost imperceptible filament of hope. The story of their rescue is the greatest epic in the history of Antarctica.

The Imperial Trans-Antarctic Expedition had set sail aboard *Endurance* from London's East India Docks on 1 August 1914, three days before Britain declared war on Germany. The plan was that a party led by Shackleton would sledge across Antarctica, starting from the Weddell Sea, while a team on the other side of the continent laid depots for them. But in January the ship was caught in the pack ice of the Weddell Sea 'like an almond in a chocolate bar'.

'Almost like a living creature', wrote Shackleton during the painful weeks of ebbing hope as he watched his ship die, 'she resisted the forces that would crush her.' When she finally went down, Frank Worsley, her skipper, recorded in his diary, 'When one knows every nook and corner of one's ship as we did, and has helped her time and again in the fight that she made so well, the actual parting was not without its pathos, quite apart from one's own desolation, and I doubt if there was one amongst us who did not feel some personal emotion when Sir Ernest, standing on top of the look-out [a platform they had rigged up on the ice], said somewhat sadly and quietly, "She's gone, boys." '

They were each allowed to take off two pounds of personal possessions, and these they buried in snowholes. Shackleton himself tossed a handful of gold sovereigns from his pocket on to the ice and picked up a slim volume of Browning's poetry. 'I throw away trash', he said, 'and am rewarded with golden inspirations.'

For five months, then, the twenty-eight drifted on ice floes for two thousand miles, tents and all, and when the chance came they travelled for six days in the three small lifeboats from the *Endurance* until they reached Elephant Island, an outpost of the South Shetlands. On this brutal journey, Shackleton did not sleep for a hundred hours.

Even then he spoke of the beauties of the sea, and of anxieties dwindling to nothing amid those splendours.

When they landed on Elephant Island, Frank Hurley, the expedition photographer, recorded that they were more dead than alive, and that many of them could no longer row. Later Shackleton, whom they called the Boss, wrote in his book *South*, 'The smiles and laughter, which caused cracked lips to bleed afresh, and the gleeful exclamations at the sight of two live seals on the beach, made me think for a moment of that glittering hour of childhood when the door is open at last and the Christmas tree in all its wonder bursts upon the vision.'

The southern winter was already upon them, and Perce Blackborow, the man who had joined the *Endurance* as a stowaway, had his frostbitten toes amputated.[1] The men took to referring to their prison as 'Hell-of-an-Island'. There was no hope of a chance rescue, so no alternative but to send one of the lifeboats to the whaling stations on South Georgia 700 miles away. From there, a vessel could be found to fetch the stranded men. Before the *Endurance* sank, its captain, Frank Worsley, a New Zealander and an officer in the merchant navy, had worked out the courses and distances from the South Orkneys and Elephant Island to South Georgia, the Falklands and Cape Horn. Of the three battered lifeboats, the *James Caird* offered the least horrifying option, and they finished caulking the seams with Marston's artist's paint and seal blood, stripping the two other wretched boats for parts. These new additions included an extra sail, which brought the total to three. The *James Caird*, named after the expedition's main sponsor, was twenty-two feet long and her height above the water was two feet two inches: not a great deal higher than a bath. She had been built to Worsley's specifications in Poplar, East London, from Baltic pine, American elm and English oak. After the *Endurance* went down, the shipwright fitted the little boat with a pump made from the casing of the ship's compass, and two men laboured over a blubber stove with canvas and needles to fashion a cover for the makeshift cabin.

Six of them went, and Worsley was at the helm. Before they left, Shackleton issued instructions to Frank Wild, the leader of the stranded party, to the effect that if relief had not arrived in six months, when the whaling station opened on Deception Island, Wild was to assume the boat had gone down and set out himself.

Worsley recorded in his diary that on the first evening, with the

---

[1] Blackborow was a man of few words, but when finally he got home to Wales he was asked to give a talk at the YMCA Boys' Club in Newport. Speaking of the period after the loss of the ship, he said, 'I like to think of our leader as I recall him at this time. His hopes and ambitions had all been shattered, yet he was cheerful and went out of his way to impart some cheerfulness to others. He had a genius for keeping men in good spirits, and, need I say more, we loved him like a father.'

Southern Cross overhead, Shackleton sent the rest in to sleep and the two of them 'snuggled close together all night', relentlessly inundated by waves and 'holding north by the stars that swept in glittering procession over the Atlantic towards the Pacific . . . While I steered, his arm thrown over my shoulder, we discussed plans and yarned in low tones. We smoked all night – he rolled cigarettes for us both, a job at which I was unhandy.' They had one compass, and it was faulty. Shackleton confided that if any of the twenty-two perished, he would feel like a murderer. Worsley's account of how he navigated by dead reckoning beggars belief. He concluded his story, 'I often recall with proud affection memories of those hours with a great soul.'

Tom Crean, a petty officer in the navy, was in charge of the 'kitchen'. He was obliged to light the primus stove while bent double and jam it between his and another man's legs to keep it steady. There was no room for anyone to sit upright and eat their hoosh, the standard Antarctic meal of a dehydrated meat protein mixture dissolved in hot water. It was usually followed by a sledging biscuit, some Streimer's Nutfood and a few sugarlumps. By the third day everything, with the exception of matches and sugar in watertight tins, was irredeemably soaked. The men's feet and legs, immersed almost constantly, were already frostbitten and swollen. They had rations, water and oil for thirty days. Apart from that, they didn't have much, except methylated spirits for the stove, a tin of seal oil, six reindeer-hair sleeping bags, a small sack of spare clothes and one chronometer. There wasn't enough room for them all to lie down at once, so they took it in turns to crawl on their chests and stomachs over sharp stone ballast, Shackleton directing the in-out operation, into a hole seven feet long and five feet wide. Then they slid into saturated sleeping bags which after a week began to smell of sour bread. The air was bad in there, and stifling, and sometimes they woke suddenly with the feeling that they had been buried alive.

By the fifth day John Vincent, able seaman and a bully, was experiencing severe pain in his legs and feet. He lost his appetite for the fight after that. It was the psychological cramp that did for him, not the physical kind. He had worked on North Sea trawlers too, so he was no stranger to hardship.

By the seventh day their faces and hands were black with soot and blubber. They needed calories, so they drank the seal oil. Two of the sleeping bags were proclaimed beyond redemption and tossed overboard, lifted briefly against the blanched sky.

On the eighth day the ice on the boat grew so thick that they were obliged to take to the *James Caird* with an axe. It was agonisingly painful work. Their thighs were inflamed by the chafing of wet clothes, and their lower legs turned a spectral white, and numb. The painter snapped, the sea-anchor was swept away and the white light of fear flashed through six souls as the biggest wave they had ever encountered crashed over the little boat. But by the eleventh day Worsley calculated that they had crossed the halfway mark. Two of the men found tobacco leaves floating in the bilges and laboriously dried them and rolled them into cigarettes with toilet paper. By the thirteenth day frostbite had skinned their hands so frequently that they were ringed like the inside of a tree-trunk. Then they discovered that the remaining water was brackish.

As sunlight leaked into the sky on the fifteenth day, someone spotted a skein of seaweed. The hours ticked by. If they had missed South Georgia, they were lost. Then, at half-past twelve, as in a vision, the turban of clouds unravelled on the pearly horizon and revealed a shining black crag. It was land. It was in fact Cape Demidov, the northern headland of King Haakon Sound on South Georgia. What they didn't know, as they celebrated, was that the worst was not behind them. It was still to come.

A gale got up. The wind and current were against them, forcing the *James Caird* almost on to the rocks. It began to snow, and roaring breakers shattered into the mist. It looked hopeless. They steered, pumped and bailed, lying to each other with encouraging phrases. Their mouths and tongues were so swollen from thirst that they could barely swallow. At one point they were driven so close to land that they had to crane their necks to look up at the top of the crag. Tension took them, then, beyond speech. Worsley said later that for three hours they looked death square in the eye, and he felt annoyed that nobody would ever know they had got so far.

The ordeal lasted for nine hours, and then they knew that they were going to live. The storm subsided. On the seventeenth day they sailed on to the entrance of King Haakon Bay and got in. It was dark by the time they spotted a cove. They carried the boat in and heaved themselves ashore, eyes fixed on the glint of freshwater pools. Shackleton wrote later that they flung down the adze, logbook and cooker. 'That was all, except our wet clothes, that we brought out of the Antarctic, which we had entered a year and a half before with well-found ship, full equipment, and high hopes. That was all of tangible things; but in memories we were rich. We had pierced the veneer of outside things. We had "suffered, starved and triumphed, grovelled down yet grasped at glory, grown bigger in the bigness of the whole". We had seen God in all his splendours, heard the text that nature renders. We had reached the naked soul of man.'

Still it wasn't over. They had hit South Georgia on the uninhabited south coast, not the north coast where the whaling stations were located. They had to penetrate the perilous and unknown interior.

Together with Worsley and Crean, Shackleton trekked for thirty miles over mountains and glaciers no man had crossed. It took them thirty-six hours, and it was winter. To give the other two a psychological boost at a critical juncture he told them they could have half an hour's sleep – then woke them after five minutes without revealing how long they had rested. On 20 May 1916 they arrived at the Stromness whaling station, 800 miles from Elephant Island. The terrified faces of two lads who fled at their wild appearance and unguessed provenance was their first contact with the outside world for seventeen months. Captain Sørlle, the manager of the station, had met Shackleton before, but he didn't recognise him.

'Who are you?' he asked.

The quiet reply came back, 'My name is Shackleton.'

Then, 'When was the war over?'

No betting man would have put odds on it. The Norwegian whalers, hard men even among seafarers, listened to the story of this journey later, and one of them came forward. He laid his hand on Shackleton's arm, and in his halting English he said, 'These are men.'

'When I look back on those days', the Boss had said, 'I have no doubt that Providence guided us . . . I know that during that long and racking march of thirty-six hours over the unnamed mountains and glaciers of South Georgia it seemed to me often that we were four, not three.' Worsley and Crean, he said, confessed to the same idea of a fourth presence. 'One feels', he wrote, ' "the dearth of human words, the roughness of mortal speech" in trying to describe things intangible, but a record of our journeys would be incomplete without a reference to a subject very near to our hearts.'

It seems fitting that the Boss inspired a stanza in the greatest poem of the twentieth century. In his notes to *The Waste Land* T. S. Eliot wrote that an experience recounted by Shackleton had inspired these seven lines:

'Who is the third who walks always beside you?
When I count, there are only you and I together
But when I look ahead up the white road
There is always another one walking beside you
Gliding wrapt in a brown mantle, hooded
I do not know whether a man or a woman
— But who is that on the other side of you?'

What T. S. Eliot did not know was that the whole fourth-presence story was a later fabrication in order to add a dash of spirituality to the story before it went to press.

Shackleton eventually got his men out, after several agonising attempts. Leonard Hussey, the meteorologist and one of the stranded, recorded in his diary that in the evenings they had occupied themselves by reading out recipes from Marston's penny cookbook and suggesting improvements and alternatives. It had been a testing time. They told Blackborow that they would eat him first, if the seals and penguins stopped coming. Thomas Orde-Lees irritated everyone; they said he was mean-spirited and tetchy. Even before Elephant Island, Shackleton had privately referred to him as the Old Lady. He had been chosen primarily for his mechanical expertise, and had tested the motor-sledges in Switzerland.

On a muggy Cambridge afternoon, under the beady eye of the archivist at the Scott Polar Research Institute, I read his unpublished diary, scrawled in pencil between food lists in a small leather bank pass-book. I had read so very many diaries by then, but when I held the tattered originals I saw worlds in the cramped, unpunctuated, spidery handwriting, splashed with blubber and seawater. Orde-Lees' reputation as a quartermaster reached beyond the grave when I found a darning needle — a precious commodity on Elephant Island — in the creased gutter of his diary. He noted, 'There is a clique up against me to whom Wild gives too much head. I am called a jew.' The diary mostly concerns skinning penguins, but it leaps to life when the rescue vessel appears. The Old Lady writes about the makeshift flagpole behind camp which jammed, with the result that Shackleton, standing on the deck of the ship and straining his eyes, thought it was at half mast, and that someone had died.

On the long journey home to England Sir Ernest travelled free; kings and presidents entertained him. He never let the crowds down: as Roland Huntford said in his biography, he had the instincts of a showman. On another Cambridge day, this time assisted by the beady-eyed archivist, I found a bunch of flimsy green and pink fliers printed in Los Andes, a town on the Chilean and Argentinian border. The sheets read, in Spanish and English, 'Shackleton is the crystallisation of human endeavour, triumphing over the forces of nature, Hosanna! Together [with Wild] they make the symbol of those lofty sentiments of Love for the Truth, of one's Country, of Science, and of Humanity, which bears Mankind onwards with ardour towards its ideal, which places men above suffering, above destiny, which makes them heroes . . . Hosanna!'

*

Shackleton watched over his subordinates like a broody hen, quietly assessing each man's emotional state. If someone was weakening physically he would order extra hot milk all round, without revealing who needed it, so that the man would not carry the invalid's burden. When Frank Wild had lost sensation in his hands, Shackleton tried to force him to take his gloves. Wild refused. 'If you don't', said Shackleton, 'I'll throw them into the sea.'

His leadership skills had been learned in the hard school of the merchant navy, not the rigid and hermetic world of the Royal Navy, and back at home he didn't fit in polar circles because he wasn't a Navy man. Throughout his life he flitted from scheme to scheme, even standing at one time as a Unionist MP for Dundee. He wasn't perfect, as a man or as an expedition leader. He drank too much, smoked too much and had affairs with other people's wives. That's why so many people like him. He's like the rest of us. Hurley noted in his diary, 'Sir Ernest's humour in the morning before breakfast is very erratic.' During one of the attempts to get the men off Elephant Island, Worsley recorded that Shackleton 'was human enough ... to become irritable with me', and he treated the gale which blew up as if it were Worsley's fault. The latter responds heroically: 'I didn't mind; I was glad that he should have some little outlet for his misery.'

Before setting out on the first great sledging journey, with Scott and Wilson, not only had Shackleton never put up a tent before, he had never slept in a sleeping bag. Yet his men were devoted to him. Frank Wild, who took over as leader of the *Quest* expedition after Shackleton's death, said this at a meeting of the Royal Geographical Society on 13 November 1922: 'I am in the unique position of having served with *all* the British Antarctic explorers of repute since my first voyage with the *Discovery* and of having an intimate first-hand knowledge of their work in the field. My opinion is that for qualities of leadership, ability to organise, courage in the face of danger, and resource in the overcoming of difficulties, Shackleton stands foremost, and must be ranked as the first explorer of his age.' Apsley Cherry-Garrard, who went south with Scott, made a comparison which has been hijacked and rearranged by almost every explorer ever since: 'For a joint scientific and geographical piece of organisation, give me Scott; for a Winter Journey, Wilson; for a dash to the Pole and nothing else, Amundsen: and if I am in the devil of a hole and want to get out of it, give me Shackleton every time.' The finest decision ever made in the Antarctic belongs to the Boss. It was when he decided, during the *Nimrod* expedition, to turn back just ninety-seven miles from the Pole.

Although Shackleton knew that the Southern Ocean was 'pitiless almost to weakness', he was an indefatigable optimist, and his power to inspire hope and courage amid seemingly desperate misery has scarcely been equalled in the rich history of human endeavour. 'It is in these circumstances,' Hurley wrote, 'stripped of the veneers of civilisation, that one sees the real man ... A born poet, through all his oppressions he could see glory and beauty in the stern forces which had reduced us to destitution . . .'

On another expedition a colleague noted in his diary that for Shackleton 'Antarctica did not exist. It was the inner, not the outer world that engrossed him.' To the Boss, the continent represented much more than a landmass. 'I have ideals,' he said, 'and far away in my own white south I open my arms to the romance of it all.' Yes boys, we will be home again, he wrote:

But our hearts will still be faithful to this Southern land of ours,
Though we wander in English meadows 'mid the scent of English flowers,
When the soft southerly breeze shakes the blossom away from the thorn,
And flings from the wild rose cup, the shining gift of the morn;
And when the scarlet poppies peep through the golden wheat,
As the stronger winds of Autumn march in with heavier feet;
And when the fields are snow clad, trees hard in a frosty rime,
Our thoughts still wander Southward, we shall think of the grey old time;
Again in dreams go back to our fight with the icy floe . . .
We shall dream of the ever increasing gales, the birds in their Northward
    flight;
The magic of twilight colours, the gloom of the long, long night . . .
And when, in the fading firelight, we turn these pages o'er,
We shall think of the times we wrote therein by that far off Southern
    shore.
With regret we shall close the story, yet ever in thought go back, . . .
Though the grip of the frost may be cruel, and relentless its icy hold,
Yet it knit our hearts together in that darkness stern and cold.

The war loomed over the *Endurance* expedition like a thunder-cloud. When it was declared, the Boss offered the services of the whole expedition to the Admiralty. The telegram came back saying simply 'Proceed'. Over the months and years on the ice, Shackleton wrote in *South*, 'The war was a constant subject of discussion . . . and many campaigns were fought on the map during the long months of drifting.' When he finally learnt of the horrors he wrote, 'We were like men arisen from the dead to a world gone mad', and in Australia, on his way home, he issued a messianic appeal to Australian men urging them to fight, draw-ing the analogy of 'the white warfare of the Antarctic and the red warfare of Europe' from his extensive and well-polished arsenal of rhetoric. Like Scott, he was used as a national icon at home to bolster morale. One newspaper wrote, after the news of the epic rescue mission had broken, 'As long as Englishmen are prepared to do this kind of thing, we need not lie awake dreading the boys of the dachshund breed.' Conan Doyle wrote, 'We can pass the eight Dreadnoughts, if we are sure of the eight Shackletons.' Every single one of the men who had sat it out on Elephant Island went off to fight when he got home, and Shackleton dedicated *South* 'To my comrades who fell in the white warfare of the south and on the red fields of France and Flanders'.

Even in peacetime, war has been used as an image for the exploration of the continent. Admiral Byrd, one of the grand old men of America's Antarctica, wrote, 'The Antarctic was like war, in one respect', and after listing names of ice camps in his book *Discovery*, published in the States in 1935, he says, 'these names were later to be burned into the minds of my men, to become as bitterly unforgettable as the localities of hard-fought engagements to the memories of soldiers.' On Frank Hurley's first night in London after the *Endurance* expedition, the city was bombed. He ends his book, 'Emerged from a war with nature, we were destined to take our places in a war of nations. Life is one long call to conflict, anyway.'

*

When I got back to McMurdo from the valley I set about making arrangements to travel overland to Cape Royds to see Shackleton's hut before the sea ice melted out. Ann, the long-haired photographer, wanted to shoot the interior of the hut.

'You go and get all the survival gear and some food', she drawled, 'and I'll score us a vehicle again.'

The food stores were run by a tall, straight-backed woman called Sarah with clear eyes, long hair and a seraphic countenance. For five years she had been in charge of what people took to their camps to eat and drink. She relied almost exclusively on dried, canned and frozen food, though some fresh goods arrived on planes from New Zealand.

'I'm pushing dried figs quite hard right now,' she said, 'as I was sent 900 pounds, rather than the 90 pounds I ordered.'

'Do people eat more down here because it's cold?' I asked as I walked up and down the aisles picking up ziplock bags of trail-mix and cartons of juice.

'Sure – they need to. And I notice that in a warm season they eat a lot less than in a cold season,' Sarah said. 'Which makes my job difficult as I have to place my order eighteen months in advance.'

Food assumes a role of abnormal importance in a place deficient in so many of life's pleasures. In his book *Life at the Bottom*, published in 1977, the American journalist John Langone mentions a submarine commander who wintered over in Antarctica and reported a group obsession with food, going on to say the men cared desperately if meals weren't up to scratch as food served as a substitute for sex. In the early days culinary ingenuity occupied a good deal of time. One man assured himself of lifelong popularity by producing minty peas, revealing later that he had squirted toothpaste into the pot. Christmas and Midwinter Day menus were elaborately recorded and printed up. During the hard times out sledging they played the game Shut-eye, or Whose Portion is This? when food was doled out. Someone named the recipient of each plate with his eyes closed, so the cook couldn't be accused of favouritism. It wasn't a game, really; it was a peace-keeping mechanism. When rations dwindled they began having food dreams, and spoke bitterly to each other about turning down a second helping of such-and-such ten years previously.

These days, the residents of Antarctic field camps deliberately hid the chocolate to stop themselves overindulging.

Packed, fuelled and ready to set off for Shackleton's hut, Ann checked out with the radio people while I tested the level of the transmission fluid. On the journey we took it in turns to get out and measure the thickness of the ice with a drill. By mid-December the sea ice in front of base was beginning to melt.

'If it's thinner than thirty inches', said Ann, 'we turn back or find an alternative route.' But it never was.

After about two-and-a-half hours, beyond the seals at Big Razorback, beyond Scott's hut at Cape Evans and beyond the Barne Glacier, striped with its layer of ash, we left the Spryte by a large berg and walked over the ice to the volcanic hillock of the cape itself, following the caustic odour of penguins. Individual birds out walking never seemed to smell of anything, but tens of thousands of them at home stank like an ammonia factory. Shackleton's neat buff-coloured hut appeared nestling in a dell as we reached the brow of the hill, and out beyond it thousands of Adelies were standing in front of a panoramic view of the Transantarctics.

A pair of penguins had nested on top of a spoke from the Arrol-Johnstone car Shackleton took south, the first motor vehicle in Antarctica, and the carcass of a dog, well picked over by skuas, had frozen to the floor of the dog-house. I unlocked the door, and entered the tiny vestibule. The hut was smaller than Scott's, about thirty feet by twenty, and as everything was arranged around a central space it seemed more open.

Like the other huts, it had been built in London, then taken down and shipped south in pieces. The walls were made of smooth wooden planks, and the room was sparsely furnished with packing cases, a low table and, at the opposite end to the entrance, a hefty cast-iron stove connected to the roof by a bulky metal flue. A set of sledge runners hung from the rafters, and an assortment of pots, pans and lamps from the rickety shelves behind the stove. A door in the corner next to the entrance led to a small, windowless storeroom. In 1916 Ernest Joyce spent three months there studying penguins, and he, or someone, had scrawled in big letters on the crates at one end of the hut *Joyce's Skinning Academy*.

'Aren't you going to sing the National Anthem, dear?' drawled Ann, nodding in the direction of a framed portrait of the King and Queen hanging in the middle of a side wall. Without waiting for a reply she stopped in front of a row of tins on a shelf behind the stove.

'What's Irish Brawn?' she asked.

'It's like a loaf of bread, but made from jellied pig's head,' I said.

'Eat that a lot over there, do you?'

'Not every day,' I said.

They had pinned postcards around the hut – a painting of an Elizabethan yeoman, and B. D. Sigmund's 'The Bells of Ouseley'. I too carried a dozen familiar images around with me on my travels. I usually propped them up wherever I happened to be sleeping. They reminded me who I was, I suppose, like the creased photographs businessmen carry in their wallets. Mine were not rosy-cheeked children but images that had moved me over the years, now comforting and familiar landmarks in the daily blur of visual stimulation. Most of them depicted some kind of universal human theme, like Botticelli's 'Birth of Venus' or Stanley Spencer's 'Resurrection',[1] but one of them was Manet's boring old 'Pinks and Clematis in a Crystal Vase'.

'I could live here,' said Ann, setting up her tripod in a corner.

'Especially if he was here,' I said. 'I'd like to have been picked for his team.'

'What, more than Scott's?' she said, feigning horror.

'Much more,' I replied. I was sitting at the head of the low table in the middle of the room.

---

[1] Spencer alone of the multitudinous Resurrection artists sends everyone to heaven. His Christ does not judge. I love this picture.

'Smile!' Ann said before letting off a puff of light.

Back in Britain, on a wet afternoon in August, I had met Shackleton's greatest living apostle. He had invited me to his home on Blackheath in south-east London, and I had been obliged to push my way through dripping branches to find his house. When I got there, he had forgotten I was coming. His name was Harding Dunnett, he was in his eighties, and he described himself as 'a bit of an ancient mariner, these days'. Like Shackleton, he went to Dulwich College, and as a schoolboy he could remember seeing the *James Caird* arrive in 1924, by then resembling an old rowing boat. It had been donated to the school by one of Shackleton's benefactors, John Quiller Rowett, another alumnus who used to walk to school with Shackleton. He had become fed up with the little boat. The schoolboys knew nothing of their famous alumnus. 'Scott was the myth,' Harding told me, 'even at Dulwich.' The boat was loaned to the Maritime Museum, and when they too grew tired of it, they returned it to the school, which had nowhere to put it, so it was shoved in with the lawnmowers.

While researching a book on eminent Dulwich alumni, Dunnett unexpectedly came across Ernest Shackleton. 'He just hit me between the eyes.' Dunnett committed himself to his hero's rehabilitation, and founded the James Caird Society, which I immediately joined and over the next year spent several happy evenings dining in the north cloister of Dulwich College in front of the restored boat itself, paying homage. I suspected that the other members were mumbling 'Down with Scott' during the toasts. In the interests of objective research I had tried to join the Captain Scott Society, too, but they wouldn't have me – or any other woman. It was based in Cardiff, and Beryl Bainbridge had been invited to one of its dinners as guest speaker. She wasn't allowed to go to the lavatory, and had her hand slapped for trying to light a cigarette. In the morning she left before anyone else was up (though she had been allowed to visit the toilet by then).

Shackleton had become Dunnett's mission. 'To hell with Scott,' he said as I disappeared into the wet bushes, and, tapping his forehead, he added, 'he lacked it up here.'

*

One day I found a note pinned to my office door inviting me to a Christmas party at the Movement Control Center. Despite the sinister name, the MCC fulfilled a benign role as a kind of on-ice airport terminal. It was the perfect venue for a bash as it was really a hangar, and they had put up a Christmas tree the size of one of those Californian redwoods people drive through. It was made out of parachutes. The party was very crowded, and people were serving beer and pizza from trestle tables. Trotsky materialised out of the gloom, laughing loudly at another feeble joke. He worked on the sea ice, and so he was packing up to go home.

'Once it starts melting out', he said, 'I haven't got anything to work on.' His LC-130 flight to Christchurch had been cancelled three days in a row.

He jumped up and began hurling a woman across the dance floor. The man selling beer raised his eyebrows.

'Once the beakers have crated up their samples they don't have any work to do,' he shouted, 'so they sleep all day and party all night.' 'Beaker' was a character in Sesame Street, but the term had been appropriated and was applied to all scientists. Whether it was derogatory or not depended on the context and the attitude of the speaker. I was becoming more acculturated to Americans by the day, but I still had linguistic barriers to cross. I thought Kool Aid was an Antarctic charity until I was offered a raspberry flavoured tin of it.

Meanwhile an outbreak of lab art had resulted in an accretion of earrings in my office. I was perceived as the link between art and science in the lab, and the scientists began competing with each other to make earrings out of their equipment. I had a pair consisting of a cluster of luminous microcentrifuge tubes, another made with two tiny vials of glacier water, several pairs of glittering plastic zigzags used as fishbait, and so it went on.

I woke up in my room at five in the morning to see my roommate standing by the window, fully clothed. Our paths rarely crossed, as we both spent more time in the field than on station and led generally erratic lives.

'Are you off?' I asked.

'No,' she replied. 'I've just come in.'

*

The vertical borders of the maps I was using were not parallel. They were heading inexorably for 90 degrees south, and I was becoming increasingly preoccupied with following them down and reaching the Pole, where they all converged. I decided to concentrate solely on getting there rather than dashing off anywhere else, and I got myself on a Fridge-to-Freezer fuel flight later in the week.

To fill in time, I practised my cross-country skiing. I wasn't very good at it, but I got to know the south of Ross Island pretty well. Fortunately, I had found a very good skiing teacher. He was a veteran Antarctic support worker called Felix, and for years he had been circumventing the strict McMurdo regulations about what constituted 'safe travel'. One day, we went out to the skiway. This is a landing strip consisting of compressed snow over glacial ice. The 'ice runway', another facility at McMurdo, is sea ice stripped of its snow. As I puffed along behind him Felix told stories of his illegal escapades on the ice. He called his exploits 'missions'.

'I always launch on a Saturday night,' he said, 'when no one suspects anything. Usually I stow my skis under a rock somewhere near McMurdo the day before, so I don't arouse suspicion.' Like all serious outlaws, he brought his own sleeping bag and bivvy sack south, plus a pair of mini-binoculars to scan the horizon for people who, if encountered, might rat on him.

'What happens if you do see people?' I asked.

'I lie low behind a snowhill till they've gone.'

Once, Felix had climbed Erebus alone.

'I took a snowmobile at midnight, and it stopped going up at three in the morning at what I later reckoned was 8,000 feet. [At about this elevation snowmobile carburettors must be rejetted for altitude.] I climbed for nine hours. On the summit, I was hallucinating. I walked halfway round the crater, and the terrain got rough; I was frightened then. I knew that if I so much as sprained an ankle I'd be dead – but it was the best thing I've ever done.'

Felix went back to McMurdo early, and I stayed out on the ice alone. It was almost midnight when I skied back, and the temperature was hovering around zero degrees Celsius. The sky was burnished blue, streaked with a twisted ribbon of alto-cumulus, and dazzling honeyed sunlight flashed off the faces of the Transantarctics. As I stopped to lift my goggles, I glimpsed something out of the corner of my eye . . .

*

Some time before coming south I had done a long line of radio interviews to talk about the publication of my book on Chile. At the first one, in Manchester, the interviewer asked me a specific question about the nature of fear. She was interested in how I could trek around alone in the high Andes, hopping in and out of antediluvian Bolivian lorries freighted with smuggled drugs. I was flummoxed by the probing nature of her enquiry, as she seemed convinced that I had some secret to impart which would empower all the women of the world, enabling them to fling down their aprons and run off to South America. I muddled through the interview, and the women of Manchester did not subsequently stampede to the airport, clogging the concourse in their frenzy to cross the Atlantic.

Over the next weeks I was repeatedly asked, 'Weren't you afraid, alone over there?', and I was embarrassed to admit that I had never been frightened, not even at the worst moments. As a result, journalists suspected I was a freak – not a troublesome freak, but a benign, barking-mad free spirit, like the tweed-skirted Victorian 'lady' travellers who rampaged across Africa with a fly-swat in their hand and three hundred heavily laden 'natives' behind them.

What I could never quite tell anyone was that I was afraid of other things – so afraid that nothing that could happen to me up a Chilean mountain could possibly worry me. All my life, or at least since a long journey returning from a holiday in Cornwall on a green leather bench seat in the front of my father's first car when I was eight, the thoughts trailing nomadically round inside my head have intermittently staged a rebellion, coalesced into a mass of far-reaching grief and paralysing fear, caused my mouth to go dry, my hands to shake and all the colour to be blanched from the sky.

It would have been hard to explain this on a 'talk' show. 'Um, what are these thoughts actually rebelling about?' the interviewers would understandably have asked, riffling through their papers to find the next item.

The misery of the human condition is popular with the Nomadic Thoughts. The catalyst might be an old man replacing a box of teabags on the supermarket shelf, having held it up to his pebble glasses and peered at the price; or a young woman with Down's Syndrome staring out of the smeared window of the day centre around the corner from my home because there was nothing else to do, on that day or any other day; or another visit to another friend in another AIDS ward, watching young men shrivel up until they were replaced by new ones, and the supply never ran out.

Like many people, I was depressed and upset about these things. They made it hard to find the energy to go on – going on seemed pointless. The setting for my anguish was not a long-forgotten byway far from home but the nearby grubby corner of a London street where someone was eating, or opening a window, or just walking dully away. Faced with incontrovertible evidence of the inescapable misery of most people's lives, and the ultimate tragedy of all of them, it was hard not to be a pessimist. Sometimes I saw my own life stretching ahead of me blighted by depression, the asphyxiating kind of depression that felt as if a hod of bricks had been deposited on my chest. I was never going to find peace of mind (I would think at these times), I was never going to be usefully creative, and, like many people I knew or heard about, I would probably end up with a nervous breakdown. Just as you suck all the way down a stick of Brighton Rock and still find the word 'Brighton' written through the mangled stub, I would never be able to escape from my melancholic nature.

This was all frightening enough, but it grew much worse when the Nomadic Thoughts arrived at their favourite watering-hole. Everything was all right, of course, if God was in his heaven; as the Catholic Church used to preach in the South American slums before Vatican Two in the sixties, 'Life in this world is a piece of shit but shut up and put up with it because in the next world everything will be fine.' (I admit they didn't actually preach that overtly, but it was what they meant.) I have never had any trouble with faith. I have believed in God for many years. It was a God who constantly redefined himself as I staggered through my life, and he seemed to live inside me, rather than in heaven or on the ceiling of the Sistine Chapel. He did not, of course, have a long white beard. If any of the radio journalists had asked me directly: 'What are you frightened of?' – I could have told them immediately, in three words. 'Losing my faith.' I had experienced intimations of it when the teabag man and the smeared window of the day centre and the AIDS ward supply-line led me too far down the long, unwinding road of despair. All I can tell you is that I felt the white heat of terror then, and the idea that a gang of Bolivian truck drivers could provoke a similar response was like suggesting that if I attached wings to my skis I could take off and fly back to McMurdo.

In Antarctica I experienced a certainty amid the morass of thoughts and emotions and intellectual preoccupations seething inside my balaclava'd head. It was what I glimpsed out of the corner of my eye. It wasn't an answer, or the kind of respite offered by a bottle of calamine lotion on sunburn. It was something that put everything else – everything that wasn't Antarctica – in true perspective. I felt as if I was realigning my vision of the world through the long lens of a telescope. It emanated from a sense of harmony. The landscape was intact, complete and larger than my imagination could grasp. It was free of the diurnal cycle that locked us earthlings into the ineluctable routine of home. It didn't suffer famines or social unrest. It was sufficient unto itself, and entirely untainted by the inevitable tragedy of the human condition. In front of me I saw the world stripped of its clutter: there were no honking horns, no overflowing litter bins, no gas bills – there was no sign of human intervention at all.

You might ask why I didn't go to the Yorkshire moors or the Nevada desert if 'all' I wanted was pristine nature. It would have been a lot easier. I had been to those places, and many others, but it was the scale, the unownedness, and the overpowering beauty that made Antarctica different and diverted the Nomadic Thoughts. It wasn't a permanent diversion. I knew I would meet my demons again and again before my life ended. Still, I glimpsed a world in which everything made sense. God didn't appear to me in any particular shape or form – if anything he became even more nebulous. But I heard the still small voice. I had never known certainty like it. I felt certain that a higher power exists, and every soul constitutes part of a harmonious universe, and that the human imagination can raise itself beyond poverty, social condemnation and the crushing inevitability of death. For the first time in my life, I didn't sense fear prowling around behind a locked door inside my head, trying to find a way out. It was as if a light had gone on in that room, and I had looked the beast in the eye.

It happened in a second. I've noticed that it is often the seconds which matter. They can be far more important than the hours.

Reason is too lumbering a faculty to operate in seconds, and it leaves the way clear for instinct, or for nothing at all except a bit of psychic energy flying across a synapse. The glimpse left me with a deep and warm sense of calm and mental well-being, like the cosmic glow after some astronomical phenomenon.

CHAPTER SIX

At the South Pole

Great God! this is an awful place and terrible enough for us to
have laboured to it without the reward of priority . . . Now for
the run home and a desperate struggle. I wonder if we can do it.

From Scott's diary, January 1912

THE ONLY other passenger on the fuel flight to the South Pole
was a physicist in his late twenties from Boston. On the way
to the ice runway he told me that he had been south before, and
was about to spend a year at the Pole, a prospect which filled him
with great joy. He reminded me of an overgrown puppy.

The sun was shining, and the ice runway was pitted with water-
holes. The following day, 17 December, air operations were shifting to the firmer skiway at Willy Field. We picked our way over
to a metal hut on stilts containing a drum of drinking water, a
quantity of padded blue plastic chairs, the usual bewildering array
of rubbish bins and a box of yellow earplugs. The walls were bare
except for two brightly coloured waste management posters, and
the blue lino floor was smudged with dirty snow. When we had
settled down, the physicist handed me a photograph of his telescope at the Pole. He was carrying a stash of them in his pocket.

We could see our plane squatting on the ice, attached to umbili-
cal tubes of fuel and tended by diminutive khaki figures. After an
hour, the pilot arrived and announced that we were 'all set'. We
made our way over to the steps of the Hercules. On the Flight
Information board in the hold it said, 'Only eight shopping days
till Christmas.' As we belted up in the red webbing seats, the pair

96

of us alone in the cavernous fuselage, a crewman appeared and said, 'As far as emergency exits go, if you have to, get out any way you can.'

They ushered me up to the flight deck immediately after take-off, and there I stayed for the whole journey. A crewman gave me a styrofoam cup of coffee, and on the side he wrote '850 miles to go'. We flew towards the Beardmore Glacier over a window in the clouds, and up ahead the tips of the Transantarctics pierced the stratocumulus. Scott and his party walked up the Beardmore to get through to the plateau, and it had become a potent name in the shaping of the legend: Nancy Mitford called her chilly upstairs lavatory the Beardmore. It was hot in the cockpit, and I fell asleep for a while, images of small figures and cold Edwardian porcelain flashing through my dreams.

The ten men of the Ross Sea party had manhauled upwards of 1,500 miles over that stretch of the continent, some of them without washing or changing their clothes for two years, and on that ice they had laid depots for men who never came; depots which were still there, strung out for 400 miles. They were members of the Imperial Trans-Antarctic Expedition, and their party, led by one-eyed Aeneas Mackintosh, were storing supplies from the coast to the base of the Beardmore Glacier for six men, led by Shackleton, who were supposed to be marching across from the other side. At Cape Evans I had seen a cross to the three who had stayed in the Antarctic; Wind Vane Hill, they called it. Back at home, nobody ever carved statues of the Ross Sea party to adorn public squares. It was partly because the survivors got home in the middle of the Great War.

Like Scott, they didn't feel they had struggled in vain. Dick Richards, the party's physicist, wrote later, 'That the effort was unnecessary, that the sacrifice was made to no purpose, in the end was irrelevant. To me, no undertaking carried through to conclusion is for nothing. And so I don't think of our struggle as futile. It was something that the human spirit accomplished.'

On 6 May 1915, before they had unloaded all their supplies, the ship blew away. They had to make trousers out of canvas tents left in the Cape Evans hut by Scott. Later, Mackintosh fell sick, and another man, Ernest Joyce, took over the leadership by default. He was a complicated character whom Shackleton engaged after seeing him ride past the expedition office in London on top of a number 37 bus. (Exactly how this occurred, I cannot say. I like to think of Shackleton glancing out of the office window and, as he catches sight of Joyce riding contentedly past on the top deck, being struck by inspiration. Recognising his man, Shackleton sprints after the bus until he is able to leap on and collar the hapless Joyce.) Mawson almost took Joyce south in 1911, but there was a row about Joyce's drinking in Tasmania, so he wasn't asked. On the first page of his book, *The South Polar Trail*, Joyce says that the hardships 'were almost beyond human endurance'. 'If there is a hell,' he wrote, 'this is the place, and the sleeping bags are worse than hell.'

Twenty-five months after they had left the fleshpots of civilisation, Shackleton came to get them, aboard *Aurora*. They never forgot what they had endured. In a footnote to his text, Joyce said that when they got home they were frequently invited to festivities in London which went on into the early hours, and afterwards they would find destitute people on the Embankment 'and line [them] up at the coffee stalls'. When he was ninety, Dick Richards said that he hadn't yet recovered.

There was a padre with them, Spencer-Smith, who died of scurvy after weeks lashed to the sledge, often unconscious. Then, when they had laid the depots and got back to Hut Point, Mackintosh, who had recovered, and V. G. Hayward, who was in charge of the dogs, their minds fogged by suffering, set out across the fragile ice for the other hut at Cape Evans. They were never seen again. It has been said that Shackleton made a rare error of judgement in choosing Mackintosh. He might have done so out of loyalty, because Mackintosh had lost his eye on Shackleton's previous expedition, aboard *Nimrod*.

When I woke up, I had spilled the coffee over my windpants. The crew were pointing out of the window. I looked out too, but I couldn't see anything. Then I spotted a smudge. It was a small patch of snow groomed as a skiway, and a cluster of black dots. Feeling confused, I looked at my watch. It had taken three hours.

The first thing I saw when we landed was a twelve-foot posterboard of Elvis and a signpost marked 'Graceland'. The geodesic dome in the middle of the station flashed in the bright sunlight. It was very noisy when we climbed down the steps, as it was too cold to shut down the engine, and the snow was knuckle-hard. A man approached me, bulky as a yeti.

'Welcome to South Pole,' he shouted in my ear, and together we walked down through a tunnel into the dome beneath a sign announcing that the United States too was welcoming me to Amundsen-Scott Station. My heart was beating fast, due either to excitement or lack of oxygen, and I sat drinking weak tea in the galley with the puppy-like physicist.

Later, the yeti directed me to a Jamesway ten minutes' walk from the dome. When I got there, I lay down on my bed and tried to think about where I was.

'The South Pole', says a character in Saul Bellow's novel *More Die of Heartbreak*, 'gives a foretaste of eternity, when the soul will have to leave its warm body.' At another point he says, 'There you saw as nowhere the features of the planet in pure forms and colours.' In reality the only two colours were white and blue – but I liked the sentiment. In Thomas Pynchon's first novel, *V,* published in 1963, a man makes this statement about the Pole. 'But I had to reach it. I had begun to think that there, at one of the only two motionless places on this gyrating world, I might have peace. I wanted to stand at the dead center of the carousel, if only for a moment; try to catch my bearings.'

I admired both writers. If they had been able to see me at that moment, supine in a tent at ninety degrees south, I imagine they would both have said, 'God, I didn't mean it *literally.*' Without going anywhere near it, Pynchon had transformed the continent into a symbol so comprehensively that when reduced to a lower-case 'a' in his book 'antarctica' becomes isolation itself – 'a beach as alien as the moon's antarctic'. I had to come, and already I knew that I would never be quite the same again; nonetheless Pynchon's character was right when he said, 'It is not what I saw or believed I saw that in the end is important. It is what I thought. What truth I came to.'

*

The twelve cots in the Jamesway were curtained off with sheets of green canvas, so we all had our own few feet of privacy. It was hot and dark inside, and when I went out to find the bathroom the glare made my eyes smart. First of all I strode into a Jamesway marked 'Women', but this turned out to be a joke, and the shift-workers asleep inside turned fitfully on their cots. The bathroom was called 'The Inferno', and it was as bright as the inside of an open fridge. In the toilet cubicles a sign read, 'If it's yellow, let it mellow, if it's brown, flush it down.'

'Showers', another sign said, were 'limited to two minutes twice a week'. Out of the window I could see a dozer trundling along carrying a load of snow, and a strange blue building on stilts.

I walked to the dome, and my heartbeat immediately quickened. My breathing was shallow. It was like being on the summit of a medium-sized mountain. The altitude at the South Pole, 2850 metres or 9,300 feet, meant I was standing on a layer of ice almost one third of the height of Mount Everest. In addition, the earth's atmosphere is at its most shallow at the Poles. The combination of altitude and shallow atmosphere means that at the South Pole the human body receives about half its normal oxygen supply.

The small thermometer which hung permanently from the zip of my parka read minus 29 degrees Celsius. This was the coldest temperature I had ever experienced, though I had once been in New York when it was minus 23. Had I spent the previous winter in the hamlet of Crask Inn in northern Scotland I would have suffered minus 29.2 degrees Celsius – the coldest temperature ever recorded in Britain. At the Pole on that first day I felt perfectly snug, bundled up in my special clothes, though it wasn't windy. When the wind whipped up it sliced through any number of layers like a pneumatically driven carving knife. The mean annual temperature at the South Pole is minus 49, and the record high, recorded in December 1978, a sultry minus 13.6. The lowest temperature yet experienced here is the minus 82.8 recorded in June 1982.

The configuration of small buildings which made up the station were dominated by the sapphire blue harlequinned dome, an aluminium structure shaped like the lid of a wok. It was 165 feet in diameter and 55 feet high, and on the top a Stars and Stripes flag was flapping among a small forest of antennae. Underneath this protective lid, half a dozen simple heated buildings housed essential facilities such as winter accommodation and the communications room. Before I went inside, I wanted to see the Pole itself. For a year I had looked at it every day, in a photograph next to the toothmug in my bathroom in the attic; and every day, as I cleaned my teeth, I had made myself believe I could get there. It was the famous photograph of Scott and the four others at the Pole. Ponting had taught Scott and Bowers to use a remote device so they could shoot photographs of themselves, and after the film had reached home he told a journalist, 'They all look so well and strong in that last picture.' But they don't. They look as though their hearts have just broken.

The marker at the Geographic Pole is shifted about thirty feet each year to compensate for ice drift. The layer of ice, basically, is moving steadily over the surface of the earth far below it, with the result that once a year a member of staff from the U.S. Geological Survey is obliged to make the trip to the Pole to pull out the marker and move it thirty feet.[1] This must be one of the best jobs of all time. Later in the season I met the person who did it, and I asked her what she said to people at parties when they came out with the usual 'And what do you do?' I was longing to hear her say, 'I'm a Pole-shifter', or something similar, but alas, she launched into a lengthy description involving geological software. At least it's guaranteed to clear the deck at the party.

A few hundred yards away from the perambulating marker, the permanent Ceremonial Pole consists of an arc of flags facing a chromium soccer ball on a short barber-striped column. Here someone had drilled a compass into the snow on a piece of canvas, every direction pointing north. I wondered how Muslims knew which way to face.

The Geographic Pole was marked by a small brass plaque and a large board quoting Scott and Amundsen (presumably they had to move this too). Whoever selected these quotes must have had a stunted imagination. Amundsen was commemorated with the immortal words, 'So we arrived and were able to plant our flag at the geographical South Pole.' Scott's quotation read 'The Pole. Yes, but under very different circumstances from those expected.'

The bathetic words conceal a welter of cultural baggage. Two nations could hardly have been further apart in their journeys when Amundsen and Scott raced one another to the Pole. When Amundsen was born, Norway didn't exist. The Norwegians separated from the Swedes on 7 June 1905, and when Amundsen planted the flag at ninety south Norway was taking its first tentative steps on the fragile slope of nationhood.

---

[1] The ice moves in the direction 40 degrees west of Greenwich ('That's Greenwich, England', I was told by the U.S. Geological Survey staff member who had landed the Pole-shifting job).

The citizens of Britain, on the other hand, had learnt that it was their right to rule. It was inconceivable to them that Britain could be wrong, or lose. Scott wrote, 'I don't hold that anyone but an Englishman should get to the Pole first,' and on the subject of Norwegian competition in the south the crusty president of the Royal Geographical Society said, 'Foreigners rarely get below the Antarctic Circle.' When Amundsen finally announced that he too was going south, *The Times* said in a leader that 'he may not have played the game', a notion which has been handed down the generations like a mildewed heirloom, resurfacing (for example) in 1995 in a biography of Scott's widow written by her granddaughter: 'At best, Amundsen's secrecy was underhand.'

In his excellent book *The Return to Camelot*, Mark Girouard points out that the code of medieval chivalry and the cultural appendages it towed in its wake were revived and adapted in Britain between the late eighteenth century and the First World War, and that the Scott myth should be seen in the context of the vanished world of late Victorian and Edwardian England. In *Westward Ho!*, as Tom swims to the North Pole Charles Kingsley conjures up the frozen spectres of dead explorers. 'They were all true English hearts; and they came to their end like good knights-errant, in searching for the great white gate that never was opened yet.' The chivalric code created ideals of behaviour. The concept of playing the game, which loomed so large in the British perception of Antarctic exploration and in the code of conduct of the English gentleman of that time, ultimately derived from that of medieval knights. Oates appears in Baden-Powell's bestselling *Scouting for Boys*, in which the scouts are portrayed as little knights, and while Scott was slugging back from the Pole the play *Where the Rainbow Ends* was packing them in at London's Savoy theatre; it was repeated, in fact, every Christmas till the 1950s – the *Morecambe & Wise Show* of its day. In this piece of deathless drama St George appears in shining armour, there is talk of dying for England and at the end audience and cast sing the national anthem together.

In the context of the British exploration of Antarctica and this chivalric code, Girouard concludes that Scott's last message suggests an attitude in which heroism becomes more important than the intelligent forethought which would make heroism unnecessary.

By and large, the war put an end to all that.

Amundsen didn't labour under such a burden. It wasn't science that motivated him; he just wanted to get there first. He wasn't eloquent, either on paper or in person, and he never played to an audience. It is revealing that he alone of the Big Four did not take a photographer to the ice. He had his own demons, however. For reasons of his own, perhaps jealousy, he humiliated Hjalmar Johansen, a polar explorer whose feats in the north with Nansen had rendered him a national hero. Johansen was a member of Amundsen's team, but was excluded from the polar party, probably because he criticised Amundsen's judgement. When Johansen shot himself in a seedy hotel room back home in 1913, his friends held Amundsen responsible.

The Norwegians had practically grown up on skis – Olaf Bjaaland, one of the five who reached the Pole, was a former national skiing champion. Luck, as far as they were concerned, had very little to do with it. When the victorious polar party boarded the *Fram* at the end of the season, the captain, Nilsen, chatted to Amundsen for an hour before asking, 'You have been there, haven't you?' Both men recorded this in their journals. 'Victory awaits him who has everything in order,' wrote Amundsen. 'Luck, people call it. Defeat is certain for him who has neglected to take the necessary precautions in time – this is called bad luck.' When the five of them set out from Framheim, their base, to ski to the Pole, the cook, Lindstrom, didn't even come out to say goodbye. In order to toast the return of the polar party he had slept all winter with bottles of champagne in his bed to stop them from bursting. In his long account of the race to the Pole Amundsen makes it seem as arduous as a day at the seaside. The food depots were so plentiful that he describes the plateau as 'the fleshpots of Egypt'.

Commentators have found Amundsen cold, but the author of *The South Pole*, published in English in two fat volumes in 1912, emerges as a warm and humorous figure. He was capable of great admiration; he said that Shackleton's sledge journey to within 97 nautical miles of the Pole was 'the most brilliant incident in the history of Antarctic exploration', and that 'Sir Ernest's name will always be written in the annals of Antarctic exploration in letters of fire.' The night before he reached ninety south he said that he felt as he did as a little boy the night before Christmas Eve. There is more than a touch of romance about his perception of the continent. He refers to it as 'the fair one': 'Yes, we hear you calling, and we shall come. You shall have your kiss, if we pay for it with our lives.'

Many pages of the book concern the dogs, some of which have more distinct personalities than the men. 'If we had a watchword', Amundsen wrote, 'it was dogs first, dogs all the time.' When the dogs were killed for manfood, Amundsen records that he turned the primus up full blast so he couldn't hear the shots. And oh, the innocent, ingenuous times! A photograph, taken by a member of the crew and depicting a man dancing with a dog, is captioned, 'In the absence of lady partners, Ronne takes a turn with the dogs.'

He tried hard to be egalitarian, insisting that all five plant the flag at the Pole, and when they arrived back at Framheim they mustered outside the hut so that they could go in together. He cherished those days. 'When everyday life comes back with its cares and worries, it might well happen that we should look back with regret to our peaceful and untroubled existence at Framheim.'

Yet there was a doubt, lurking somewhere in the shadowy recesses of his mind. He left a letter for King Haakon in the tent at the Pole, for Scott to deliver should the Norwegian party fail to return. They talked of Scott daily. Amundsen must have known that he himself had made a terrible mistake by setting off too early in the season and almost killing his men and himself.

Amundsen also used a camera, and the images in his surviving lantern slides are artless, immediate and authentic, revealing, in the self-portraits, a long face, enormous nose and the gleaming, lugubrious eyes of a basset hound. He was lonely and unhappy at the end. He knew that the English had all but expunged his achievements from the records. His autobiography tells of the son of a prominent Norwegian living in London who reported that English schoolboys were taught that Scott discovered the South Pole. As Roland Huntford commented in his introduction to a 1987 edition of the lantern slides, 'It was as if he had been called upon to pay the price of achieving all his goals; beware, as Teresa of Avila said, of having your prayers answered.'

*

I entered the dome through the wide tunnel. Underneath, it was a couple of degrees warmer than outside. Following the sound of laughter, I crunched over the same knuckle-hard snow and stopped in front of a construction like a large mobile home with a freezer door. At that moment a woman appeared behind me dragging a banana sledge loaded with cardboard boxes. She was wearing a white apron underneath her parka, and on her head she had a purple hat with enormous earflaps.

'Ha!' she said. 'You must be Sara. I'm Kris, one of the Galley Queens. That means I cook your meals. Pleased to meet you!' She extended a bearpawed hand.

'Go on in.'

I helped her to carry in the boxes. They contained frozen peas.

A small vestibule was piled with vermilion parkas, white bunny boots and multi-coloured hats, and beyond it a group of women were unpacking boxes of Christmas decorations in a brightly lit and well-heated room spread with tables. As I watched the snakes of tinsel uncoiling, childhood memories rose like milk to the boil.

'The other Galley Queens,' said Kris, waving her hand at the women.

At that time there were 130 people at the Pole, 40 of them scientists. This made for an extremely crowded station. Besides the dome, and the dozen Jamesways, the station consisted of a handful of science buildings on stilts (some sporting bulbous protrusions or spherical hats), a few metal towers vaguely resembling electricity pylons, and long neat lines of construction equipment and shipping containers that trickled over the plateau. Despite the webs of antennae and the clumsy cargo lines, and the fact that the buildings constituted an unsightly jumble of shapes and colours, I cannot say that the station was ugly. It was too small and insignificant in such a vast landscape to seem anything but vulnerable.

Later in the day, I borrowed a pair of skis and spent a while alone on the ice. A high-tech hut which had lost its roof stood on the bare plateau, a testament to some modern Ozymandias. The sun moved steadily, always at the same elevation, and the ice glinted secretively, shimmering in the distance like heat. The surface was creased with tiny ridges and embossed with minuscule bumps. It was so quiet I heard the blood pumping round my head, and I had the same sense of immersion in a different world that I've experienced scuba diving. The silence was like the accumulation of centuries of solitude. I was shocked that such emptiness could inspire me with awe, but it did. It was the purest landscape, the grandest, and, so it seemed to me, the most exalted. I had a powerful sense that I didn't exist at all. The sublime grandeur of nature can strip away layers of the ego – I had experienced it once in the Australian outback, lying under an immense purple sky as the heat rose off the sun-cooked earth.

Later, I stopped at the ASTRO building to see Tony. ASTRO stood for Antarctic Submillimeter Telescope and Remote Observatory, and Tony was an astrophysicist I had met on the plane from Los Angeles to Auckland. After telling me casually that he was going to Antarctica, he had looked punctured when I revealed that I was too. He resembled a bear, and the label on his parka said *Ironman*, which was not a conceit but an endearing attempt to recapture the spirit of the old days (the name had been bestowed upon him in 1986, when everyone wrote nicknames in magic marker on their parka labels) and a clue to what lay below the scratchy exterior. He had designed the building himself in 1987. His telescope, which weighed six tons, was on the roof, and he showed it to me as a parent might reveal an infant in a cot, pointing to the damage sustained when the truck conveying it was rearended in Arkansas. (I had heard about this harrowing episode in some detail on the plane.)

'It detects short wavelengths known as submillimetre radiation,' Tony told me as his beard iced up. The instrument could look into distant galaxies, and its detectors were cooled to three degrees above absolute zero (minus 273 Celsius) with liquid helium to damp down the machinery's own submillimetre-wave radiation. Talk of minus 273 degrees made me feel less cold.

When I asked how it was going, he ran a finger over his icy beard and said, 'Astronomy in Antarctica is full of disappointments.'[1]

'You must have great faith,' I said, 'to keep you going through these long and gruelling years, never knowing if you're going to learn anything.'

'That's what science is about,' he said. 'It's usually presented to

---

[1] The ASTRO project went on to achieve notable success, including the first detection of atomic carbon in the Magellanic Clouds.

the public as unrelentingly upbeat and optimistic, and I think that's a fundamentally false picture. Science properly done should often result in ostensible failure.' He patted his telescope, as if for reassurance.

'I'm not saying scientists are this special breed of people who alone can accomplish things, either. In fact, science and scientific thinking are things anyone can do, but they are difficult and usually require considerable struggle to accomplish anything worthwhile. The presentation of scientists as a priest caste of semi-infallible beings is a disservice to the public and to scientists. It's the root of much misunderstanding and resentment – especially in Antarctica. Let's go in. I'm cold.'

Tucked away in a small room under the dome I found a contraption which looked as if it might have been installed by Scott. It was called a gravimeter and sat in a huge glass and wood cabinet like the ones you see at the Smithsonian or the British Museum. A solid 1950s alarm clock, which wasn't working, stood next to it. It was recording data in ink, on a spool of paper, and although someone on station regularly changed the paper, no one could tell me what this instrument was doing. It was rather gratifying, after Tony's window on the cosmos.

The Skylab tower was one of the largest buildings at the Pole, and from the outside it resembled a giant orange Tardis which had just landed from another planet. It was reached through a tubular under-ice corridor off the back of the dome. To get to the top, I climbed a series of staircases, walked along narrow corridors past mysteriously labelled doors which no one ever went through, and the final assault consisted of a ladder. Three men worked up there making spectroscopic and interferometric studies of airglow and auroral processes in the upper atmosphere. They seemed to be struggling against almost insuperable odds. The project leader waved desperately at the humidity barometer, which was hovering between zero and one.

'We are working here', he said in a tone of quiet desperation, 'on top of thousands of feet of ice, so we are not grounded, or earthed as you British say. Every instrument works when you pack it into the box at home, but it's not working when you get it out of the box here. It's a conspiracy.'

*

When I came out of my Jamesway one evening I crossed paths with a man carrying a case of beer. He said, 'Want to come for a beer with us?' In another Jamesway, half a dozen people were draped over a sofa and a few armchairs, or leaning on a wooden bar, grasping cans and smoking in the gloom while Eric Clapton pumped out of the speakers. A huge video screen dominated one corner, and the walls were graffitoed with the signatures of previous residents. 'John F. Baker, summer '90–'91. So long guys, it's been a party.' It was the South Pole's equivalent of the Corner Bar. I was gratified that it hadn't taken me long to find it.

A construction worker with hair the colour of custard was sitting on a stool at the bar. She had grown up on the coast, but she said she only realised how much she missed the ocean when she saw it again. They often talked about sensory deprivation. One of their favourite topics was the rush of arriving in New Zealand after leaving the ice, and they always mentioned specifically darkness, trees, colours and smells. (I had noticed how much the absence of smell affected people at Fryxell, when one day I had put on a dab of perfume from a sample bottle I found in the bottom of a bag. When I went into the Jamesway they reacted as if I had poured a bucket of Chanel over my head.) On three separate occasions over the past decade a pair of skuas had flown to the Pole in midsummer, stayed a day or two and disappeared. As they were the only wild living creatures ever seen on the polar plateau these birds were a topic of perennial interest at ninety south.

A tall man who had been leaning silently on the bar picked up his parka and left without a word.

'Man, is he toasted,' said the woman with custard hair.

'What does toasted mean?' I asked.

'It means you've been here too long!' she said. 'You kind of wander off when people talk to you.'

'How long has he been here then?' I asked, gesturing at the empty space recently occupied by the tall man.

'Thirteen months. He's a science technician. Leaving this week.'

It was a long time to go without any topographical features to look at.

'You know what, though?' custard-hair went on, leaning towards me. 'I bet you he comes back next season. Everyone leaves saying they're never coming back. But they do. They get home and realise they haven't got a life anyway, so they might as well come back here. We have a saying at Pole that "never" means "yes".' With that she disappeared underneath the bar to fish out more beer.

'By the end of January', I overheard someone say behind me, 'there's no such thing as an ugly woman here.'

*

That this place – the South Pole – was discovered at all was probably due more to the Norwegian explorer Fridtjof Nansen than to any other single figure. He looms over the Heroic Age like an Old Testament prophet, though he never went south. Everyone who followed learnt from him: even Scott asked his advice. Nansen boosted Norwegian national pride at a crucial juncture in the country's history, and the role model he provided gave his countrymen the confidence to pull it off in the south. When he was welcomed back from his epic attempt on the North Pole in 1896, he was greeted by Bjørnson, the national poet, in front of a crowd of 30,000 enthusiastic Norwegian nationalists, with the words, 'And the Great Deed is like a confirmation for the whole nation.'

Nansen was practical and romantic – even mystical. What drives men to polar regions, he said, is *the power of the unknown over the human spirit.* He was a formal, aloof man, but his frailties were very human. He fell in love with Scott's wife, and of course he had wanted the South Pole for himself. But Nansen was drawn into other areas, becoming Norway's ambassador to London, and felt, eventually, that it was right to give way to the younger man, and that it was best for Norway. He lent Amundsen his ship, the *Fram*, and years afterwards he said that when he saw Amundsen sailing away in her it was the bitterest moment of his life.

One story about Nansen illustrates the importance of choosing companions carefully. He decided he could only have one man with him on his longest and most arduous journey in the north, and selected Hjalmar Johansen. Long afterwards Nansen confessed that at the very first camp after leaving the ship he realised that he had chosen a man without any intellectual interests whatever. It must have been a bleak moment.

*

I signed up to help in the kitchen before Sunday brunch. The galley was the heart of the community, and the six Galley Queens made it beat. The food they prepared was delicious too; my first meal was calzone with spinach and cheese and lentil salad. Sometimes a Hercules brought freshies, but the station was largely dependent on the frozen food stacked in boxes under the dome. (Freezers were unnecessary, though elsewhere on the continent I saw scientists using fridges to stop things from freezing.) During the winter, when the station was isolated for over eight months, they had no fresh food at all except whatever came on the midwinter drop, when a C-141 plane flew over from Christchurch and dropped cargo on the plateau. The previous season the crew had pushed out one hundred dozen individually bubble-wrapped eggs, and only two had broken.

I was taken over to view the COBRA telescope by an electrical engineer who always wore a cowboy hat. The COBRA project (Cosmic Background Radiation Anisotrophy) looked for minute deviations in the smoothness of cosmic background radiation, itself the after-effect of the early years of the expanding universe. The telescope was positioned ten feet off the ice on a wooden platform, and looked like an enormous inverted fez.

The engineer was taking care of the telescope for the astronomers who built it. It was not an easy job.

'If a part goes down on the telescope at forty degrees below, it takes three people an hour to fix it,' he said, pushing back his cowboy hat. 'At home it would take one man no more than five minutes.'

'Why bother then? Why not do it at home?'

'The thin air here means we have less stuff to look through to see into outer space.'

'You must hate this thing sometimes,' I said, unfreezing my eyelashes with my fingers.

'Hell, no. Most people go to the office, I go to the telescope. It's just another instrument to me – like a toaster.'

*

In the evenings people sprawled on the sofas in the library under the dome, swathed in candlewick bedspreads. It was like a nest. Once a week, fifteen of them went off to the station poetry group. They each put a word into a box, and everyone had to write a poem about the one which was pulled out. All the words were white, like marshmallow, or cloud, or chalk.

The pool room next to the library was festooned with framed letters celebrating the establishment of the station. After Scott and his party left the Pole in January 1912 it was abandoned until 31 October 1956, when Admiral, George Dufek stepped out of an R-4D plane called *Que sera sera*. The following month Americans began parachuting in materials, and construction of the first South Pole station began. In 1947 Admiral Richard Byrd had flown over the Pole. It was his second attempt, and he said it was like flying in a bowl of milk. Byrd was a towering figure in the short history of Americans in Antarctica, though not a popular one, and several of his claims, such as his 1929 'flight over the South Pole' are regarded with suspicion. People told stories about him falling drunk out of planes. He made five journeys to the ice, and when asked what men missed most on Antarctic expeditions, he would reply with the single word, 'temptation'. Harry Darlington, an American who took his wife south some years after Byrd, was asked the same question. He replied also with one word. It was 'variety'.

Byrd's second expedition, only twenty-two years after Scott, was the most spectacular. *Discovery*, the book he wrote about it,[1] includes an account of the return to Little America, Byrd's base on the Bay of Whales, after four years. Together with several companions, he dug down into the mess hall. As they were standing there under six feet of accumulated snow, the telephone rang. It was an internal system, of course, and a colleague in another part of the base had found the button and pressed it. 'If Haile Selassie had crawled out from under one of the bunks,' said Byrd, 'we couldn't have been more taken aback.'

Alone is Byrd's best book. It tells the story of four-and-a-half months alone at Bolling Advance Weather Base in 1934. It was night all the time he was there, and very cold; he was living in conditions 'like those when man came groping out of the last ice age'. He injured his shoulder before the support team left and almost died of carbon monoxide poisoning. It taught him, he wrote, 'how little one really has to know or feel sure about'. Only when he became almost certain that he was going to die did

---

[1] The British edition is called *Antarctic Discovery*.

he understand Scott's last words, 'For God's sake look after our people.'

This is how he described the departure of the sun.

Above me the day was dying; the night was rising in its place. Ever since late in February, when the sun had rolled down from its lofty twenty-four hour circuit around the sky, it had been setting a little earlier at night, rising a little later in the morning. Now it was just a monstrous ball which could barely hoist itself free from the horizon. It would wheel along for a few hours, obscured by mist, then sink out of sight in the north not long after noon. I found myself watching it as one might watch a departing lover.

... Here were the imponderable processes and forces of the cosmos, harmonious and soundless. Harmony, that was it! That was what came out of the silence – a gentle rhythm, the strain of a perfect chord, the music of the spheres ... This is the way the world will look to the last man when he dies.

The decision to inaugurate an International Geophysical Year in 1957-8 encouraged the Americans to build up their Antarctic programme. In addition, the Soviets were known to be nurturing a desire to build a station at the Pole. When the U.S. government learnt of this, the project was quickly hustled down the corridors of bureaucracy and out on to the ice. The station was completed in February 1957, and no more was heard of the Soviet plan.

Paul Siple, Byrd's protege, took on the old man's mantle. He oversaw the construction of South Pole station, was among the first to winter there, and invented the wind-chill factor. A biologist and geologist, Siple wrote a book, published in 1959, called *Ninety Degrees South*. The subtitle was 'The Story of the American South Pole Conquest', and in it he wrote, 'One striking characteristic of my six Antarctic expeditions is that almost all the men were of the he-man type.' Siple regularly worked himself into a fury on the subject of the fecklessness of young people. No alcohol was permitted on his expeditions, and on one occasion, when chief scientist and second-in-command Tom Poulter discovered thirty cases of liquor smuggled in by the doctor he poured it all on to the snow. The doctor then declared himself sick (presumably from a broken heart). Shortly after this, they ran out of tobacco, though Siple himself no longer smoked, of course, and spent much of their time searching for discarded cigarette ends. One man held butts to his lips with long-nosed pliers.

Smoking is a leitmotif of polar expeditions. Shackleton understood the hardship of tobacco famine, and when he arrived at Elephant Island to rescue his men he threw bags of it ashore before he landed. The stranded men had been smoking penguin feathers, and one of them, the proud possessor of two pipes, had tried to smoke the wood of one in the bowl of another. Viktor Ignatov, the geophysicist in command of Vostok from 1959 to 1960, recorded that at the beginning of the year four smokers signed the pledge and gave up. Not only did these men soon crumble under pressure – the non-smokers took up the habit as well. During the bitter periods between resupplies they smoked tea.

In the modern era the shortage of tobacco is rarely an issue. It is the restrictions on smoking that annoy the nicotine addicts. All round the continent men and women huddle outside huts and tents inhaling furiously like office workers on the streets of Manhattan. When finished, they can't throw their butts on the ice. They have to put them in their pockets, if there isn't a receptacle to hand. We were always finding butts in our pockets, and once, in the field, I saw a scientist's parka catch fire.

*

Dave Grisez kicked six barrels of fuel out of a C-124 fifty feet over the Pole in 1956. He was a construction worker in the Navy, and he spent fourteen months on the ice putting up what was to become McMurdo. If the public has only a vague awareness of Antarctica now, in the fifties the continent existed only in the realm of fantasy. Before leaving his small town in Indiana Dave wrote in his black vinyl diary, 'Auntie Doris thinks it's hot at the South Pole.' On 26 October 1956, his twenty-first birthday, Dave wrote in the same diary in a cold tent on Ross Island, 'A C-124 took off to fly over the Pole this afternoon. They are afraid that Russia is at or near the Pole.' He had been working all winter flattening ice for a runway. On 4 September he recorded, 'Sky was pink, blue, green, turquoise, gold, yellow and lime. Would trade it all for a moonlit night with a farm girl in Indiana.'

One day, forty years after this was written, I walked into the Heavy Shop at McMurdo to get a litre of transmission fluid. Dave Grisez was standing in the corridor wiping oil from his hands. He had just taken a job as a machinist in the Heavy Shop. He had got the girl in Indiana, but he had come back. 'Call of the quiet land,' he said.

*

I met a man who had been assessing the long-term build-up of global pollutants in the atmosphere. He was trying to get home for Christmas, but the incoming plane from McMurdo had been delayed, one painful hour at a time, for the past two days, and all he could do was hover close to his suitcases like a wasp around a jamjar. He had been travelling for thirty years.

'I want to sit at home and think about it now,' he said. 'I want to ask myself why I went to all those places.'

I, too, often ask myself why. A small, white worm of doubt wriggled away in the dungeons of consciousness, fidgeting over the unanswerable question about escape or pursuit. Travel represented either a journey of discovery concerned with pushing forward all kinds of boundaries, or an easy-access escape hatch to a primrose path. It was a treacherously familiar stretch of the psychic landscape.

I had never understood the appeal of remaining within earshot of the tinkling bells of the parish church – *campanilismo*, they call it in Italy. Travelling gave me and all the other compulsive travellers a new identity away from that place called home; at least, ostensibly it did. As everyone who has done it has discovered, and as many writers have written since Horace (though no one has ever done it better than him), *Caelum non animum mutant qui trans mare currunt* – You can run away as far as you like but you'll never get away from yourself. Knowing that was no reason to stop, even if it could be a little disappointing to find oneself lurking in the corner of the Taklamakan Desert after all the effort it took to get there. For me, it meant I was still trying. That was how I saw it.

Somehow, somewhere in a dark, voiceless place in my heart, I sensed that one day I would find something more important than myself lying in wait – something that would put all those other places I had tramped through in perspective. It was not that the other places had disappointed me. I had fallen passionately in love with many landscapes. If you don't know what you're looking for, it's difficult to be disappointed.

I began travelling at the age of sixteen when I took a train to

Paris with a friend. I had just sat for my O-Levels, and had been working in a clothes shop to raise the cash for the trip. My friend had been an usherette in a cinema. We camped for a week at a site in the Bois de Boulogne, strolled aimlessly along Hausmann's wide boulevards, discovered Impressionism, *Livre de Poche* existential novels and *pains au chocolat*, met some Finns and drank a lot of vodka. Before that, holidays had been taken in Cornwall, Devon or south Wales with my brother, mother, father and sometimes a pair of grandparents bringing up the rear. Two features of these holidays have taken up residence in my memory. First of all, the sun was always shining, a phenomenon I can only explain as a trick played by my retrospective imagination. Second, I clearly recall that our daily collective aim was always to *get away from everyone else*. We were, at that stage, a reasonably happy family; or so I remember it. My brother, eighteen months younger than I am and similar in temperament and looks (though thinner, damn him), has been brain-damaged since before his first birthday, probably as the result of a vaccination against whooping cough. We spent most of the time steering him away from other children's elaborate sandcastles, upon which he enjoyed descending in an impressive flying leap, or from the pointed mountains of buns on cafe counters which tended to come crashing to the floor when he appeared in front of them.

So I had no role models – I didn't know any travellers. I followed my instinct. On the last day of the camping holiday in Paris I woke up in our small tent, in which we had inexplicably been joined by a pair of stertorous Finns, and I didn't feel sorry that it was over. I felt as if it had only just begun.

Seventeen years on, when I reached the South Pole, I had got as far, geographically, as anyone can go on this earth. In retrospect, it seems like a natural conclusion to all the places that preceded it. It was as if one great long journey was coming to an end, and I looked over my shoulder at the miles that had unravelled since the tent in Paris. There were none I wished I hadn't covered. Yet there was a payback; the attrition of which climbers are so aware. I wanted freedom more than I wanted a partner or children, and on the road I was free. Back at home, increasingly, it seemed a tough choice to have to make.

In Antarctica I met many people who were struggling with this dilemma. The pressures of separation had always been present on the ice. During the first Operation Deep Freeze in the fifties the enlisted men used to hold Dear John parties when the mail arrived. At the Pole now, letters were strange and obsolete artefacts of the past, replaced by electronic mail. Email was as much a part of life there as food and drink. The problem of long-distance relationships, however, could not be solved by technology. One individual told me his girlfriend had just dumped him by email. On station anxiety was concealed behind a mask of humorous resignation and encapsulated in the apocryphal email message they had pinned on the wall of the computer room: 'Yours is bigger, but his is here.'

I was thinking about this as I stepped out of the science building and was accosted by my new friend Nann. She was a large woman from Chicago who looked as though her hair had been arranged with a blowtorch, and she had her own reason for making the journey. She had come to the Pole to get away from her husband. Her responsibilities as general factotum on station included cleaning the toilets, and she called herself a porcelain engineer.

'I'm going to see a balloon go up,' she said. 'Come along, why don't you?' With that, she took my arm and pulled me along.

The balloons released each day by a meteorologist called Kathy captured atmospheric data which could then be used to compile weather records. It happened to be the summer solstice, but it was hard to celebrate the longest day at a place where day never ended. In the inflation room at the top of the balloon tower Kathy spread the translucent fabric over a large table and began pumping it with helium.

'What happens to them when they're up there?' I asked.

'Sooner or later – depending on the type of balloon – they expand so they can't hold the pressure within them any more, then they burst and come tumbling back to earth.'

'Which is your favourite type of balloon?' I asked, shouting over the loud hiss of helium.

'Well, size matters,' she said.

'As in all things,' interrupted Nann.

'The bigger balloons take more preparation, go up more slowly and gracefully, and you feel you've accomplished something. Could you give me a hand getting this out?'

The balloon was now ten feet in diameter, and as I held the

small styrofoam box attached to the bottom, Kathy opened a pair of metal doors and stepped on to a platform.

'I give you life!' she shouted as she flung her balloon away, and we watched it float peacefully off into the blue, like an Ascension.

'It looks like a condom,' said Nann.

At that moment, a voice crackled over the loudspeaker.

'We have seen black dots on the horizon, assumed to be the Japanese,' it seemed to be saying.

'God!' I said, imagining that the Second World War was about to be re-enacted on the ice sheet. 'What the hell's that about?'

'It's an expedition coming in!' said Nann gleefully, pulling on her parka. 'Let's get out there, to see 'em come in.'

On the way she told me that a Japanese called Susumu Nakamura had skied from Hercules Inlet on the Ronne Ice Shelf. He had covered 775 miles, and it had taken him thirty-nine days, four of which were rest days. He was accompanied by a navigator and three television crewmen on snowmobiles.

Japan had first involved itself with Antarctica in 1910 when Nobu Shirase set out from Tokyo in the *Kainan-Maru* (Southern Pioneer). He reached the Ross Ice Shelf, which he thought looked like 'a series of pure white folding screens', and marched 160 miles inland before sailing over to the Bay of Whales. There his team stumbled upon the *Fram*, which they thought was a pirate ship. The Norwegians, in turn, were horrified by the wanton slaughter of seals perpetrated by the Japanese, and when they were invited aboard the *Kainan-Maru* to drink tea and eat slices of cake they said in hushed tones that they wouldn't have got halfway to Antarctica in such a crummy ship. While in the Bay of Whales Shirase and his men unloaded their stores from ship to shore wearing traditional Japanese straw boots. 'We wound our way upwards', said the expedition report, 'like a string of pilgrims ascending Mount Fuji. It was without doubt the worst of all our trials and tribulations since the moment when we had left our mothers' wombs.'

It was difficult, as a Japanese in those days, to venture on to the world stage. When the *Kainan-Maru* stopped in Wellington the *New Zealand Times* referred to the men as 'a crew of gorillas'. Japan none the less went on to launch scientific expeditions to Antarctica and was an original signatory of the Antarctic Treaty, the international agreement protecting Antarctica from exploitation.

The second Asian country to sign it was India, which in 1983 became the first developing nation in Asia to become a full Treaty member. India's involvement in Antarctica had emerged largely as a result of prime minister Jawaharlal Nehru's vision of his country's global position several decades previously.

Susumu skied up to the Ceremonial Pole, his cheeks 'burnt as black as lacquer', as the *Kainan-Maru* expedition reported theirs had been. A single tear froze as it emerged from a corner of his eye. After handshakes all round (anyone would think they were English), the party began unfurling corporate flags for the inevitable sponsorship photographs, and later we saw all their small yellow tents pitched in the distance.

The frostnipped faces and frozen beards reminded me of other images of exhausted men at the end of punishing journeys across Antarctica. The point of these treks appeared to be to see how dead you can get. Well, *chacun a son gout*. I could understand the appeal of answering the question, 'Can it be done?' If you did it, no one could ever ask the question again. It was yours. All the journeys made by the almost-deads were treks through monomania. They were undertakings of the mind. Yet writing a book was like that, so perhaps we were doing the same thing, only in different ways.

*

The Race around the World was the most enduring Christmas tradition at the South Pole, and it began at four o'clock in the afternoon on Christmas Eve. The two-mile course involved three circuits around the Pole. They had rigged up a starting line and engaged a couple of timekeepers, and participants could complete the course however they liked. One skied, one sat on a sledge towed by a snowmobile, someone else rode a hobby horse and a bunch of committed drinkers were driven round on the back of a dozer. The most imaginative competitor had taken the rowing machine from the weights room, loaded it on to a sledge and was towed round the course, rowing all the way.

I jogged around and developed a violent headache which, aggravated by the altitude, slid seamlessly into migraine. I was obliged to sneak off to the medical facility under the dome and lie down. The doctor was a descendant of Otto Sverdrup, the distinguished Arctic explorer and the captain of Nansen's *Fram* on the *Farthest North* journey. Her name was Eileen, and she put me on oxygen for two hours.

I was marooned in a large consulting room hung with posters of Neil Armstrong wobbling about on the moon. In the radiography room alongside it, Eileen had kept the unwieldy equipment from the sixties, in case the new set broke. My mother is a radiographer, and as a small child I used to go to work with her in school holidays. The smell of the chemicals, the labels ('*Stop Bath*') and the wire racks on the walls for hanging up the X-rays to dry – well, they took me back. It seemed odd that my childhood should catch up with me at the South Pole.

In 1961 a Soviet doctor at an Antarctic station had removed his own appendix. 'I've trained the others to do mine,' said Eileen, as if she were talking about having her hair cut. 'I'd have a spinal anaesthetic so I could talk them through it.' She had also done a short dentistry course.

'The low temperatures make people's fillings and crowns fall out,' she said. 'The glue dries out, you see.' You had to use your initiative. Forty years ago a Swedish doctor took out a man's eye. He had never seen an eye operation before, but he was coached by wireless by an ophthalmic surgeon in Sweden.

Nann came to visit me. She was furious that her husband had failed to send her a Christmas present. Before she left, I asked her to fetch my Walkman and two particular cassettes from the Jamesway. I had been storing up a treat in the event of a miserable moment, and I decided its time had come.

'What are they?' Nann asked when she returned, watching me rip the cellophane off the cassettes.

'They're a talking book,' I said. 'The diary of a man called Alan Bennett. He's a living institution in England.'

Nann thought about this.

'You mean, like Ronald Reagan used to be?'

'More like the Queen Mother,' I replied.

Fortified by a dose of Bennett, which worked rather better than the oxygen, in the evening I asked Eileen's permission to go over to the galley and sit quietly in a corner for the Present Exchange.

Everyone put a wrapped gift on a table and drew a number out of a hat. Number one would then pick a present, which he or she had to open in front of everyone else. Number two could then either pick a present from the table or steal number one's gift, at which point number one chose another, and so it went on. Gifts ranged from knitted hats and an oil painting of the Southern Lights to a box of cigars and a handful of rocks. Before leaving home, I had been tipped off about the gift exchange and had carefully wrapped up a signed copy of one of my books. Having been carted halfway round the world, it looked as if it had been towed from Hercules Inlet on Susumu's sledge. Nann got it – she stole it from someone else. I had my eye on a handmade journal someone had already unwrapped. It had a felt cover bearing a white applique map of the continent with a red arrow at the Pole bearing the words *You Are Here*. When my number was called, I stole it. I was drinking weak tea while everyone else slurped buttered rum punch, but virtue did not save me. The pain in my head returned like a freight train and drove me back to my invalid's bed. Eileen was wonderful. She gave me a massive Demerol shot at two in the morning, and at four she came back, telling me that she'd thought I might be dead.

The Demerol worked, and I dreamt of rain. I was able to walk over to the galley to sit in, at least, on Christmas dinner. They were playing carols on the tape deck, and candle flames were flickering in the foil bands around the crackers. It felt as if someone had cranked up the heating. When they pulled the crackers, however, they did so unilaterally, I mean they each gripped their own cracker with both hands and pulled it. Was this another quaint American custom? They obviously didn't know what a cracker was. (Where the crackers appeared from, I never discovered.)

'Who's that?' I asked Nann as we put on our paper crowns. A tall woman with a weathered face was sitting at the end of the table, engrossed in conversation. There hadn't been any planes. Where had she come from?

'Didn't you hear?' replied the oracle. 'Her name's Liv Arnesen. She's Norwegian. Skied alone from Hercules Inlet, pulling all her stuff on a sledge. Took her fifty days.'

'That's amazing,' I said. 'It's the *second* expedition that's arrived during the short time I've been here!'

'Not a coincidence,' Nann replied, still grappling with the contents of her cracker. 'There's only a small weather window in which you can trek on the plateau. Given the distances involved, that means if more than one person sets out in one season, they're almost bound to reach the Pole around the same time.'

'That's why at home we get a flurry of Beard stories in the press at Christmas,' I said.[1]

'You got it,' said Nann. 'Hey, the joke in this cracker isn't funny.'

'They're not supposed to be funny. That's the point of crackers – unfunny jokes.'

When everyone had finished eating I moved around the table and met Liv. She was sitting next to Ironman Tony, who was plying her with technical questions about the trip. She had begun with a load of 222 pounds, 132 of which was food, and her radio had failed.

'God,' said Tony. 'That must have been a disaster.'

'Actually, it wasn't,' she said guiltily. 'I was so happy not being able to communicate!'

Liv was forty-one years old. She spoke excellent English with the quiet, vibrant confidence of someone who has attained their goal and thereby dislodged all their anxieties in a stroke. Unlike Susumu, who had spent his thirty-nine days arguing with the television crew, she had developed an inner peace during the long weeks of solitude.

'Were you ever lonely?' asked Tony.

'Once. At the beginning of the last week I awoke one night in the tent, and thought "What is wrong? I feel like I am in a dream." Then I realised the wind had dropped. I had been in this wind for six weeks, and you know, it had been a companion.'

'It must have been odd walking straight into Christmas lunch here.'

'Amazing . . .'

'What was your first impression?'

'I go into a bathroom for the first time in fifty days and see myself in the mirror. I see my grandmother's face. It is a shock – how much I am aged by this trip.'

'What made you do it?'

'When I was twelve years old my father was working in Nansen's house in Norway. The caretaker showed me round one day

---

[1] David Hempleman-Adams, a Briton, arrived at the Pole in a similar flurry the following year. When he flew out of Antarctica, to Punta Arenas in Chile, he telephoned home at once, eager to share his triumph. At his home in Swindon he heard his own voice on the answering machine, so he tried his grandmother. She refused to accept the call.

– and that was the start of it. I began reading all the explorers, and it became a dream to reach the South Pole. I grew up on skis, so I knew I could make the trip. The worst was raising the money. I think that comes more easily to Americans, don't you?' She looked at me conspiratorially.

'What does your husband think?' asked Tony.

She bristled amiably.

'Did anybody ask Susumu about his wife?'

'Did you read at all in the tent?' I asked.

'I read Ibsen's *Peer Gynt*, and skied to its rhythm in my head. And I had a volume of Norwegian poetry with me. One line echoed in my mind as I crossed the plateau – how shall I translate it? "A country in my heart that no one can take from me." '

After dinner, we read out passages from the journals of the early explorers. There was a Swede on station, near enough to a Norwegian, we thought, and he had been pressganged into playing Amundsen. Ironman Tony did Scott with gusto, though it was difficult to imagine anyone less suited to an American accent than Scott. During the march to the Pole, Bowers was cooking on their last Christmas Day, and he scraped together two spoons of raisins for each man's tea, five sticks of chocolate, and 'a good fat hoosh, two-and-a-half inches of plum duff, four caramels each and four squares of crystallised ginger.' For once, snug in the tent, they ate until they were sated. 'We shall sleep well tonight,' Scott wrote, 'no dreams, no tightening of the belt.' On an earlier occasion, in the Cape Evans hut, Bowers had rigged up a Christmas tree from a ski pole and skua feathers. Shackleton, out sledging one Christmas, boiled a six-ounce plum pudding in an old sock and served it garnished with a sprig of holly he had found on the ship.

After the readings we rampaged through a few carols. Then we went downstairs to dance, and someone remembered it was traditional to smoke cigars at the Pole on Christmas Day, so the box of cigars was found underneath a pile of wrapping paper and we rushed outside into the dazzling sunshine. It was all an elaborate hoax to stop us feeling sad that we weren't at home.

CHAPTER SEVEN

Feasting in the Tropics

We came to probe the Antarctic's mystery, to reduce this land in terms of science, but there is always the indefinable which holds aloof yet which rivets our souls.

Douglas Mawson

SEISMIC MAN had sent me a letter on a resupply plane returning from the deep field. In it, he asked when I was going to visit. He even wrote in a Texan drawl. I also received a letter from my grandmother in the west of England. She commented, 'I suppose even you are beginning to feel that youth has passed you by.'

The day after I arrived back at McMurdo it was snowing, so nobody could go anywhere. Scotty, the Scott Base cook, invited me to the Kiwis for dinner. They put on an Italian night, and even produced *ciabatta*. An Andres Segovia tape was unearthed; they admitted he was Spanish, but Antarctica taught you to improvise. Afterwards we took the flexikites out behind the pressure ridges, an area out of bounds to McMurdo residents. As a red parka betrayed a trespasser for miles, I had borrowed yellow and blue Kiwi kit.

'You'll have to pretend you're not American,' Scotty said.

With two or three kites on one cord we could sit down and ski on our bottoms. The kites twisted in arcs, whirls and vertiginous turns, confounding the salt-encrusted pupils of a Weddell seal. The clouds melted into shifting layers of gauzy gold, and between them glimpses of the Royal Society range appeared, like the suggestions of heaven shimmering behind the trees in a painting

123

by Botticelli. The Royal Society was the sponsor of the *Discovery* expedition, and these mountains were cursed with its name. It reminded me of Fitzroy Maclean crossing the Oxus in a boat called *Seventeenth Party Congress*.

I wanted to get out to Seismic Man's camp for New Year's Eve. He was working at a remote deep field site on the ice sheet called Central West Antarctica, a place so notoriously difficult of access that its acronym had been elongated into Continually Waiting for Airplanes. Either the weather had closed in at CWA, or a system was about to descend upon Ross Island, or the planes were broken. The camp was regularly resupplied – at least in theory. I went to the skiway four times to hitch a ride on one of these resupply flights, only to languish for hours on the padded blue plastic chairs and scuff my feet on the sky-blue lino smudged with dirty snow. I even took off once, but the Hercules, which was older than I, had problems with its landing apparatus and boomeranged after five minutes in the air. On base I had said goodbye so many times that people began laughing when I reappeared. I developed an intimate relationship with the two other prospective passengers, both support staff assigned to relief work at CWA. Evelyn, was a woman in her forties with biscuit-coloured hair and Jose, also in his forties, was a diminutive Mexican-American biker who grinned like a satyr and called me Kid.

In good spirits, I checked in for the fifth time for my flight to CWA, but after a long morning had drained away it was postponed all over again, this time for at least a week, as the one Hercules on station had developed a serious ailment. I felt interminably depressed, as I didn't want to spend New Year on base. I retrieved my bags and decided on impulse to call into Helicopter Operations to see Robin, the helicopter queen and the personification of American can-do culture.

I had been intending to visit a group of geologists at Lake Mackay, and decided to try to get out to them while waiting for the next plane to Seismic Man's camp. Ross, the project leader, had invited me, and as it was only an hour away by helicopter at 76 degrees south 162 degrees east I knew I could catch a lift fairly easily. Ross had listened patiently to garbled radio messages from various parts of the continent announcing my imminent arrival, an event which had never taken place. Robin studied her schedule for a few moments, seized a pencil and inscribed W-002 in large letters on the manifest of one of the last helicopters before the holiday. It was heading for a camp further inland. 'They can drop you off,' she said cheerily. 'Happy New Year.'

An hour later I was clamped into the back of a helicopter following McMurdo Sound in the direction of Terra Nova Bay and listening to the pilots arguing about whether an eruption of Erebus would offer better odds than either of them scoring at the McMurdo New Year's Eve party.

The small camp was empty when I arrived, a *Marie Celeste* of the ice, and before I took off my headset the pilot asked doubtfully, 'Will you be okay?', shouting out of the window as an afterthought, 'Mind the crevasses, won't you?' It was a still and cloudless day, only five below, and the surface of the ice was hesitantly yielding, like a block of butter on a spring morning. I took off my parka, hat and gloves and contemplated the scene.

They had pitched camp in a large embayment covered by sea ice facing the Mackay Glacier Tongue. Mount England and the granite and dolerite cliffs opposite, striped in glossy chocolate browns, cast squat shadows over the streaky cliffs of the glaciers and the frozen folds of sea, and in the middle five small tents spread into a crescent. Above, an arc of lenticular clouds floated against the Wedgwood sky. I cannot say it was beautiful; it was beyond all that.

Like all the best camps, there was no generator. After a few minutes, however, I heard the buzz of a snowmobile. When I turned around I saw a bearded figure riding along towing a sledge loaded with pans of ice.

'Welcome to the tropics,' he said as he got off, hand extended.

The other four were working out at their dive hole, so we unloaded the sledge and drove across. It was only five minutes away, near the walls of the glacier, and they were crowded around a bright yellow machine which looked like a large lawnmower. I soon learnt that this contraption ruled camp with an iron rod. Operated by remote control, it went down to the seabed and took pictures, and all their science depended on it. They were studying the release of debris from the glacier and its dispersal into the marine environment. The vehicle was the only thing in camp which ever got a wash.

Everyone had sunburnt faces and white eyelids. One of the three graduate students (who described themselves as 'pipettes') was a Lancastrian studying for his doctorate in the States. Mike was six-and-a-half feet tall and taciturn, though when he spoke it was through a wry grin, and he was committed to Wigan, his home town. He had found a spot on the map not far away called Black Pudding Nunatak, and was terribly pleased to find this little piece of Lancashire so far from home. He asked me to guess where he came from by his accent, and then told me that if I had said Yorkshire he would have given me smaller portions on all his cookdays, clearly the most dire threat he could imagine. Besides Ross – the project leader – and the students, the fifth member of the team, the man who had met me, was camp manager. John was softly spoken and looked after the others like a benign scoutmaster.

I was used to the initial awkwardness of being a stranger in camp. It never lasted long so I didn't worry about it any more – quite the reverse, as I relished the thought that these unknown people were about to define themselves to me, as I to them. It was like a lens coming into focus. It was an odd way to live, I suppose; but it didn't strike me as odd at the time.

Every day they lowered the yellow vehicle through a hole in the sea ice covered by a canvas hut. Once the vehicle hit water, Ross controlled it from another hut. He sat in front of a pair of screens which transmitted images from two cameras attached to the vehicle. A hydrophone next to the cameras sent up a beep as regular as a heartbeat. Images of diatoms,[1] skittering by as the vehicle moved along the seabed 450 feet below us, shone out from the screen in the darkness of the hut. It was like being an extra in *Star Wars* in there. I could see a jellyfish with long, undulating strings threaded with tiny lights, and shrimpy crustaceans circling a tall sponge among luminous branches of hydroids. When Ross tipped the vehicle, the cameras peeked inside a sponge. It was hollow, and dimpled, and when pushed gently, it folded like a ballerina.

'You know what?' he said. 'No one's ever seen that before.'

As we got back to camp, I saw that John had put up my bottle-green and maroon tent. I hadn't brought a board to avoid getting soggy in the night, but he had found one in the science crates. We had dinner in another small canvas hut underneath a sign which said 'Floggings will continue unless morale improves.' The

---

[1] A diatom is a microscopic unicellular alga.

graduate students were engaged in eating contests. Mike had recently won a night off cook duty by swallowing a bowl of cold potatoes and three cans of coke after his dinner. Ross smiled beatifically as they argued over past ignominies and future victories; the dynamics of the group were predicated on an easy and harmonious equilibrium, well oiled now as a long, hard and successful season drew to a close.

On New Year's Eve we went off to make the last dive of the season. The wind was up, so it was chilly. I helped to scoop up platelet ice which had formed over the hole, then settled on a crate in the dark hut. When the yellow machine was travelling to the surface, the screen looked like a bank of rain on a grey day. 'Like Wigan in November,' Mike said.

I had volunteered to cook a New Year's Eve banquet. They were about to strike camp and return to the real world, so we had a double cause for a celebration, and besides, they had only had one day off all season. People in Antarctica were always looking for an excuse for a party. The first American team at South Pole station threw a birthday party for a dog, and baked him a cake with a candle. In the early days, the Australians made such effective use of *Whitaker's Almanack* that they staged a major feast to celebrate the Anniversary of the Lighting of London by Gas.

I found the absence of any trace of home more refreshing on New Year's Eve than at any other time. I was spared the sickening realisation that once again, despite the passing of another year, nothing had changed except the things that had got worse. None of us at Mackay began spawning good intentions just because a new year was upon us. We were set free from all that.

While rooting around in the iron-hard cardboard boxes next to the dining hut I uncovered four bulbous pink packages labelled Cornish Hens, a misleading name as the birds had clearly never been east of Newark. With these, assorted dried vegetables and a tin of condensed tomato soup I contrived to make a casserole. Once cooked and jointed, the hens produced enough meat to satisfy one hungry scientist, thereby necessitating the deployment of three emergency tins of 'new' potatoes. I concocted a salad from one flaccid head of lettuce, a tin of olives, a tin of kidney beans and three lethargic carrots. The discovery of a packet of dehydrated strawberries seemed like a small personal triumph, and with dehydrated egg, powdered milk, a tin of butter and a packet of ginger biscuits I made a strawberry cheesecake in a saucepan and left it on the ice to set. Finally I made flowers for the table out of a cardboard box, and napkin rings for the toilet-paper napkins out of the silver powdered egg bag.

The food was enthusiastically despatched, and the occasion proved that a meal is much more than the sum of its parts. Someone had brought a Walkman with speakers, and we listened to Vangelis's *Antarctica*. Jim suggested that at midnight we should go outside to see in the New Year in silence; it would be the first and almost certainly the last silent one in all our lives. Jim, one of the graduate students, was quiet, and handsome, and the others tormented him as his was the shortest beard. The sun was immediately behind the peak of Mount England, and we stood apart from each other, lost at that moment in our own private worlds.

Various bottles – the dregs of the season – appeared among the kerosene tins, and we tried somewhat ineffectually to warm them up before disposing of the contents. At two or three in the morning Ross said he had to listen to Georg Solti's live recording of Beethoven's Fifth with the Chicago Symphony Orchestra before going to bed, so we went outside to hear it soaring over the ice. The glaciers sent the sound up like the walls of a cathedral. All the ice ridges opposite were edged with gold, and I wondered how Beethoven could not have been looking at the same scene when he wrote the music. He had probably made his own journey, but in a different way.

*

I woke late on New Year's Day, sweating in the bag; the tropical weather had returned. I lay there with the tent flap open, the bottle-green and maroon walls suffusing light over my possessions like a stained-glass window. I could hear the others talking, and when I went to get coffee I found a fried breakfast left for me in the pan. I couldn't face it, and when no one was looking I crept over to our waste hole in the sea ice and watched the food and its puddle of grease slide silently into the depths. Then I took the coffee back to my tent and lay half-in, half-out on my thermarest mat and snapped Alan Bennett into the Walkman as a New Year's treat. He was visiting New York, and described walking past a sign in the Village offering ear piercing 'With or Without Pain'.

Mike was sitting at an open-air desk made of crates, labelling data. The others were packing up. Then Steve appeared, asking if I wanted to go and collect water with him on the south side of the glacier tongue. He was small and garrulous – the antithesis of Mike – and permanently astounded by the fact that he hadn't washed his hair for seven weeks. Steve spent most of his time at Mackay sitting on the ice feeding out coils of pink tubing attached to the vehicle.

Alistair F. Mackay, Shackleton's doctor on the *Nimrod*, had one of the best glaciers. He went on to die in the Arctic, but in 1908 he had manhauled to the South Magnetic Pole with Mawson and Edgeworth David, and on the way they camped near our spot. It is clear from Mawson's diary that Edgeworth David drove him almost mad. It was Edgeworth David's approach to the mundane detail of daily life that grated – if they had been at home, they would have quarrelled over who left the cap off the toothpaste. Mawson was a fine geologist, and all the scientists I met revered him. It is this which sets him apart from Shackleton, from Scott, from Amundsen and even from Nansen. He is the scientist's explorer. We were discussing this as we prepared the sledges, and when we filled up the snowmobiles, Steve shouted:

'Mawson was the greatest in the south, and Nansen in the north.'

Douglas Mawson was born in Shipley, in West Yorkshire, but his parents emigrated to Australia when he was two. He went south four times. The most legendary solo trek on the continent was his, and it always will be, no matter how many Beards sally forth. On the Far Eastern Sledging Journey across King George V Land in 1912–13, after the death of his two companions, Xavier Mertz and B. E. S. Ninnis, this naturally enormous man staggered back to Commonwealth Bay at almost half his normal weight. The first person who saw him was a member of the expedition who knew Mawson very well. This man screwed up his face, peered at the wreck in front of him and said, 'Which one are you?' Mawson had watched almost all the food go down the crevasse which had killed Ninnis, so he was forced to eat the dogs, eyes and all. He had witnessed the agonised ravings of Mertz, watched him bite off his own finger and cleaned up his acute dysentery. He noted on 11 January that his own body was rotting through lack of nourishment.

Australians tend to speak in awed tones about meeting members of the great man's family, and a Mawson research industry has fuelled the development of the legend. While I was studying the period I received a letter from a distinguished Australian which included this: 'Mawson, on one of his outback trips, during which the blokes open up under the vast night skies, confessed to an Australian scientist called Madigan that he had eaten part of Mertz's corpse. The story has it that Madigan wrote all this in his diary, which is now locked away so that Mawson's reputation will not be tarnished by the unpalatable revelation that he was a cannibal.'

Mawson was a man of action, little given to introspection and with none of Shackleton's romanticism and poetic flair. His diaries, admittedly not written for publication, are a litany of irritation. Twenty years after Edgeworth David had rendered Mawson apoplectic, Captain Davis provoked even more abundant outpourings of venom. (Davis took the *Aurora* back to pick up Mawson and his team and didn't leave the bridge for seven days and seven nights.) Only after Ninnis has disappeared down the crevasse does Mawson refer to Mertz by his Christian name in his diary. Frank Hurley, who went south with both Mawson and Shackleton, summed up the difference between the two men like this. 'Shackleton grafted science on to exploration – Mawson added exploring to science.'

The sea ice was flat and free of sastrugi.[1] Beyond the seals on the other side of the tongue, in front of the Minnihaha Ice Falls and Cuff Cape, Steve stopped abruptly, raised his goggles, pushed out his neck like a tortoise and pointed ahead. Three glossy emperors were standing in a row on the ice, looking expectantly into the middle distance as if a bus were about to appear to transport them to a fish shop. They saw us, and approached immediately. One of them was taller than the other two, though they were all over three feet. Their sleek, deep yellow collars and the mandarin streaks on their lower beaks were glowing in the sunlight, and when they were very close I could see the New Glacier reflected in their soot-black eyes.

Their feet looked as if they didn't belong to them: they were grey, scaly and reptilian, ancient-looking, feet made for standing

1 Wind-carved ridges of ice.

on the ice throughout the polar winter with an egg balancing on top. The tall penguin was squawking and flapping his flippers.

'The edge of the sea ice is over twenty miles away,' said Steve. 'I wonder why these guys came all that way?' We thought about this for some time, but neither of us came up with an answer.

The emperor penguin is the world's largest extant diving bird, and the adult weighs seventy pounds. (Fossils reveal that prehistoric penguins were as tall as six feet.) On land he knows no fear. He has no predators: Antarctica's largest permanent terrestrial resident is a wingless midge half an inch long. I knelt on the ice next to the tall penguin, close enough to watch the nictitating membranes close across his eyelids like camera shutters, and I saw how it could have been, between human beings and animals.

*

That evening, we ate outside. It had been so warm that the streams were flowing. At midnight the boys began throwing a rugby ball around. I sat on a fold-up chair like Old Mother Time as a mist stole over the glacier. I was reading a biography of T. S. Eliot. His asperity, attenuated sensibility and dapper dress sense were a perfect foil for the vast scale of the continent, our wild appearance and the primal face of nature all around us, and his uncertainty stood at the opposite pole to the fastness of the ice. Besides that, he had written that in hot places, like the Caribbean, 'the spirit sleeps'. The implication was that cold places were conducive to spiritual alertness, and this was my experience. I had been on assignment in Jamaica some months previously and could clearly remember lying on a beach straight out of a tourist board brochure, fanned by a sultry tropical breeze while the lapis ocean sussurated under a blazing midday sun and a six-foot waiter stole soundlessly across the hot sand bearing another vat of some treacherously agreeable cocktail. Think? I don't believe I managed a subordinate clause the whole week I was there.

*

Over the last two days a battalion of jobs presented themselves for attention. John dispensed tasks from long lists inscribed in a red spiral-bound notebook.

'When I get on the last helicopter,' he told me, 'I like to look back and see it looking just as it did the day we landed.'

I packed up the foodboxes, and took the others mugs of Lipton's Hot Spiced Cider. All camps had a suspicious proliferation of this. It came in teabags, and the packet proclaimed 'Contains No Apple Juice', as if this were a selling point. As I carried a mug across the ice a tall figure dived in front of me with his pants around his ankles. It was Mike, and he slid to a stop at my feet, arms flailing. 'Shit!' he said.

The latrine at Camp Mackay was a hole in the sea ice. It was protected by a small windbreaker and offered a panoramic view of the landscape. On this occasion, a seal had emerged through the hole and exhaled in his usual manner while Mike was engaged in the task at hand.

Lavatorial stories were part of the fabric of camp life in the south, as they are in all camps. Fortunately the Incinolet variety of Antarctic outhouse had been abandoned. Like many of their kind, the Incinolets only accepted solids, but unlike the other types they were powered by electricity, with the result that if liquid was deposited in error the donor received an electric shock and the Incinolet shorted out.

We made such good progress with the cleaning up that Ross declared a half day and we took off on an excursion to Botany Bay and Granite Harbour. John didn't come; he took his work very seriously. I think he was glad to have us out of the way.

I travelled lying in a trailer behind a snowmobile. It wasn't very comfortable, but I preferred it to the back of the snowmobile as it was easier to lose yourself when you didn't have to concentrate on hanging on. We trawled round the sea ice and stopped beneath the cliffs at Granite Harbour, climbing over pressure ridges to zigzag up a hill coated with spongy black lichen and lash out at swooping skuas. Glacier ice cascaded down the granite cliffs like ice cream down a cone, and the boys paused to argue the toss between the conflicting theories of glacial stability and glacial dynamism.

Granite Harbour, discovered in January 1902 when the *Discovery* steamed in, was an embayment about eleven miles wide which marked the seaward end of a deep valley between Cape Archer and Cape Roberts, and it was backed by high mountains. Frank Debenham, T. Griffith Taylor, Tryggve Gran and P.O. Robert Forde, the Second Western Party, set out from Cape Evans on 14 December 1911 to geologise in the area of Granite Harbour, and they built a rock shelter which they called Granite House, a name they took from a Jules Verne story. They used it as a field kitchen, because the blubber stove exuded too many fumes to be kept in a tent. They even sprouted sea kale in a kitchen garden outside. In 1959 an American party discovered two books in perfect condition in the shelter. One was by Poe and the other by Verne, and when they opened them they saw from the flyleaves that Griffith Taylor had owned one and Debenham the other. As both men were still alive, the Americans sent the books back.

*

Everyone gathered in the canvas hut at seven the next morning, the day of our pull-out, lured out of sleeping bags by John's tactical promise of maple-syrup pancakes. As the stove had been purged it was very cold, and the hut had been stripped, so it was like sitting down at home for the final cup of tea on the day you move house. The discussion revolved around the weather and potential competition for helicopter time, and our spirits rose during our radio schedule with McMurdo as we heard that a number of other camps were weathered in.

I was sent back on the first trip, wedged between Ross and three plastic trash sacks. I couldn't see anything at all, and teabags leaked on my shoulder.

CHAPTER EIGHT

The Response of the Spirit

Even now the Antarctic is to the rest of the earth as the Abode of the Gods was to the ancient Chaldees, a precipitous and mammoth land lying far beyond the seas which encircled man's habitation, and nothing is more striking about the exploration of the Southern Polar regions than its absence, for when King Alfred reigned in England the Vikings were navigating the ice-fields of the North; yet when Wellington fought the battle of Waterloo there was still an undiscovered continent in the south.

Apsley Cherry-Garrard, from *The Worst Journey in the World*

IN 1911, in the heart of the polar winter, the saintly Bill Wilson, Scott's right-hand man, pulled a sledge from Cape Evans to Cape Crozier with Birdie Bowers and Apsley Cherry-Garrard in order to collect emperor penguin eggs. No human being had yet seen such eggs. The temperature dropped to minus seventy-seven degrees Fahrenheit, the tent blew away, and when they finally got back to the hut after five weeks the others had to use tin openers to get their clothes off. 'I for one had come to that point of suffering at which I did not really care if only I could die without much pain,' wrote Cherry-Garrard.

When three eggs reached England, the men in starched collars labouring in the Gothic scientific institutions sniffed and said that the Crozier trip 'had not added greatly to our knowledge of penguin embryology'. In *The Worst Journey in the World*, a book which deals with the whole expedition, though the title refers to the march to Crozier, Cherry-Garrard artlessly turns the journey into the quest for truth and the penguin eggs into a symbol of its spiritual goal. It is the archetypal transmogrification of failure on a human plane into success on a higher one. He said this:

> Superficially they failed. I have heard discussions of their failure. The same men would have discussed the failure of Christ hanging upon the cross: or Joan of Arc burning at the stake . . . To me, and perhaps to you, the interest of this story is the men, and it is the spirit of the men, 'the response of the spirit', which is interesting, rather than what they did or failed to do: except in a superficial sense they never failed. That is how I see it, and I knew them pretty well. It is a story about human minds with all kinds of ideas and questions involved, which stretch beyond the furthest horizons.

Cherry wrote the book after he had been invalided home from the Western Front, and by then the war had shattered illusions like so many eggshells. 'Never such innocence, never before or since,' Philip Larkin wrote of 1914. For Cherry, the trek to Crozier became a one-way journey out of prelapsarian innocence. Nobody needed to believe the mythical elevation more than he did. His two companions, Wilson and Bowers, had gone on to die with Scott, and he tortured himself with the thought that he might have saved them had he taken the dogs further before the next winter closed in.

For Cherry, as for the dying Scott, the whole business became an apotheosis. He ends the book like this:

> And I tell you, if you have the desire for knowledge and the power to give it physical expression, go out and explore. If you are a brave man you will do nothing: if you are fearful you may do much, for none but cowards have need to prove their bravery. Some will tell you that you are mad, and nearly all will say, 'What is the use?' For we are a nation of shopkeepers, and no shopkeeper will look at research which does not promise him a financial return within a year. And so you will sledge nearly alone, but those with whom you sledge will not be shopkeepers: that is worth a good deal. If you march your Winter Journeys you will have your reward, so long as all you want is a penguin's egg.

His prose is divine, its mournful echoing cadences reminiscent of a great badly-lit railway station where people are saying goodbye.

Among the youngest of Scott's men, Cherry was a typical Edwardian landed gentleman, a classicist and a rower, and he was very popular in the south. Despite shockingly bad eyesight, besides being one of the best sledgers, he was the editor of the *South Polar Times* and Wilson's indefatigable zoological assistant. The transmogrification he effected did not keep his demons at bay, and he spent a large part of his later years suffering from depression.

Shortly after I had returned from Chile, I found a battered copy of *The Worst Journey* in a secondhand bookshop. Knowing almost nothing about Antarctica, I lay in the hammock on my roof for an hour's respite after a murderously frustrating morning in front of the word processor. With a duvet over me, I grasped the book in one hand so that it hovered in mid-air above my face. I had been invited to a birthday party that night, and in a burst of organisational zeal I had already ironed my frock, which was hanging, ready for duty, from the picture rail in my bedroom. But I never went to the party. I closed the book at four in the morning – by then inside on the sofa, though still under the duvet. 'This journey had beggared our language,' Cherry wrote, but he had searched within himself and produced a masterpiece.

The Worst Journey has slipped the shackles of its period and entered the immortal zone. It has influenced countless people, and pops up unexpectedly in volumes of memoirs and essays by writers from Nancy Mitford to Paul Theroux. George Bernard Shaw, a friend of Cherry's, had cast his eye over an early draft, and in his biography of Shaw, Michael Holroyd wrote, 'In Shaw's imagination the appalling conditions of the Antarctic became a metaphor for the moral climate of Britain between the wars, and Cherry-Garrard's survival a triumph of human will over social adversity.'

Cherry, Wilson and Bowers had built a rock shelter they called an igloo near the Cape Crozier emperor penguin colony. This was where the tent had blown away. I had an overpowering desire to lie in what was left of their shelter. There, I thought, I could pay homage.

I heard that a pair of scientists had to be picked up from their camp further down the coast of Ross Island and ferried to and from the Adelie colony at Crozier. By this time I had honed the skill of appearing at judicious moments in the Helo Ops room. Soon I had successfully insinuated myself on the flight manifest.

The day before I left for the Crozier pilgrimage I attended the weekly science lecture. It was about evolutionary biology, and the Catholic priest, appearing for the opposition, sat in the front row. 'This is what Antarctica looked like for much of its geological history,' intoned the lecturer. By the time he got down to the palaeontological nitty-gritty the priest had nodded off, effectively registering his protest.

*

We set off in a helicopter early in the morning and proceeded up the coast to Cape Bird, where two Kiwi biologists were waiting next to their small hut. From there, it took us half an hour to reach Crozier. I saw from the map that we were in James Clark Ross's territory: he had sprayed names everywhere. Cape Crozier was named after his best friend Francis Crozier, who captained the *Terror*, one of the two ships Ross took south. Its first lieutenant was Archibald McMurdo.

The pilot pointed across the Sound. In the distance a red dot was stationary in the heavy pack ice. It was an American ice-breaker, trying to cut a channel for a tanker which would refuel McMurdo. Beneath us crevasse fields streaked the snow like cellulite.

'See those?' said the pilot over the headset. 'You could drive a double-decker bus in there.'

Then, like a handful of ash, fragments of black metal appeared on the snowfields. On 28 November 1979 a 200-ton DC-10 on a sightseeing flight crashed into the lower slopes of Erebus, killing all 257 aboard. The passengers on Air New Zealand Flight 901 were tourists. Like Americans and the assassination of John F. Kennedy, every Kiwi can tell you what they were doing when they heard the news. They could all remember, too, seeing the familiar Maori koru, the airline's logo, protruding from the snow on the DC-10's tail engine pod. The effect of the disaster on the national psyche was incalculable. 'The fact that it was in the Antarctic made it particularly obscene,' someone said. Sixteen years on, I happened to mention to a table of New Zealanders in Wellington that someone had attended a McMurdo Halloween party in an impressive Mount Erebus costume. Silence descended like a fog. It was like telling a British gathering that someone had dressed up as Lockerbie.

We dropped off the biologists and arranged to pick them up two hours later. Having purposefully inflamed the crew with stories of epic heroism, I experienced no difficulty in persuading them that we should try to find Cherry's rock shelter. They threw themselves enthusiastically into the search.

'You mean to say that they dragged their sledges over *that?*' asked the pilot, looking at the gnarled pressure ridges.

'Yes,' I said, keen to maintain his interest. 'They said their necks were frozen into the same position for hours.' It took three aborted landings and several radio conversations to establish the exact location of the rock shelter. I had read in *The Worst Journey* that it was two miles from the emperor colony. As we knew exactly where the emperor colony was, I had assumed that a swift aerial sweep within a two-mile radius would reveal the shelter. I didn't know that the colony had shifted four miles since Cherry man-hauled to it.

We got out and looked over the pressure ridges from the top of a hill.

'Look at that,' said the crewman. 'Forty miles of crevasse fields and cracked, craggy ice – we could never land on most of that, and they pulled their sledges all this goddam way. Damn sure I wouldn't do it.'

When I spotted the remains of the shelter, my heart contracted. It was as if they were going to appear from behind a rock, their necks frozen, smiling through cracked lips. As the ground came up to meet us, my eyes filled with tears. I pulled down my goggles. I hadn't realised how close we had become, these dead explorers and I.

'Can you believe those suckers built a shelter in such an exposed saddle?' said the crewman over the headset as the blades whirred to a stop and the wind buffeted the helicopter like a rocking chair.

'They chose the site in complete darkness,' I said, instinctively springing to their defence.

They had built a kind of igloo out of stones, about seven feet in diameter. Most of it had been carried off by the wind, but a ring of stones about ten inches high had survived. 'This is the House that Cherry Built,' an anonymous contributor had written in the *South Polar Times*, their expedition newspaper. It went on,

This is the Ridge that topped the Moraine
That supported the House that Cherry Built.
These are the Rocks and Boulders 'Erratic',
Composing the Walls – with lavas 'Basic' –
That stood on the Ridge that topped the Moraine . . . [1]

The interior of the shelter was covered with snow, and through
it poked a small wooden crate and a pair of frozen socks. People
told me these items had belonged to Cherry, Bowers and Wilson,
but I was sceptical about that. It was blowing so hard that in order
to walk forward we had to mould ourselves into the wind. I found
the small entrance in the crumbling wall of the shelter, lay down
and closed my eyes.

Cherry had prepared to die as he lay there. He did not rue the
past; he said only that he wanted those years over again. The
comradeship between the three men never faltered, even at the
worst moments. Cherry exults in the dignity with which they
emerged from their ordeal. 'We did not forget the please and the
thank you,' he wrote. 'I'll swear there was still a grace about us
when we staggered in. And we kept our tempers, even with God.'
People have said that this is an easy thing to write, after the event,
especially when no one is alive to gainsay it. This may be so – but
Cherry's prose sings with conviction. Lying in the remains of his
shelter, I felt something approaching awe, as he had taught me so
much. From him I had seen that it was possible to do anything
two ways, whether a five-week dance with death or an hour-long
business meeting. You could do it with dignity and loving kind-
ness, keeping your temper with God, or with ambition, self-
interest and greed, allowing the world to sweep you away like an
Antarctic wind. It was a simple choice. As he said, there were no
promises attached – the effort brought its own rewards. I had made
myself believe I could get to Cape Crozier, as he had done, but
what mattered was 'the response of the spirit'. It is surely the same
whatever your personal Crozier – summiting without oxygen,
building a garden shed, telling someone you love them.

The crewman and pilot leapt over the low wall and landed on
top of me.

---

[1] The same issue of the paper included a reworking of *Henry V* in which
Lieutenant Evans strides in declaring 'Once more unto the beach, dear friends,
once more.'

'Bit cramped in here, with three,' the crewman shouted over the wind. Indeed. Cherry's party had bulky reindeer sleeping bags to contend with, too, and the stove. One night a glob of boiling blubber had sizzled from the stove and landed in Wilson's eye. He was temporarily blinded, and in excruciating pain. Needless to say, they were dangerously underfed. 'Night after night', Cherry wrote, 'I bought big buns and chocolate at a stall on the island platform at Hatfield station.'

'Let's go,' said the pilot, jumping up. 'We've got a sustained twenty-five knots here and it's slicing through this gear like a knife.'

The manhauling winter journey to Crozier has been repeated once, though only one way. What Mike Stroud, Roger Mear and Gareth Wood accomplished when they pulled sledges to Crozier during the private Footsteps of Scott expedition in 1985 was a remarkable achievement. Mear, however, who went on to make an aborted attempt at a solo crossing of the continent a decade later, acknowledged in his book that the trip had been dominated by tensions and hostility. 'We came out of it anxious and hurt,' he wrote. So Cherry had been right. For him, what counted was 'the response of the spirit', but we are living in an age which doesn't give a fig about the spirit, an age fatally compromised by ambition and worldly success. Cherry knew, somehow, that the men who walked in his footsteps wouldn't be interested in 'gold, pure, shining, unalloyed' companionship. It seemed unbearably sad.

When Mear and his companions returned to their Cape Evans hut, a twelve-pound tin of strawberries exploded and could easily have killed them. Imagine doing all that and being killed by a strawberry.

*

Bill Wilson, who went south with Scott on both the *Discovery* and the *Terra Nova* expeditions, was the leader of the Crozier trek. He was a deeply religious man, even a mystic. That he was called by God, he had no doubt. This is an extract from one of his poems.

> And this was the thought that the silence wrought,
> As it scorched and froze us through,
> That we were the men God meant should know
> The heart of the Barrier snow.

Wilson was a doctor, a naturalist and an accomplished artist; a renaissance man. He admired Ruskin, and had a volume of Tennyson's poems in his pocket on the last sledging journey. He had Scott's ear, so he was a natural confidant for the men. As the great southern journey grew nearer, an increasing number of them came to him with their grievances, whether against Scott, other colleagues or the world in general. 'My goodness!' he wrote, 'I had hours of it yesterday; as though I was a bucket and it was poured into me.' Yet back at home he found normal social intercourse so difficult that he confided to his diary that he took sedatives before going to parties, and one of his biographers wrote that it required far more courage for him to face an audience than to cross a crevasse.

Everything served a grand purpose for Wilson and was a component of an embracing and harmonious philosophy. Art functioned to help science, which in turn enhanced faith. He was an ascetic. Between expeditions he wrote to his wife from somewhere in England that he had begun to enjoy hotel dinners and to prefer hot water to cold, and that it was a bad sign.

Many people are mystified by Wilson. After their first meeting, Mawson noted in his diary, 'I did not like Dr Wilson.' While I was having lunch with Roland Huntford in Cambridge, he put down his knife and fork on the long table in the dining hall smelling of boiled cauliflower and said, 'I can't *stand* Wilson.' Mike Stroud, one of the three who repeated the Winter Journey in 1985, once told me, 'Wilson's books are so strange. He was a very odd bloke. I don't know what to make of him.' Robert Graves said he had wanted to put Wilson into his autobiography *Goodbye to All That*, but couldn't find space. The two met in 1909 and Graves was much tickled by the story of a penguin who tried to mate with Wilson, though in fact all the bird did was drop a stone at his feet, which is quite a long way from mating, though perhaps not to a penguin.

In the south Wilson experienced the peace which passes all understanding. He spent the happiest times in the crow's nest, communing with his God together (as he felt) with his beloved wife Ory. Towards the end he appears already to have worked himself beyond the earthly plane. 'This is the most fascinating ideal I think I ever imagined,' he wrote on the plateau, 'to become entirely careless of your own soul or body in looking after the welfare of others.' If this is true – and I have no reason to suppose that it is not – Wilson must have overcome the most powerful of instincts: survival. In that case, it is not so surprising that he didn't survive.

Bowers, the third member of the team, was called Birdie because he had a beak nose. He was a peerless worker, indomitably cheerful, never felt the cold and shared, though to a lesser degree, Wilson's spirituality. That he had bought the fatal British prejudice concerning the moral virtues of dogless travel is revealed in a letter he wrote to Kathleen Scott. 'After all, it will be a fine thing to do that plateau with man-haulage in these days of the supposed decadence of the British race.' He gave his horse, Victor, a last biscuit from his own ration before shooting him.

He was devoted to his mother, and wrote this in a letter to her from the south.

Have been reading a lot and thinking a lot about things. This life at sea, so dependent upon nature, and so lonely, makes one think. I seem to get into a quagmire of doubts and disbeliefs. Why should we have so many disappointments, when life was hard enough without them? Everything seems a hopeless problem. I felt I should never get out, there was no purpose of it.

One night on deck when things were at their blackest, it seemed to me that Christ came to me and showed me why we are here, and what the purpose of life really is. It is to make a great decision – to choose between the material and the spiritual, and if we choose the spiritual we must work out our choice, and then it will run like a silver thread through the material. It is very difficult to express in words what I suddenly saw so plainly, and it was sometimes difficult to recapture it myself. I know, too, that my powerful ambitions to get on in this world will conflict with the pure light that I saw for a moment, but I can never forget that I did realise, in a flash, that nothing that happens to our bodies really matters.

We arrived early to pick up the biologists, and sat down to eat our sandwiches. The skuas complained bitterly about this flagrant trespass. The sandwiches were peanut butter and jelly, a particularly American combination and very nasty indeed. The whole of the Cape Crozier area was characterised by the dull background roar of the Adelie colony – some 170,000 breeding pairs. The chicks were sixteen days old, about ten inches tall and very lively. From a distance they looked like grey puffballs.

The Kiwi beakers, who were monitoring the Adelie diet, came trudging up the hill carrying their buckets like children coming home from the beach.

'Know what's in those buckets?' asked the crewman.

'No,' I said.

'Penguin vomit!' he announced triumphantly.

'Krill[1] dip, anyone?' shouted Bruce, the younger Kiwi. The pair of them had climbed into the helicopter when we first picked them up and begun chatting over the headsets as if they had known us all their lives. In fact, none of us had ever seen them before. They had a straightforward and pragmatic approach to whatever the day threw at them, and viewed the world with a healthy perspective that I had observed in many New Zealanders.

'What exactly do you do to the penguins?' I asked dubiously over the headset after we had taken off.

'Put catheters down their throats, introduce a little ambient temperature salt water and apply pressure to their abdomens,' said Jack cheerfully. He was the project leader. 'They throw up pretty quickly.'

Hardly surprising, I thought. The crew made gagging noises.

'What do you do with the vomit?' I continued in spite of myself.

'Bottle it,' said Jack. 'And take it back to New Zealand to have a closer look. Or sell it as chutney.'

When we landed at Cape Bird, everyone agreed that we should shut down and climb out for a turn on the cape.

The wind had carved the band of twisted ice fastened to the shore into a series of apocalyptic shapes, and the Adelies waddled among them like spectators at an art exhibition.

'There's between thirty and forty thousand breeding pairs here,' said Bruce, 'and see how well they blend in with the environment.' It was true – they melted into the snow-streaked black volcanic rock. Penguins were everywhere. Antarctica was the antithesis of the jungle or the rainforest, where everything burgeoned and

---

[1] A krill is a small, shrimplike marine crustacean, and a vital constituent of the Antarctic food chain. The word comes from the Norwegian noun for a young fish.

mutated and thousands of species and tens of thousands of subspecies co-existed. (I remembered fungus forming on my rucksack in the Amazon Basin as quickly as ice did in the south.) As the biologist David Campbell wrote in *The Crystal Desert*, 'A paucity of species but an abundance of individuals is a recurring evolutionary motif in polar areas.'

Everything was so simple in Antarctica. Even the food chain was simple. Phytoplankton, the primary producers, took light and made matter. Phytoplankton were eaten by krill, and krill were eaten by everything else.

Bruce, a man of Pickwickian geniality and an alarming orange beard, was showing off his new electronic weighbridge over which a sub-colony of Adelies were obliged to strut on their passage to the sea. The parents took it in turns to swim out, swallow a meal and return to regurgitate it to their offspring. There was a good deal of argument over it all. When a leopard seal began his late afternoon patrol hundreds of penguins porpoising through the water shot out vertically as if propelled by a tightly coiled spring. After landing, they shook themselves off as if they hadn't expected to land quite so soon. The water, reflecting the pearly silver blues of the sky, was thick with drifting pack, and suddenly the dark arched backs of a large pod of killer whales appeared, proceeding with rhythmic perfection in front of the cape. It was an identical scene to that of Herbert Ponting's finest hour, when, not far from this spot, he was apprehended on a floe by eight killer whales – but not until he had got the shots he wanted. He makes much of this episode in his book.

Ponting was the official photographer on the *Terra Nova* expedition, though he pressurised Scott to let him be called Camera Artist. Besides the famous stills of Scott writing purposefully at his desk in the Cape Evans hut and the ship perfectly framed by an ice cave, images now engraved on the national consciousness, Ponting shot a 'kinematograph', or moving-picture film, and twenty years later reissued it with a commentary and soundtrack, calling it *Ninety Degrees South*. Teddy Evans appears at the beginning in front of a creased black curtain in full evening dress and, hands in pockets, plays with his balls for some minutes while introducing 'Ponto', who slides into view resembling a large stuffed animal. What follows is a brilliant piece of film.

Ponting was a cold fish. He abandoned his wife, daughter and son to become a photographer, and never saw any of them again. Scott deplored his commercialism, and Ponting was always moaning that Scott had got the publicity wrong. In the south he irritated the others by asking them to pose all the time, like many photographers after him, and in later years never attended reunions. His prose is stiff and pompous, yet often revealing. 'We felt like boys again,' he wrote, 'and acted, too, like boys.'

Frank Hurley, the other great photographer of the Heroic Age, went south with Shackleton and took the famous picture of the crippled *Endurance* balancing on the ice like a ballerina. As a record of the death of a ship it will never be surpassed. Hurley, an Australian with none of Ponting's pomposity, ran away from home and didn't see the sea until he was fifteen. He met a French opera singer in Cairo and married her ten days later. Besides hundreds of images of Australian troops, Hurley took pictures of monolithic columns in the Church of the Nativity in Bethlehem with beams of light falling in pools on the flagstones (he called one 'I am the Light of the World'). He has left fewer remarkable Antarctic landscapes than Ponting; his Antarctica is less frigid and more human. The pack ice in his best picture is like a field of white carnations. In life Shackleton and Scott had found the appropriate photographers, just as in death they had got the Societies they deserved.

*

By the time the helicopter landed at McMurdo, it was already eight o'clock. I was supposed to be moving over to Scott Base. Many months before I had engaged in a long correspondence with the people who ran the New Zealand Antarctic Programme, and they had invited me to spend a few days at their base while I was on Ross Island. Shortly after arriving in McMurdo for the first time I had walked the two miles over the hill to Scott Base to meet Malcolm Macfarlane, at that time the senior representative of the NZ programme. We had almost collided before, we discovered. Three years previously Malcolm had been working on a cruise liner in the Southern Ocean when a passenger died while the ship was off Cape Horn. I was hanging around in Tierra del Fuego at that time, and in order to get a glimpse of the Horn I had hitched a lift on a supply boat delivering an empty coffin to a cruise ship. The coffin had been covered with a candlewick bedspread, and the sailors played poker on it for most of the trip. When we got to the Horn, where a gale was raging, I had helped lower the coffin into a zodiac, and must have seen Malcolm hanging over the rail in the stern of the ship, assisting the embarkation of the coffin.

I arrived at Scott Base later that evening, and repaired to the bar with Malcolm. A sign on the door said, '*Remove boots, jacket and hat or buy the whole bar a drink*.' Someone had to tell me that, as the sign was in Japanese. It was a cunning Kiwi ploy to stitch up passing strangers and force them into buying a round.

There were only thirty or so people on base, so I had a room to myself. It was a small, windowless room with a set of bunk beds, but it was very comfortable. There was a mug on the bedside table bearing the slogan '*Party Till You Puke*', a caption which went some way towards summing up the off-duty philosophy of the base. The Kiwis on the ice had a culture all their own. They held three-legged ski races and painted their toenails blue.

It snowed for two days, and scientists paced the corridors. A trio of microbiologists were trying to get to the crater of Erebus to collect high-temperature bacteria. One of them, a tall man with wild eyes which peered over his glasses and down his nose, had hair shooting from his head like the flame of the Olympic torch. He flung his arms around when he spoke.

'I work', he told me one day, jiggling his left hand and slicing the air with his right forefinger, 'on bacteria for which the tropics are too cold. They like it best at 105 degrees Celsius. This is a theory of evolution – that life began with these creatures. They form the very roots of the tree of life! That is my belief. A theory of evolution must be like a belief.'

On my third day Bruce, the Pickwickian biologist with the orange beard, turned up from Cape Bird. He got on to the subject of the Husky Hugging Club. Initiation into this august institution had involved stripping naked in front of the base, walking a hundred yards and hugging a husky. The last huskies left Antarctica in 1994 as a result of Antarctic Treaty regulations banning all alien species, although they hadn't been used as working dogs for some years before that. I wondered why humans had not qualified for the same exclusion. Bruce talked fondly of the dogs, while the Americans seemed to have forgotten their existence.

Much of the human culture of Antarctica was caught up in the mystique of 'the old days', for every nationality. I wondered how many stories I had heard Americans telling about the Biolab which preceded the Crary, and its crappy lounge with the beaten-up sofas and benches where everyone worked next to each other, and about walking past Art DeVries' bench and being offered a bowl of fish soup? It was like some Homeric age in which men larger than ourselves bestrode the continent, replaced now by the etiolated figures of bureaucracy.

The legends were even more vividly drawn in the collective memory of Kiwi veterans. They reached their acme in the exploits of the Asgaard Rangers and their bitter enemies the Vandals. The former were nomadic hydrologists who had been roaming the Asgaard mountains in the Dry Valleys since the late sixties, and the latter were the sedentary scientists of the Lake Vanda camp on the valley floor. One of the Asgaards had just arrived at Scott Base, and he was extremely keen to extol Asgaard virtues and Vandal frailties. Pete was a rogue with a gleam in his eye and an infectiously enthusiastic manner; once he spotted a joke he pursued it like a hound after a hare.

'Tell me about your work,' I said.

'We measure water flows', he replied quickly, 'and compare the rate of glacial advance and retreat here with glacier movement in New Zealand. They move much more slowly here.' He didn't seem very interested in talking about this.

'What you have to understand,' he said, clearing his throat and leaning over the dining table towards me, 'is that Vandals are inferior to Asgaards in every way.'

The passage of almost thirty years had not diminished their rivalry. Mock battles continued to be staged, and if the Vandals raised their flag from the bamboo pole at their camp, an Asgaard Ranger would be sure to ski down from the top of the valley and slice it off.

'Asgaards pride themselves on the theft of as much issue clothing as possible,' said Pete, adding quickly, 'though of course, we Rangers don't actually need to wear many clothes, as we barely feel the cold.'

'What else rates highly then?' I asked. 'I mean, in the Asgaard-versus-Vandal rivalry?'

'Stealing food from Americans but ratting on Vandals who do the same is highly regarded,' he said, warming now to the theme.

'I remember hijacking a leg of ham from a helicopter once. We were only talking about that at a reunion last month.'

'Where do you hold the reunions?' I asked.

'Strip clubs, usually,' he said.

I could imagine how much the bureaucracy and safety regulations of the contemporary Antarctic programme must have crucified him. The affection with which he recounted his stories made me realise what an important part of his life Antarctica had been. When I commented on that, he paused reflectively.

'Well, relationships here are especially close,' he said eventually. 'It's obvious, isn't it – you can't share it with anyone else. I hardly ever talk about Antarctica at home. No one would understand. There's no place like this, and because of that it becomes emotional.'

Some time later I caught sight of Pete strolling around McMurdo wearing his tatty Rangers jacket, and he made me think of an amiable dinosaur tramping the streets of Milton Keynes or the malls of New Jersey.

On the fourth day the Kiwis went into a huddle, and when they came out of it, a camping trip had been arranged. As soon as they asked me along, I sent a message to McMurdo to say I wasn't coming home.

The team consisted of four men and five women. 'Here,' said Jaqui before we left. She was the base cleaner. 'Take this.' With that, she bundled a yellow parka into my arms. 'So you won't feel the odd one out,' she said. The Kiwi women had raised their collective wing and taken me under it. It was like coming home.

We set off in high spirits and a Hagglunds tracked vehicle, bound for an old hut on the ice shelf. The Kiwis had been maintaining the hut for years – it was only a few miles away, but it was off-station, and that was what mattered. We stopped en route at the skiway on the southern side of Hut Point peninsula for a couple of hours downhill skiing. They had fixed a towrope to the back of an old truck, and imported some juggernaut tyres for tubing downhill.

After exhausting ourselves on the slopes we drove on to the hut. Lighting the Preway always constituted something of a drama in Antarctic huts, but once we had done it there was nothing further to do but snuggle around it and sip mulled wine. The hut, in full view of Erebus, was hard by the snowfield used by the New

Zealanders for survival training. Besides building igloos, snowholes and snow walls, they had carved a lifesize bar, complete with barstools, draught pumps and glasses.

'It makes us feel at home,' someone commented.

On the spur of the moment I decided to sleep in an igloo, as the ambient temperature was above zero and the wind had fallen to a whisper. When I woke up next morning sky-blue sunlight was trickling through the bricks and splashing on to the blue-and-yellow sleeping bag. I crawled up the tunnel and watched the plumes of Erebus dissolving into the limpid sky. The sun had warmed the motionless air, the clouds had fled, and nobody else was awake.

I lay down on my parka. Sometimes I lost myself so thoroughly in Antarctica that I felt as if I had fallen off the planet and forgotten who I was. It was as if all my points of reference had dissolved like the Erebus plumes, or I had wandered off into some country of the mind to which I alone had a passport. When I felt it most acutely I had to close my eyes and think about something that was still going on in the inhabited world. It was a device to ensure I didn't lose my grip on reality, like looking up through a periscope on a submarine for reassurance that the world is still there. The image that leapt most readily into my empty mind was that of a beak-nosed nun crouching on a chequered floor in a tiny Byzantine chapel. A single oil-lamp in a niche cast flickering light around the entire biblical cosmogony, and on the chipped fresco at the back a mass of faces were permanently twisted into the tormented screams of the damned.

The nunnery was high on a mountain in the middle of the Greek island of Evia. I had spent several weeks there five years previously staying in a bare room above a courtyard filled with geraniums bursting from terracotta flowerpots. The rims of these flowerpots were regularly whitewashed by the beak-nosed nun. It was an operation modelled on the painting of the Golden Gate bridge, for when she had finished, she started at the beginning again. The Sisters spent at least half their waking hours in the chapel, and services were punctuated by brief hiatuses during which an argument stormed to and fro over which psalm was to be sung.

In the years since I had walked back down the mountain, I often found myself thinking of the nuns. They represented something solid and permanent when everything else seemed to be sliding away like loose scree.

*

Unlike the United States, New Zealand claims sovereignty over a slice of Antarctica. The Antarctic Treaty neither endorses nor refutes this claim, or indeed the claims of six other nations (Chile, Argentina, Australia, Britain, Norway and France). The Treaty evolved to preserve the fragile balance of ownership and non-ownership and to protect *Terra Incognita* from the depredations of exploitation and warfare. It states that 'Antarctica shall be used for peaceful measures only . . . in the interests of all humanity', and gives all parties free access to the whole of the continent, fostering science as the legitimate expression of national interest. Initiated during International Geophysical Year and applicable to all territory south of sixty degrees south, the Treaty was signed by twelve nations in 1959 and came into force in 1961. Since then the number of signatories has more than tripled. The accession of India and Brazil in 1983, and China two years later, meant that the Treaty was no longer the exclusive territory of rich, developed nations. The document subsequently expanded. The Protocol on Environmental Protection, signed in Madrid in 1991, imposed a fifty-year moratorium on extracting oil and mining minerals. It has been called Pax Antarctica.

In the early days, everyone wanted some of this unknown land – or at least, they didn't want to be left out. Doris Lessing wrote that to non-Europeans thinking about the Antarctic in the decades before the First World War, 'there was little Europe, strutting and bossing up there in its little corner, like a pack of schoolboys fighting over a cake.' Just before the Second World War, Hitler decided that Antarctica too was to be part of the great Nazi empire. He ordered several thousand steel-barbed swastikas, loaded them on to planes, put the planes on a ship and sent the whole lot south, telling the pilots to drop their cargo over a vast tract of the icefields. After the war, people were still optimistic that the continent could be made to earn its keep. In 1949 a journalist called Douglas Liversidge went south to visit British bases and witness the relief of Fuchs and his expedition from Stonington Island. In his book *The Last Continent*, published in 1958, Liversidge suggests that Antarctica might provide 'cheap, large-scale refrigeration of grain, meat and other supplies' – that it might function as a global freezer, in other words. By the late eighties, a coalition of Third World nations led by Malaysia accused Treaty members of 'modern day colonialism'.

The political situation often belied reality. I observed on my first visit south that the Antarctic can erase national boundaries. An Argentinian arrived for a minor operation at a Chilean base which included a relatively sophisticated medical facility. The man was greeted with slaps on the back and urgent petitions about a forthcoming radio chess tournament. I had never heard that kind of talk in Chile, only spiteful jokes about loud-mouthed neighbours who rolled their 'r's. The geopolitics of Antarctica – complex, potentially explosive, deadly serious and ice cold – were played out not on the snowfields but in the ring of the international circus of conferences they engendered and the carpeted corridors of capital cities.

CHAPTER NINE

Igloos and Nitroglycerine

I don't really mind science – I just seem to feel better
when it's not around.

Observed on latrine wall,
Central West Antarctica deep field camp

RESUMING THE QUEST for Seismic Man and his group, I wheedled my way on to a fuel flight to Central West Antarctica, and after a series of false starts I was transported to the skiway with four members of a science project staging at CWA en route to Ice Stream B. The West Antarctic ice streams – fast-flowing currents of ice up to 50 miles wide and 310 miles long – are cited as evidence of possible glacial retreat and the much-touted imminent rise in global sea levels. The project leader pulled out *The Road to Oxiana*, the greatest travel book ever written and one which lies so close to my heart that it gave me a shock to see it there, as if the paraphernalia of home had followed me. He was a beatific man in his mid-fifties with a round, mottled face like a moon, and his name was Hermann. Ten years previously, he had climbed out of a crashed plane in Antarctica.

Later, when we were airborne, the scientists retreated into the hoods of their parkas, jamming unwieldily booted feet among the trellis of rollers, survival bags and naked machinery. I loitered on the flight deck for a while, but I couldn't see much. It grew colder.

The previous evening, in the galley at McMurdo, I had run into a mountaineer from a science group which had recently pulled out of CWA.

'Hey!' he had said when I told him I was on my way there. 'You can sublease the igloo I built just outside camp. It's the coolest igloo on the West Antarctic ice sheet.'

When we landed at eighty-two degrees south, the back flap lifted and light flooded into the plane. Tornadoes of powder snow were careering over the blanched wasteland like spectral spinning tops. There were no topographical features, just an ice sheet, boundless and burnished. Lesser (or West) Antarctica is a hypothesised rift system – a jumble of unstable plates – separated from the stable shield of Greater (or East) Antarctica by the Transantarctic Mountains. On top, most of Lesser Antarctica consists of the world's only marine-based ice sheet. This means that the bottom of the ice is far below sea level, and if it all melted, the western half of Antarctica would consist of a group of islands. The assemblage of plates which make up Lesser Antarctica have been moving both relative to one another and to the east for something like 230 million years, whereas Greater Antarctica, home of the polar plateau, has existed relatively intact for many hundreds of millions of years. In Gondwanaland, the prehistoric supercontinent, what we now know as South America and the Antipodes were glued to Antarctica. Gondwanaland started to break up early in the Jurassic Period – say 175 million years ago – and geologists like to speculate on the relationship of Antarctica to still earlier super continents. Most exciting of all, Antarctica once had its own dinosaurs.

The crewmen began rolling pallets off the back of the plane. We walked down after them, and the wind stung our faces. The engines roared behind us as we struggled to pull our balaclavas down around our goggles.

In the sepulchral light ahead I could see a scattering of Jamesways, a row of sledges, half a dozen tents, and Lars, the shaggy-haired Norwegian-American from Survival School. He was looking even shaggier, and proffering a mug of cocoa. We hugged one another. Lars led the way into the first Jamesway, where half a dozen weatherbeaten individuals were slumped around folding formica tables.

'Welcome, Woo!' somebody shouted. I had brought them cookies and a stack of magazines, and as I handed these over we all talked at once; a lot seemed to have happened in two months.

'Guess what?' said Lars. 'We saw a bird.'

The CWA field camp was probably the largest on the continent. Fifty people were based here for most of the summer season, working on four separate geological projects. Often small groups temporarily left camp, travelled over the ice sheet on snowmobiles or tracked vehicles, pitched their tents for a few days and tried to find out what the earth looked like under that particular bit of ice. They were creating a relief map of Antarctica without its white blanket.

Seeing Seismic Man's lightweight parka hanging on a hook in the Jamesway, I suspected he was away working at one of these small satellite camps. I was thinking about this, just as Lars produced another round of cocoa, when a familiar figure flew through the door of the Jamesway and clattered to a standstill beside me. It was Jose, the diminutive Mexican-American biker who grinned like a satyr and with whom I had failed to get to CWA on my first attempt. He had made it here a week before me. In one long exhalation of breath he said that he had heard I'd come, that he and two others were about to set off to strike a satellite camp thirty miles away, that it would take about twenty-four hours and they wouldn't be sleeping, that I could go too if I wanted ... and then he trailed off, like his bike running out of fuel.

Having trekked halfway across the continent to find Seismic Man, I left immediately without seeing him at all. It was the idea of the quest that had appealed to me. Feeling vaguely irritated about this, as if the whole expedition had been someone else's idea, I climbed into the back of a tracked vehicle and shook hands with a tall loose-limbed Alaskan in the driver's seat.

'They call me Too-Tall Dave,' he said as he pumped my hand, crushing a few unimportant bones. 'Pleased to meet you.'

The man next to him – a medical corpsman on loan from the Navy – looked as if he had just got up. His name was Chuck, and apparently he had forgotten the American president's name one day and asked Too-Tall Dave to remind him. Jose and I spread out over the two bench seats in the back of the vehicle. It was a temperamental Tucker which only liked travelling between eight and ten miles an hour, and we were towing a flat, open trailer and a sledge loaded with survival gear. As we were following a flagged route to the small camp you couldn't really call what Too Tall was doing driving: it was more a question of stabilising the steering wheel with his elbow and looking at the dash every so often to make sure he was maintaining the correct rpm to keep the water and oil at a stable temperature. It was very warm in the Tucker. The ice was dappled with watery sunlight, and the sky pale, streaky blue.

'This', said Jose, 'is what travelling in a covered wagon across the United States must have been like.'

After five hours, we reached a weatherhaven and a Scott tent.

'Is this it?' I asked.

'Yep,' said Too Tall, swinging nimbly out of the Tucker.

When I saw the tent, its flap still open, sunlit against the white prairies, an image flashed across my mind, and after a moment I recognised it as J. C. Dollman's painting of Titus Oates staggering off to die, arms outstretched and wearing a blue bobble hat. The lone tent in the background of the picture was identical to the one I was looking at, except that Dollman painted something which looked like a Land Rover parked outside. The painting was called 'A Very Gallant Gentleman', and the previous summer I had gone to see it at the Cavalry Club in London's Piccadilly. The Patron of my expedition, Jeremy Lewis, came along in an attempt to expiate his guilt at fulfilling none of the duties performed by more experienced Patrons such as the Duke of Edinburgh or the manufacturers of Kendal's Mint Cake. Jeremy said he thought Oates was probably wearing a tweed jacket under his parka with a copy of the *Symposium* in the pocket.

In its clumsy way the picture captures the most luminous moment in Antarctic history – when a desperately weak Oates announced that he might be some time and, without putting on his boots, crawled out of the tent. The episode has inculcated itself so effectively into the national psyche that the phrase, 'the Captain Oates Defence' is now bandied around the financial press when a senior figure leaves a troubled company to save his colleagues. At the time, Oates's deed unleashed a good deal of excruciating sentiment disguised as art. I was especially taken by two stanzas of 'Omen Pugnae', a poem by Hugh Macnaghten, vice-provost of Eton College, Oates's school, published in 1924.

So, on the day he died,
His birthday, one last gift was his to give
For him to perish that his friends might live
Was 'just to go outside'.

Just two and thirty years
But O! thy last farewell, a household word
And all that we have seen and we have heard,
There is no room for tears.

In the *Daily Telegraph*, on 8 April 1995, Beryl Bainbridge took a more robust approach, suggesting that Andrew Lloyd Webber might like to stage a musical of Scott's expedition including a number sung by Oates, 'I'm just stepping outside and may be some time'.

Oates was in charge of the ponies on the *Terra Nova* expedition. They were a bunch of old crocks from Siberia and a disaster from the start. He had not selected them himself, and described his charges and the dogs on board the ship as 'the most unsuitable scrap-heap crowd of unfit animals'. Nicknamed Titus after the seventeenth-century intriguer, Lawrence Oates was the only expedition member from the army, and consequently he was also known as 'the Soldier'. He had money, and his father had written 'gentleman' in the Paternal Occupation box on the infant's birth certificate. As a young man Titus was Lord of the Manor at Gestingthorpe in Essex, and the whole village celebrated feudal-style when he returned from the Boer War a wounded hero. He was reserved, measured and a cheerful pessimist, the archetypal Action Man whose only pin-up above his bunk was a portrait of Napoleon. In many ways he was the polar opposite of Scott. He received a toy gun for Christmas in the south, and went around shooting people with it *for the rest of the evening*, asking them to fall down when hit. His creed was 'Down with Science, Sentiment and the Fair Sex', and he once confided to Wilson that his mother was the only woman he had ever loved.

He was a popular officer. I read a pile of letters sent to his mother after the news had broken. One said, 'Dear old Titus took my brother's place when he died in the Transvaal and I loved Titus as a brother and now he is gone. What it must mean to you God alone knows.' Indeed. She burnt his diaries, though his sister, alerted to the imminent conflagration, stayed up all night to copy out as many of the handwritten pages as she could.

He was a stereotypical upper-class twit, in many ways, and twits were no different then than they are now. Despite that, I liked him. His no-nonsense approach appealed to me, and so did his fierce opposition to prevarication or cant.

*

I packed up the contents of the weatherhaven while Jose and Too Tall set about dismantling it from the outside. Fortunately the wind had dropped, but it was bitterly cold.

'Why didn't the beakers do this themselves?' asked Too Tall irritably. 'Next time they'll be asking us to wipe their butts.'

By the time we had finished loading the gear on to the trailer it was six o'clock in the morning. We squatted in a banana sledge we had forgotten to pack up, and opened three cartons of orange juice and a large bag of trail-mix.

As we rearranged our own gear in the back of the Tucker afterwards I noticed that fuel had leaked all over my sleeping bag, not for the first time or the last. I wasn't the only one in Antarctica who smelt like an oil rig.

I drove for the first three hours on the way back to camp. It was a mesmerising occupation, and as I wandered into a reverie or stared blankly out at the ice sheet, the needle crept up on the rev. counter dial.

'Less gas!' Too Tall would then say, delivering a karate chop on my shoulder from the bench in the back. The monotony was broken by the appearance of a bottle of bourbon. Jose set up a Walkman with a pair of speakers.

'We need tortured blues,' said Too Tall. He was right. It was the perfect accompaniment to the inescapable monotony of the landscape and the hypnotic rhythm of the Tucker.

I got accused of picking all the cashews out of the trail-mix, a crime of which I was indeed guilty. Everyone started talking.

'Are you married?' Jose asked me.

'No,' I said. 'Are you?'

'No.' There was a pause, which something was waiting to fill.

'Go on Jose, tell her!' said Chuck.

Jose cleared his throat.

'Actually, I married my Harley Davidson,' he said.

I choked on the last cashew.

'Oh, really?' I said, in an English kind of way. 'Who performed the, er – ceremony?'

'Owner of my local bike shop. He does it a lot.'

This information was almost more than the human spirit could bear. Fortunately an empty fuel drum chose that moment to fall off our trailer and roll over the ice sheet, and after we had dealt with that, the topic was forgotten.

A fresh one, however, was looming.

'You know that Captain Scott,' said Too Tall in my direction as the bourbon went round again. 'Was he a bit of a dude, or what?'

I had just begun to grapple with a reply to this weighty question when Chuck, his face puckered in concentration, chipped in with 'Hey, is that the guy they named Scott's hut after?'

'No,' I said, quickly grasping the opportunity to divert the conversation away from the dude issue. 'That was Mr Hut.'

It took us eight hours to get back, and then I had to put up my tent. It was snowing lightly, and I was too tired to dig out the igloo. I chose a place at the back of camp, facing the horizon. My metal tent pegs weren't deep enough, so I hijacked a bunch of bamboo flagpoles, and after the bottle-green and maroon tent was up I collapsed into a deep sleep.

When I woke up, a face was hovering a foot above mine.

'Hi Woo,' it growled. 'Didn't want to wake you.'

'This is a funny way to go about not waking me,' I said as the face drew closer.

*

They were using explosives to find out what the ground was like under 6,000 feet of ice. 'We're not particularly interested in ice,' someone commented breezily. Because of the inconvenient ice cover, most Antarctic geology can only be studied by remote-sensing methods like seismology. This involves setting off explosions, bouncing the soundwaves down through the ice to the earth's crust, and recording them on their way back up.

Before they could be detonated, the explosives had to be buried, and twelve itinerant drillers had been travelling around the ice sheet within a 200-mile radius of CWA boring a series of ninety-foot holes. They began each hole using a self-contained unit which heated water and sprinkled it on the ice like a shower head.

This unit fulfilled a secondary function as a hot tub, and we got in four at a time, draping our clothes carefully over the pipes to prevent them from turning to deep-frozen sandpaper. This was a task requiring consummate skill. A square inch of fabric inadvertently exposed to the air could have excruciating consequences.

Five members of the drill team were women, and in the hot tub one day I found myself next to Diane, a lead driller. She was tall and willowy with long hair the colour of cornflakes. I asked her how long she had been away.

'Thirty-five days,' she said. 'And my feet were never dry.'

'What did you do out there?' I asked. 'I mean, when you weren't drilling?'

'Well, just living took all our time. We worked twelve-hour shifts on the drill, and then we'd have to set up the cook tent and all that. We had to plan what we were going to eat carefully, as even if it was going to be a can of peaches it had to be hung up in the sleep tent overnight to thaw.'

'Was it your, er, ambition to do this kind of work?' I asked, struggling to grasp the concept that a woman could enjoy spending weeks in sub-zero conditions manipulating a drill for twelve hours a day.

'I do love it,' she said. 'I think this is the most magical place in the world. People say – "But all you can see is white!" That's true, but I could never, ever get bored on the drill when I can watch the dancing ice crystals, and the haloes twinkling round the sun. It's another world.'

The evening before they flew back to McMurdo, the drillers brought in ice from a deep core and hacked it up on the chopping board in the galley. It was over 300 years old, and packed with oxygen bubbles. It fizzed like Alka-seltzer in our drinks. Diane was baking cinnamon rolls. When she opened the oven door a rich, spicy aroma filled the Jamesway. It was like a souk.

Diane inhaled deeply. 'Heaven!' she said.

The next day I moved into the igloo. It was at the back of what they called Tent City, and it took me two hours to dig out the trench leading down to the entrance. Like all good igloos, the sleeping area was higher than the entrance, thereby creating a cold sink. Inside, there was a carpet of rubber mats, and a ledge ran all the way round about six inches off the floor. I spent a further two hours clearing away the pyramids of snow that had accumulated through the cracks. When my new home was ready, I spread out my sleep kit and sat on it. The bricks spiralled to a tapering cork, filtering a blue fluorescent light which threw everything inside into muted focus. I was filled with the same sense of peace that I get in church. Yes, that was it – it was as if I had entered a temple.

The previous inhabitant had suspended a string across the ceiling like a washing line, so after hanging up my goggles, glacier glasses, damp socks and thermometer, I fished out the beaten-up postcards that I always carry around. These could be conveniently propped on the ledge. The blue light falling on the 'Birth of Venus' highlighted her knee-length auburn hair with an emerald sheen, and the flying angels had never looked more at home. I felt that Botticelli would have approved.

*

In the mornings I sat underneath rows of cuphooks at one of the formica tables in the galley Jamesway, watching the beakers making sandwiches and filling waterbottles before setting out to explode their bombs. The cooks were the fixed point of camp. Bob and Mary were a great team. Every morning they dragged banana sledges over to what they called their shop, a storage chamber seventeen feet under the ice from which they winched up filmy cardboard boxes on a kind of Antarctic dumb waiter. Mary was relentlessly cheerful, and she loped rather than walked. Bob had an Assyrian beard, a penguin tattoo on his thigh and a reputation as the best cook on the ice. He was hyperenergetic, very popular, and seven seasons in Antarctica, including two winters, had left him with a healthy disrespect for beakerdom.

'What's going on out there?' someone asked one day after an explosion of historic volume.

'They're just trying to melt the West Antarctic ice sheet,' Bob said, scrubbing a frozen leg of lamb. He could seem abrasive, but really he was as soft as a marshmallow.

*

Seismic Man had spent so long in the field over the past six weeks that he said 'Over' as he reached the end of whatever he was saying. When he had to set off an explosion we rode far out from camp on the back of Trigger, his snowmobile. The ice was mottled and ridged like a relief map, and a hint of wind blew a fine layer of white powder over the surface. You could almost absorb the psychic energy out there.

'You know what?' I said to him one day as I unpacked orange sausages of nitroglycerine. 'People call this a sterile landscape, because nothing grows or lives. But I think it's *pulsating* with energy – as if it's about to explode, like one of these bombs.'

'Hell, yes,' he drawled. 'I've often felt as if it's alive out here. Hey, look at that,' he said, pointing to where the china-blue sky grew pale.

'It looks like a bunch of fuel drums,' I said.

'Ha!' he replied. 'It's the distorted image of camp, thrown up by refraction of the light. It's caused by temperature inversion in the atmosphere.'

Every few minutes a sharp tirade would issue forth alarmingly from somewhere within the folds of Seismic Man's parka. The beakers were forever gabbling to each other over the radio. They had developed their own language, and entire conversations took place between Lars and Seismic Man consisting of acronyms, nicknames and long-running, impenetrable jokes.

I had never met anyone who found life as effortless as Seismic Man. He approached everything with a positive attitude, and saw something to laugh about in every situation. As a result, everyone loved him. In addition, he was disarmingly perceptive. He seemed to have got me taped, anyway. He exemplified the easy-going languor I associate with Texas, without any of the cowboy-hat brashness.

'Can you tape the explosives into bundles of three?' he said, handing me a roll of tape. 'I have to set up the shotbox.'

The drillers had already made a hole, and after attaching the first two orange bundles to an electric line, we lowered them both into it. Then we tossed down the other 400 pounds of explosives. When the time came to initiate the detonator, I pressed the button on the shotbox and a black plume shot up like a geyser. A sound that could have come from Cape Canaveral followed in a second.

'Wow,' I said.

'That's it, Woo!' said Seismic Man, throwing an empty tube of explosive into the air and heading it like a football.

'How are we measuring the soundwaves, then?' I asked. 'When they bounce back up from the earth's crust?'

'Well,' he said, packing up the shotbox, 'what we're trying to do here is image the geology under 6,000 feet of ice. Seismology is the tool we use, and it operates either by refraction or reflection, the difference between the two being largely a function of scale in that reflection facilitates the imaging of a smaller area in greater detail. With me so far?'

I nodded.

'What you've just been doing is refracting. The soundwaves we send down are refracted back to the surface from the earth's sediment and recorded by a line of Ref Teks, the soundwave equivalent of the tape recorder. The Ref Teks contain computers hooked up to geophones, and we have 90 Ref Teks 200 yards apart on a line right now, recording away. So all you and I have left to do is pack up!'

On the way back we stopped about ten miles from camp to eat our sandwiches (tinned ham and mustard). A narrow strip of incandescent purply blue light lay on the horizon between ice and sky, looking for all the world like the sea. It seemed to me that it would be almost impossible, in this landscape, not to reflect on forces beyond the human plane. Here, palpably, was something better than the realm of abandoned dreams and narrowing choices that loomed outside the rain-splattered windows of home.

'You're right,' said Seismic Man when I mentioned this. 'It's like plugging yourself in to the spiritual equivalent of the National Grid out here. Wasn't it Barry Lopez who wrote that Antarctica "reflects the mystery that we call God"?'

I called what I sensed there God too; but you could give it many names. It was more straightforward for me than it had been for some, as I brought faith with me. I can't say where the faith came from, because I don't know; it certainly wasn't from my upbringing, since neither of my parents have ever had it. I remember first being aware of it when I was about fourteen, the same time that a lot of other things were happening to me. At first, it embarrassed me, like a virulent pimple on the end of my nose. I have no problems of that kind with it now, though I have persistently abused the giver by following the siren voices of the opposition, also dwelling in the rocky terrain of my interior life and determined to fight to the death.

Despite a good deal of high-mindedness and a sprightly ongoing dialogue with God, in the day-to-day hustle I constantly failed to do what I knew to be the right thing. A sense of spirituality all too often stopped short of influencing action. I was a hopeless case. But I believed that what mattered to God was the direction I was facing, not how far away I was. Sin, it seemed to me, was the refusal to let God be God. I admit that it was a handy credo to espouse – but I did it from the heart. The inner journey, like my route on the ice, was not a linear one. It was an uncharted meandering descent through layers and layers of consciousness, and I was intermittently tossed backwards or sideways like a diver in a current.

Not everyone agreed that Antarctica functioned as a transcendental power station. When I asked Ranulph Fiennes about this aspect of the Antarctic experience he said, 'I do not believe that Antarctica brings out spirituality. It didn't bring out any religiosity in Mike [Stroud], did it? I prayed for help there, but I would have done so in Brixton. Mr Lopez writes about it but he's hardly been there at all.'[1]

*

On Friday 13 January a Hercules appeared in the sky. It was going to take the drill team and a few others back to McMurdo. When it landed, incoming mail was borne inside in a metal turquoise-and-red striped crate like a crown before a coronation. Everyone leapt up, plunging their arms into the crate and calling out names as packages were passed eagerly from hand to hand.

My own mail was supposed to be waiting back at base. It could have been worse: Shackleton and the crew of the *Endurance* missed their mail by two hours when the ship sailed out of South Georgia, and they got it eighteen months later. Then I heard my name being called. Someone in the post room must have known where I was and slung my bundle into the metal crate. It was like a minor Old Testament miracle. The bundle included eight Christmas cards, three of them featuring polar bears, two pairs of knickers from my friend Alison and a bill from the taxman, the bastard. I took the cards to the igloo later and put them up to block the cracks between the ice bricks, and blue light shone through the polar bears.

---

[1] Lopez is an established and highly respected author who has visited Antarctica five times. His trips were not exercises in seeing how dead he could get – he went to see, and to learn.

We went out to wave goodbye to the drillers. The plane attempted to take off four times. It was too light at the back, so the drillers, we heard over the radio, had to stand in the tail.

That night I found a hillock of snow on my sleeping bag and was obliged to reseal the igloo bricks from the outside. It was perishing cold in there all the time and getting to sleep was an unmeetable challenge. I tried to listen to my Walkman to take my mind off the pain but the earphones got twisted under my balaclava and the batteries died in minutes. All my clothes froze in the night. Besides the waterbottle, I was obliged to stow my VHF radio and various spare batteries in between the bag liner and the sleeping bag to prevent them from freezing.

'It's like sleeping in a cutlery drawer,' said Seismic Man, who had made valiant efforts to stay in the igloo. 'Why are you putting yourself through it, when there are warm Jamesways a few hundred yards away?'

It was the romance of it, if I was honest. I liked the idea of living in my own igloo, slightly apart from camp, on the West Antarctic ice sheet. Besides that, during the periods when I didn't have to devote every ounce of energy to maintaining my core temperature, I did love the blue haze very much. I had noticed that when the sun was in a certain position it was faintly tinted with a deep, translucent claret. The surface of the bricks gleamed like white silver all around me. When I crawled out in the mornings (this had to be accomplished backwards) and twisted round on my sunken front path, I looked up and blinked at a pair of pale sundogs[1] glimmering on either side of the sun, joined by a circular rainbow.

Each night, however, produced a new torment. That evening my knees got wet (this was caused by a rogue patch of ice on the bag liner), so I moved the windpants doing service as a pillow down under them. This meant that the mummy-style hood of the bag flopped down over my head, raising the problem (they were queuing up for recognition now) of imminent suffocation. The digital display on my watch faded. Out of the corner of my eye I spied a fresh cone of snow on the floor near the entrance. Forced out of the bag to plug the hole with a sock, I brushed my head

---

[1] A sundog, or parhelion, is a bright spot near the sun formed by the diffraction of light by ice crystals in the atmosphere.

against the ceiling and precipitated a rush of ice crystals down the back of the neck. I began nurturing uncharitable thoughts about Eskimos.

The morning after the departure of the drillers I went straight to the galley to thaw out, noting that I had forgotten to stand the shovel upright with the result that it was now lost in accumulated snow. Camp had shrunk from forty-five to twenty-two overnight. Patsy Cline was blaring out of the speakers and Bob and Mary were playing frisbee with a piece of French toast.

In the end, the igloo defeated me. As I walked back to it the next night I eyed the drums nestling in cradles outside the Jamesways, pumping diesel into the Preways. Sneaking guiltily into one of the two berthing Jamesways, I lay on the floor behind a curtain. It was so easy.

*

Ice streams A, B, C, D and E were located on the West Antarctic ice sheet. There was also a little F, but no one ever talked about that. Hermann, the moon-faced *Road to Oxiana* scientist, was investigating Ice Stream B. He wanted me to go out there with him and his team – they were staying for a week – but I knew I wouldn't be able to get back easily, and I couldn't risk being stranded anywhere at that point in the season. I was sad.

'Just come for the put-in,' he said. I looked at him. It was an extraordinarily kind gesture: the put-in involved two Otter flights, and taking me along would seriously complicate logistics. 'You must see it,' he said. '*I must support you as a writer.*'

Hermann was buzzing around his pallets like a wasp as the Otter arrived. When we took off, I sat in the back of the hold with him. The Whitmore Mountains appeared in the distance. Hermann's eyes lit up.

'Look!' he said, pointing to a hollow above a deeply crevassed area. 'The beginning of Ice Stream B!' The ice there looked like a holey old sheet. Hermann pressed a hand-held Global Positioning System unit against the pebble window and said solemnly, 'We are entering the chromosome zone.' It sounded like the opening sequence of a science-fiction movie. 'The crevasses change direction as the glacier moves,' he said, 'and they turn into thousands of Y chromosomes.'

After that we entered the transition zone between the moving ice and the stable ice. It was called the Dragon, a highly deformed, heavily crevassed area streaked with slots. Hermann tapped his propelling pencil against the thick glass of the porthole and held forth. 'The ice streams are not well understood. The boreholes we have drilled to the bottom of this stream reveal that the base of the stream is at melting point. So they move' – tap, tap, tap – 'these motions provide a process for rapid dispersal and disintegration of this vast quantity of ice. I mean that most of the drainage of this unstable western ice sheet occurs through the ice streams. The mechanics' – tapping – 'of ice streaming play a role in the response of the ice sheet to climactic change. In other words the ice streams are telling us about the interactive role of the ice sheet in global change.'

So it seemed that if the ice melted, resulting in the fabled Great Flood of the popular press, water would pour out of the continent, via the ice streams, on to the Siple Coast, virtually the only part of Antarctica not bounded by mountains.

Hermann settled back in his seat. 'The aim of investigating ice-stream dynamics', he concluded, 'is to establish whether the ice sheet is stable.'

'Geology', Lars had told me, 'is an art as well as a science.'

Hermann stowed the pencil in his top pocket, my ears popped and we landed at a few dozen ragged flags on a relatively stable island in the middle of Ice Stream B. This island, shaped like a teardrop, was called the Unicorn, and Hermann's eye glittered like the mariner's at three or four flags flapping on bamboo poles in the distance. 'The flags mark our boreholes,' he said, 'and we have left equipment down in these holes, gathering data. Those two boreholes' – he pointed to a pair of ragged red flags – 'are called Lost Love and Mount Chaos.' It was like entering a private kingdom. The Dragon, which resembled a slender windblown channel of ice you could walk over in five minutes, was really a two-mile-wide band of chaotic crevassing running for forty miles down one side of the Unicorn. It was a dramatic landscape, its appeal sharpened by the fact that fewer than twenty people had ever seen it.

Hermann's longstanding field assistant, who had travelled with us, was a gazelle-like woman called Keri. When the plane took off and the sound of the engines faded she began spooling out the antenna.

'You be my deputy field assistant,' Hermann said to me. We crunched off to a flag where he dug around until he found a plywood board encrusted with crystals. Fishing out a skein of wires from underneath it, and attaching them to a small measuring device, he began sucking up data. After a few minutes he beamed, an expression he retained until I left the camp, and possibly much longer. He started inscribing a neat column of figures in pencil in a yellow waterproof notebook.

'These bits of data', he said, 'are all little clues to the big puzzle.'

*

Back at CWA they were detonating the last blasts of the season. Everyone went outside one morning to watch 750 pounds of explosives go up half a mile away. The blaster was close to the site. A black and grey mushroom cloud surged 500 feet into the air, followed, seconds later, by a prolonged muffled boom.

'One less for lunch, Bob,' said Jose.

I skied out to see the crater. It was forty-five feet in diameter with a conical mound in the middle, and a delicate film of black soot had settled over the ice. The blaster was admiring his work. 'My hundredth of the season,' he said proudly.

He was taciturn, as cold as the ice in which he buried his explosives, but once I showed an interest in his bombs his face mobilised and he began opening boxes to show me different kinds of powder and expounding on the apparently limitless virtues of nitroglycerine.

'Largest charge I've used this season,' he intoned with the treacly vowels of Mississippi, 'was 9,000 pounds,' and I tut-tutted admiringly as he ran his fingers through baby-pink balls of explosive which looked like candy and smelt of diesel.

It was here, above all other places, that Antarctica resembled the grainy images of the moon's surface. After man had reached both Poles (or it was believed he had), Everest was called the Third Pole, and when it too was conquered in 1953, interest shifted to the moon. Space became an arena for the international race, just as Antarctica was before it: when Yuri Gagarin went up in 1961, three weeks before a U.S. manned rocket, the Americans attempted to turn their failure into success by claiming that their astronauts actually 'drove' the spaceships whereas Gagarin just sat there. Dogs, oxygen, actual control of the craft . . . *plus ça change*.

But NASA failed to provide the world with heroes who could keep hold of the public imagination, and only two years after the hysteria attendant upon the first moonwalk, the U.S. public displayed such overwhelming lack of interest in Apollo Thirteen that the networks dropped the live-from-space broadcast filmed by Jim Lovell and his two colleagues. Houston got prime-time only when the mission was aborted and the astronauts were in danger of dying in outer space.

As the days were slipping away from me, I decided I ought to catch a lift back to McMurdo in the Otter, rather than wait for a Herc which might not come. I whipped up a bread-and-butter pudding as a farewell gift. While they were eating it, Jen, a feisty individual working her second season as a field assistant, filled a tin bowl with hot water, rolled up her long-johns and perched on a chair in the galley shaving her legs.

'But who's gonna see those legs, Jen?' someone yelled. This was followed by a ripple of laughter.

'Get outta here,' she called. 'I wanna be a girlie for once.'

I went over to the igloo and lay down one last time, looking up at the spiral of bricks and the blue haze.

Everyone came over to the Otter to say goodbye. 'See you in Mactown,' said Seismic Man, squinting into the sunlight.

I watched them get smaller and smaller until they disappeared into the ice. However much the mountains and glaciers furnished the most conventionally beautiful Antarctic landscapes, the flat, white wasteland had a power all of its own. One of the Beards whom I interviewed before I left England had said something similar, and conveyed a sense of spirituality in a particularly idiosyncratic way. Robert Swan walked to the South Pole in 1985. He was obsessed with Scott, and his romantic vision sustained him on the long one-way trek. 'We walked', he told me, 'knowing that they [Scott and the polar party] were under us, not looking a day older than when they died.' He had a vision of Antarctica. 'To me it is a symbol of hope,' he said, 'because – thank God – nobody owns it.' He had spent a good deal of time in Scott's hut. 'The horror of the last winter, when every time the door rattled the ones who were left behind thought it was them coming back – that atmosphere was still alive, and I thought our expedition could put it all to rest.' As we talked in his cavernous Chelsea offices, and he alternately bit the stumps of his nails and drew deeply on a cigarette, I was disarmed by his identification with Scott. (In fact Swan was much more like Shackleton.) When I mentioned the infamous biography, he snarled. 'Has Roland Huntford ever walked to the bloody South Pole?' Turning the concept of heroic failure upon himself (as he did most things, though I didn't dislike him for it), he said flatly, 'I am less known because I get there. Sir Ranulph Fiennes is better known because he keeps on almost getting there, with lots of dramas.'

More than anyone else I talked to, Swan appreciated the staggering effort Scott must have made to write the lapidary last diary entries. 'In those circumstances, which I know,' he said, 'when you can barely pick up a pencil, I would have just written, Oh, fuck it.'

*

The pilot wanted to play cards with the air mechanic, so I moved into the cockpit. A stack of cassettes were jammed between the front seats – most of it was 1970s stuff I hadn't heard since school, and it was perfect cruising music. *Crime of the Century*, *The Best of the Eagles*, early Bowie, that Fleetwood Mac album we all had. A good deal of joking took place over the headsets as the crew and I were about to set off for Rothera, the British station on the Antarctic Peninsula. The Otter's route, straight across the continent, was about 2,000 miles, whereas mine was ten times that as I had to leave the ice and find my way to a military airstrip in the south of England before starting all over again. I was obliged to take this absurd and deeply frustrating course of action as there is simply no way of travelling from one side of the Antarctic continent to another – short of manhauling, that is. I couldn't hitch a lift on the Otter, as it didn't have an inch of space available. Furthermore, it was too expensive, time-consuming and complicated to attempt to fly from Christchurch to the Falklands on commercial airlines. In the end I had no choice but to buy the cheapest return ticket between Heathrow and Christchurch, and rely on the Royal Air Force to get me down to the Falklands in time to meet a Dash-7 plane from the British Antarctic Survey.

Looking down at the earth from 12,000 feet, I felt then that my life was in perfect perspective. It was a sense of oneness with the universe – I belonged to it, just like the crystals forming on the wing tip. At that moment I knew that all my anxieties and failures and pain were shadows on the wasteland. Admiral Byrd, an unbeliever, experienced something similar in Antarctica, in his own way. He described it as 'a feeling that transcended reason; that went to the heart of man's despair and found it groundless'. It seemed to represent the ultimate destination of all our journeys.

CHAPTER TEN

Icebreaker

Men are not old here
Only the rocks are old, and the sheathing ice:
Only the restless sea, chafing the frozen land,
Ever moving, matched by the ceaselessly-circling sun . . .

Lighten our darkness, oh Lord;
And lettest thou thy servants depart in peace,
For peace is here, here in the quiet land.

Frank Debenham, geologist on Scott's last expedition

AN ALASKAN MOUNTAINEER returned from the field with scabbed cheeks and duct tape stuck round the metal frame of his glasses. He was very gloomy, for he had lost his snowmobile. I said I thought losing a snowmobile was quite a feat.

'Well,' he said glumly, 'you have to tie the throttle down, otherwise over long distances your hands freeze. So if you hit a sastrugi and fall off without your safety cord connected to kill the motor, the thing just keeps going until it runs out of fuel – could be a hundred miles.'

I wondered what the occupants of another remote field camp would make of an unaccompanied snowmobile careering across the ice sheet.

My office was permanently adrift with heaps of polypropylene underwear, a tangle of crampons, rolls of film, ziplocks of trail-mix, tents, tent pegs, insulated mugs, waterbottles, pee bottles and neoprene bottles of Jack Daniels. One day, I was kneeling on the floor repacking my survival bag when the grey silence of the lab

171

was shattered by an explosion of voices next door. Imre Friedmann and his team had arrived. Hungarian by birth, Imre was a distinguished microbiologist and, at 73, an old Antarctic warrior. He had a valley named after him. Shortly before coming south he had performed 500 squats in the office of some senior bureaucrat to prove that he was fit enough to join an expedition heading for the Siberian permafrost later in the year. Besides studying the cryptoendolithic microbial communities of the Dry Valleys, he was a fertile source of Biolab lore.

'It was very cramped,' he said one day, *but we all had space*. It was before the days of Walkman, and my graduate students used to listen to loud rock music. I retaliated on the other side of the partition by playing classical music, and the volume wars would break out. When I was really desperate I turned to Schoenberg.'

He was an endearing eccentric with a heavy East European accent and a big heart. He rang his mother every day on the satellite line (she was 98) and fussed over the other members of his group like a hen. One of them was a well-known Russian geocryologist called David who had spent much of his life drilling into the Siberian permafrost. He was a colourful, chain-smoking character with wild eyes and ink-black hair which hung over his eyes like that of a sheepdog. He referred disparagingly to 'You Americans', and when I issued a disclaimer, he said, 'That's better.' His sidekick was a Russian biologist called Sasha, who was as placid as David was irascible, and the team was looked after in the field by a genial Kiwi called Al, who wore a thin plait down his back.

Imre invited me on a day's geologising at Battleship Promontory in the Convoy Range, where he was collecting rocks colonised by microbes. We arranged to meet for breakfast at seven the next day, and climbed into a helicopter shortly afterwards. It took an hour to reach the Convoy Range, flying through vast rock tunnels formed by soaring sandstone ziggurats. When we landed, my heart was singing.

We were deposited in a shallow snowless dell on the promontory, our survival gear heaped around us. The sun was shining: the microclimate was so mild that the previous season a scientist had found a primitive worm in the soil. (The worm was only visible under a microscope, but it was indubitably a worm.) We were standing in a baroque landscape of rich red and old gold rock formations eroded by tens of millennia of wind and microorganisms and mottled by lichen growing under the crust.

'Like an ancient city,' said David.

'Underneath here,' said Imre, gesticulating triumphantly at an outcrop of sandstone turrets, 'just one centimetre under, the rock is singing and dancing with LIFE!' He shouted the word 'life' and performed a little dance himself.

When I first met him at the conference in Virginia, he had talked of 'painful beauty', and about his emotional relationship with the Antarctic landscape, which could be expressed 'only by the German word *heimweh*, a kind of painful longing for a lost home'.

We ate our sandwiches standing up and proclaimed the Republic of Battleship Promontory. David was president, Imre prime minister, Al in charge of home affairs and Sasha KGB officer. I was crowned Queen (it was an unusual kind of republic). The national anthem was the 'Ode to Joy' from Beethoven's Ninth Symphony. This was Imre's suggestion. 'You stand here,' he said, 'and your soul is full of joy.'

I labelled specimen boxes later while Imre and Al shuffled around wielding a geology hammer.

'In this quarter inch of rock', said Imre, holding aloft a red splinter, 'we have compressed version of whole rainforest canopy. The micro-organisms slice off rock layer by layer, like salami. One slice of salami takes 10,000 years to cut. So you see here biological and geological timescales overlap.'

The micro-organisms deep froze in the winter. Like desert creatures, they had the ability to suspend life.

'This rock provides a foothold for life in an extreme environment,' continued Imre, tapping his foot in time with the beat of Al's hammer. 'If micro-organisms can live through the hostility of the Antarctic winter, there might be some which can live in the Martian permafrost. If there is no life on Mars, it is a bad day for biologists.'

Imre was deeply involved with what he called the 'quest for life on Mars'. He believed it would answer the most fundamental questions of biology.

'Will we find life on Mars in our lifetime?' I asked.

'Maybe in yours – not mine. The limitations are not technological now. They are financial.'

173

'What do you think about life on Mars?' I asked Al, still wielding his hammer.

'It'd be a hell of a field trip,' he said.

David and Sasha were lying on their bellies in a sunny spot, smoking and looking very Russian.

'This is why the Soviet Union collapsed,' said Imre, waving an arm in their direction.

David was interested in microbial adaptation. 'If you had been living in Russia for past five years,' he said, 'you believe in the adaptation of anything.'

The helicopter was due at four, but it was after eight when we finally saw the Battleships spiral away below us. We had covered feminism (this was not a success), religion (Imre said, 'I know there is no God'), the Nicaraguan debt crisis, and methods of avoiding frostbite while taking a shit. Sasha had done a Russian dance. We finished the second thermos of hot water with the famed spiced ciderbags 'Containing No Apple Juice', and ate fig rolls containing figs like shrapnel. There was talk of putting up the tents. Imre nodded off. Al strung out the antenna and tried to radio his girlfriend, who was working in a national park hut in New Zealand. This failed. Sasha said, 'Try another girlfriend.'

*

Everyone was coming in from the field, and the Crary was swarming with burnt faces and duct-taped parkas. Tribes of the dispossessed were a feature of the Crary. Boots formed queues outside offices, thermal jackets draped themselves over chairs in the lounge and picked-over ziplocks of trail-mix littered the kitchen. Over at Scott Base, the mad microbiologist, his hair still shooting upwards like the flame of the Olympic torch, had been to the top of Erebus to collect his high-temperature microorganisms. He peered down his nose over his glasses and thrashed his arms around as he told me about it.

'I've been in the tropics, and all sorts of places, but I tell you, up there on Erebus it was like hell.'

I began the ineffably sad task of returning my kit to the Berg Field Center. Afterwards, I sat glumly in the office. The icebreaker had finally struggled in to McMurdo, and it was squatting on the Sound opposite the station, a trail of cracked ice like a runway behind it. Everyone took a great deal of interest in this bright red thing from the outside world. Few in Antarctica were ever interested in actual news from home – world events were like 'noises off' – but a concrete reminder of life on the other side of the glass, such as the appearance of a ship, that was something else. In the old days the arrival of the ship was the major event of the season. The Australian Charles Laseron was Mawson's assistant biologist on the 1911–14 expedition, and in his rumbustious account of the experience, called *South with Mawson*, he records that when the ship arrived news from the outside world was conveyed to them in the following order. One: Australia had lost the Test. Two: the *Titanic* had sunk. Three: the Balkan War had been waged. Four: Scott was spending another year on the ice.

The captain of the shiny red icebreaker invited me aboard for a couple of days, and he sent a helicopter over to fetch me, which was very decent of him. Thirteen miles offshore, stationary opposite Erebus, the *Polar Sea* was a regal scarlet vision casting its crenellated shadow over the sea ice. It was a Coastguard ship with a crew of 131, and it had just come from the North Pole. We landed on the ice, and I was winched aboard on a crane. The crew, who had just been granted 'ice liberty', were setting up goalposts on the ice, and soon an enthusiastic game of football was under way. I had watched Scott's men doing exactly the same thing not far from here in Ponting's moving-picture film. Describing ice liberty on the Japanese 1911–12 expedition, a seaman wrote, 'We were like little birds let out of the cage.'

I loitered around the decks. The crew were unenthusiastic about the south. It had been a long trip, the ship was dry, and they had expected to be home for Christmas. They showed me photographs of initiation ceremonies on the dateline, and when I asked them what it was like in the north, they said the ice was dirty up there.

The Captain had written a book on Soviet Maritime History. 'Are you more interested in the south?' I asked hopefully as we sat in his private quarters sipping Coca-Cola. He had a drawing of a polar bear by Nansen on the wall.

'No,' he said. 'I am bipolar.'

In the wardroom an engineer talked about icebreakers over a bowl of spaghetti. He had previously referred to scientists as 'customers'.

'Icebreakers have smooth bottoms, so they roll more,' he said.

'You can tell she feels at home when she hits the ice. The more effective an icebreaker you make it, the worse ride it gives you in open seas. So icebreaker design is all about compromise.'

It was a sunny evening, and the brash ice in the trail behind us sparkled. The crew milled around, and a pod of killer whales obligingly popped their heads through a hole, revealing flashes of their shiny pebble-grey underside. Skuas landed on the floes, their spindly legs slithering, and behind us, in the distance, the tanker struggled along in the channel we had broken like an elderly relation taken out for an airing.

I sat in the Captain's chair on the bridge, poring over charts with the officers. Finally, at about nine o'clock, the *Polar Sea* began to break ice. The writing in my journal gets very shaky at this point. It was as if a mysterious power had breathed life into the ship. The vibrations made our ears pop, and the officers laid bets on whether particular seals escaped, running out to look behind. 'You always expect them to burst like a pimple,' someone said. I went on deck to watch jagged chunks of ice with opaque white crusts and translucent blue bellies being squeezed upwards as the ship moved implacably on. Teddy Evans wrote about the noise of the *Terra Nova* breaking ice. 'The memory of the pack ice hissing around a wooden ship is one of the voices that call,' he wrote. 'I sometimes feel a mute fool at race meetings, society dinner parties, and dances, and the lure of the little voices I know then at its strongest . . . It is surely that which called Scott away, when he had everything man wants . . .'

*

The next morning, we woke up near Cape Evans. It had been like sleeping on top of a washing machine. I wandered out on deck to another spectacular day, and the water in our wide trail was as blue and calm as a field of mulberries.

There was another Evans, besides the one who commanded Scott's *Terra Nova*, but he did not have a cape, despite the fact that his sacrifice was greater. Petty Officer Edgar 'Taff' Evans went south twice with Scott, and was chosen for the final haul to the Pole despite disgracing himself in New Zealand where he had got so drunk that, while trying to lurch back aboard *Terra Nova*, he had missed the ship altogether and plunged into the water. He was the first to die on the trek back from the Pole, and since he was the only team member drawn from the ranks of the 'men' as opposed to officers, the unsavoury notion that he lacked the moral fibre of the superior classes was whispered in gilded corridors back at home. In the making of the myth, Taff has been conveniently manoeuvred into a corner, and he is barely remembered outside his native Rhossily. He was not represented on a set of twenty-five cigarette cards depicting Antarctic characters and scenes issued by John Player & Sons, though the other Evans got two cards and the manufacturers even deigned to include a mugshot of Amundsen. One of Taff's rare appearances as anything but the Fifth Man is in Beryl Bainbridge's *The Birthday Boys*, a novel published in 1991. Hanging on the end of a rope with Scott in the *Discovery* days, Taff clings to the formalities of rank. 'Being down a crevasse together', he maintains, 'is no excuse for stepping out of line.' When I asked Bainbridge why she gave Evans an erection at that point she produced scientific evidence that, when suspended down crevasses, men do get erections. That may be true, but I didn't believe for a moment that she had flung in the detail for technical authenticity. It served to distinguish the working-class Evans from the four toffs – and besides, she couldn't resist the joke.

*

Back at McMurdo I had to pack for my flight to Christchurch the next day. I couldn't believe I was leaving. I felt exhausted, depressed, miserable and demoralised, and I had a week's hard travelling off the ice before I got to the British base on other side of the continent. I received a note from Seismic Man, written on graph paper. He said he wasn't going to make it back to McMurdo from CWA before I left. 'So long, Woo,' the note ended.

I had planned great things for my last night, but in the end I walked to Hut Point and looked at the mountains one last time. The thought that I wouldn't see them again almost broke my heart.

The next day, I took the pictures off the office wall and the W-002 sign off the door, peeled the stickers from the ice axe and the taped label from the goggles, ripped the velcroed name off the parka, unstuck the coloured tape from the neoprene waterbottle and pulled the badge off the yazoo cap. I packed the microcentrifuge earrings, as no one would understand them off the ice.

The flight to Christchurch was delayed six times. Twenty of us were scheduled to leave, and the scientists spent all day playing patience in the Crary. I thought of T. S. Eliot when Auden asked him why he played patience so much. He reflected for a moment and said, 'Well, I suppose it's the nearest thing to being dead.' The rest of us trailed around like the Ungone, commuting up and down to the Movement Control Center. I tried to count the number of people I had hugged goodbye. At midnight, Art De Vries, the fish biologist, brought me sashimi cut from the cheeks of his *mawsoni* fish. He gave me the earbones, to make into earrings. People lay on my office floor. David the Russian came in to present me with a ring made from the tusk of a north Siberian mammoth.

'Are you ready to go?' he asked, fiddling with a fresh packet of cigarettes. 'I mean, ready with your emotions?'

'No,' I said, feeling the tears well up.

When we drove to the skiway, rays of the butterscotch light of late summer were shining through the stratocumulus. We were travelling on a C-141 Starlifter, and it had taken off for what the pilot described as a 'test run'. At four o'clock in the morning, after being handed our bagged meals, we boarded the matt grey, windowless plane. We wedged ourselves in, and the man opposite me fished out a battered copy of Aristotle's *Poetics*. The crew retired behind the cargo. It was very hot, and the most exciting moment of the journey was when a Kiwi stripped to his bare chest. I opened my brown bag. The chocolate pudding was there, but at least my last round of American sandwiches weren't filled with peanut butter and jelly.

PART TWO

When you look upon such things there comes surging through the confusion of the mind an awareness of the dignity of the earth, of the unaccountable importance of being alive, and the thought comes out of nowhere that unhappiness rises not so much from lacking as from having too much . . . And you guess the end of the world will probably look like that, and the last men retreating from the cliffs will look out upon some such horizon, with all things at last in equilibrium, the winds quiet, the sea frozen, the sky composed, and the earth in glacial quietude.

Or so you fancy. Then along comes a walloping Antarctic blizzard and knocks such night dreaming into a cocked hat.

Richard E. Byrd, from *Discovery*

THE ANTARCTIC PENINSULA

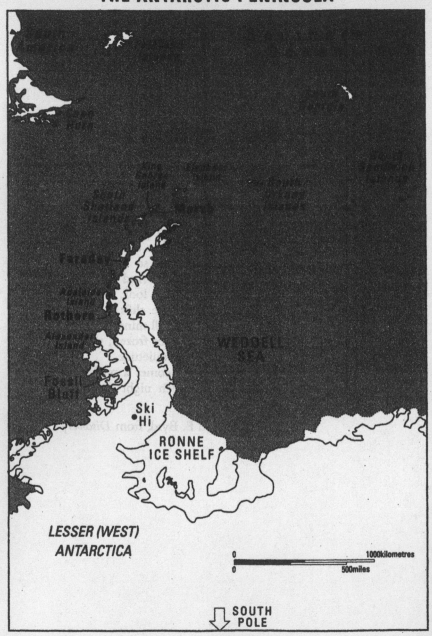

South
America

South
Pole

King
George
Island

South
Shetland
Islands

Marsh

South
Orkney
Islands

Faraday

Adelaide
Island

Rothera

Alexander
Island

Fossil
Bluff

Ski
Hi

RONNE
ICE SHELF

WEDDELL
SEA

LESSER (WEST)
ANTARCTICA

0   1000kilometres
0   500miles

SOUTH
POLE

CHAPTER ELEVEN

From New Zealand to the Falklands

It's just that there are some things women don't do. They don't
become Pope or President or go down to the Antarctic.

Harry Darlington, chief pilot on Finn Ronne's
1946–8 Antarctic Research Expedition

WE LANDED at Christchurch at half-past eleven in the morning
on 25 January. When the aircraft door opened, the smell of
trees and green things filled the plane. To us, it was as if we had
come to the middle of a jungle. A 747 had just arrived from
Singapore, and we all cleared customs together. The Singaporeans
looked clean, elegant and ironed, as well as very little. They eyed
us, a shaggy tribe of overdressed primates with matted hair and
exhausted faces. The traffic even within the airport compound
was overwhelming. I ordered a cappuccino at a cafe with the
Swedish scientist who had read the part of Amundsen at the Pole
on Christmas Day, and we both drooled over the frothy cups.

'It's really too good to drink,' he said. 'We should just look at it.'

Later, Roger took me to turn on the streetlights of Christchurch at SouthPower, where he worked. It was still possible to
do it manually, and I flicked a switch and watched the city fizz
to life. On the first night, savouring the darkness, I slept in the
garden.

'It's so *warm*,' I said to Roger the next morning when he
returned from his daily run up the nearest hill.

'What d'you expect?' he said. 'It's the end of January – midsummer, practically.'

When I went into town, I wanted to buy something in every shop. I ran into people I knew from the ice, and we quickly parked ourselves in coffee shops. It was as if we were looking for each other.

I wore a skirt, walked in the chequered shadows of trees, had my hair cut and opened my bag without being bitten by a crampon. I caught a bus to Lyttelton Museum, an overstuffed old building smelling of linoleum. The small Antarctic gallery displayed a vermilion parka identical to the one I had taken off the previous day, and curled photographs of the *Terra Nova* black cat, inevitably called Nigger, in the hammock specially made for him on the long voyage from Britain to New Zealand. Next to the pictures of Nigger, a little girl was riding Rumba through shafts of sepia sunlight. Rumba was one of Shackleton's ponies, only he never made it south – he was left behind to live out his life in Waikiri.

On my last night in Christchurch I was invited to a soiree in the Polar Room, the repository of an impressive collection of recent Antarctic memorabilia. It was presided over by the most assiduous keeper of the flame, an author, historian, eccentric and *bon viveur* called David Harrowfield. The Polar Room was tucked away at the back of his neat suburban house and clipped garden, and its trophies included the escape hatch from the first Scott Base bar and a bicycle modified with skis. Peter, the Asgaard Ranger I had met at Scott Base, arrived to model his original and much abused Ranger parka, which he had donated to the Polar Room, and large quantities of wine and sausage rolls were disgorged from the fridge. It was the centenary of the landing of the *Southern Cross* on the Antarctic continent, so David put on a special cape (I can't remember why it was special, if I ever knew) and declaimed from Borchgrevinck's diary until we had drunk the wine and eaten the sausage rolls. Then we went home.

Roger made me tomato on toast for breakfast as his last gesture of 'NZ Operational Support', as he referred to himself. On my way out to the airport I found a sausage roll in my pocket. I stopped off at Canterbury Museum to meet the Antarctic curator and historian Baden Norris. They were cutting the grass in Hagley Park, and the air smelt sweet. Baden was waiting in the foyer for me when I arrived. He was a short, middle-aged man with a diffident manner and an encyclopedic knowledge of Antarctica. I took to him straight away. He had spent six weeks alone at

Shackleton's hut in 1963, making sure American helicopters didn't land too close to the Adelie colony, which had halved since the first landing.

'I felt I was never alone,' he said. As we walked around his gallery he told me that he had grown up in Lyttelton. 'Antarctica was always part of my life,' he said, running his fingers through his grey hair. 'My next-door neighbours were children of people who'd been on the early expeditions.'

He pointed out Spencer-Smith's ecclesiastical stoles, neatly folded in a glass cabinet. 'Extraordinary man,' he commented, more to himself than to me. Spencer-Smith was a member of the Ross Sea party of Shackleton's *Endurance* expedition, and in his unpublished sledging journal, which came to light in 1981, a neat pencil hand records the laborious work of depot-laying and the powerful influence of the continent upon the human spirit. 'All the old questionings seem to come up for answer in this quiet place,' he wrote, 'but one is able to think more quietly than in civilisation.' He was a priest, and a polymath (he had 'a long argument' with Stevens about the essential nature of a preposition), and his spirit was relentlessly cheerful until he died from scurvy and exhaustion lashed on the back of a sledge. When they had to leave him alone and sick in his tent for days he had delivered a sermon in French to occupy himself, and on All Souls' Day he recorded, 'More trips around London this evening.'

*

I flew to Auckland on a Hawker Siddely, and the man sitting next to me asked where I'd been. When I told him, he said, 'Oh, my cousin went there.' Everybody in New Zealand knew someone who had been south, even if it were the milkman's brother. It brought the continent into their sphere of consciousness, and made it less remote, whereas in Britain and America what I had done was akin to going to the moon. 'Antarctica does sit in your imagination more if you live in the south of New Zealand,' someone said. 'Also, on a global scale, New Zealand is involved, for once.' A friend of Roger's remarked that he needed 'to go for an Oatie', which meant visit the lavatory. The phrase had evolved from Oates's famous departure from the tent, with which everyone in New Zealand was familiar. Most revealing of all, a Maori waitress who had sat down at a truckstop to join me for a mug of tea said, 'You know, when we feel a cold wind on our faces, we know where it's coming from.'

Perception of place is bound to be conditioned by nationality. The race to the North Pole was an American race, whereas there were no Americans in the south when Shackleton and Scott were manhauling across the ice. This partially explains why Antarctica's role in the American national psyche is less significant than its British counterpart. The media in America has tended to orientate public interest towards the Arctic, whereas the British press, generally, has done the opposite. An American scientist I met stooped over a seal hole on the Ross Sea remarked, 'Antarctica seems to have been like the Wild West for Brits,' and after a pause he added, 'Maybe it still is.'

None the less, to many people at home the Arctic and the Antarctic are indistinguishable. I had observed it when people issued warnings to me about polar bears and asked, as they frequently did, 'When are you going back up there?' In reality, the two could hardly be more different. First, the Arctic is not a landmass, and the North Pole is on floating ice. Second, the Arctic Circle has an indigenous population. People can live within it unassisted. Musk oxen wander within 800 miles of the North Pole. Things grow.

Despite the fact that the outer edges of the Arctic Circle are able to sustain life, all the Frozen Beards agree that trekking to the North Pole is a much harsher business than its southern equivalent. Everyone who had been on northern expeditions remembered immediately how bad it had been, whereas – like an irresistible lover – Antarctica had seduced them into forgetting the pain. Mike Stroud, who had made three attempts with Sir Ranulph Fiennes to walk unaided across the sea ice to the North Pole and manhauled across the southern continent via the South Pole, was in no doubt about which he preferred. 'The Arctic is an evil place. It's infinitely more threatening. You have to trek in winter, for a start – that's the only time it's frozen over – and getting to the North Pole doesn't have the same appeal as getting to the South Pole. Why is that? Is it a British thing? It occurs to me that it might be a remnant of Scott's influence. Antarctica is still very special in the British consciousness. Also, Antarctica was a mystery for much longer than the Arctic.'

Robert Swan, who has walked to both Poles, was characteristically exuberant on the subject. 'The Arctic is dour and bad-tempered. It's a bastard kind of place. It drip feeds you arsenic in your tea. The Antarctic is far more beguiling – though it's more of a bastard in a way, as it lulls you into a false sense of security and then bangs you from behind with a sledge-hammer. It all looks much softer, but crevasses lurk – it's more psychopathic.' He anthropomorphised both places relentlessly. 'Antarctica is like meeting a mass-murderer who looks nice. At least in the Arctic you *know* you're meeting a mass-murderer.' Before I left his huge Chelsea office he tipped his chair back, paused for a moment and, neatly reversing the biological distinction that separates the two places, said quietly – as quietly as he could say anything, that is – 'The Arctic is a bit dead. The Antarctic is definitely much more alive. In the Arctic, it's as if someone has said, "FREEZE!", whereas when we went up the Beardmore it was as if the landscape were saying "Hi, how's it going?".'

*

Even in Auckland, I found Antarctica. It was one half of the city's largest tourist attraction, called 'Kelly Tarlton's Underwater World and Antarctic Encounter'. I rode a sno-cat through a penguin colony, though the birds were still in transit from San Diego zoo and workmen were crouched on the fibreglass bergs, eating sandwiches, their thermos flasks balancing on the smiling heads of plastic seals. People were videoing the videos. They had even erected a replica of Scott's hut in which a piano occasionally broke spontaneously into the national anthem. The whole place endorsed the old imperial notion that this was part of Kiwi culture too, a particularly obsolete idea in the muggy, sub-tropical north island. Ed Hillary, though, had made a nice introductory film about Antarctica which played on a continuous loop, and he ended by saying, 'It belongs to you.' I liked that.

I flew to LA, and thence to London. A sales rep from a computer company attached himself to me for the whole journey. He was wearing an Armani suit, and his face possessed none of those small wrinkles produced by thought. I last saw him next to the luggage carousel at Heathrow, the Armani looking as though he'd had a fight in it.

'Nice to be back on Terra Cotta,' he said.

I spent two days in London, feeling like a visitor in my own life. When I turned up for mass at St Mark's on Regent's Park Canal, always one of my first ports of call, I was shocked to find a cardboard arrow pinned to the locked doors. It was pointing to the stone steps which led to the crypt. When I got down there, a dozen people squeezed into Sunday School chairs were gathered round a trestle table, bare save for a plain wooden cross. Mass had not yet begun.

I stood in the narrow doorway, baffled.

'My dear,' said Father Tom as he strode towards me, arms outstretched. 'You won't have heard.'

A gang had broken into our church the night before Remembrance Sunday and piled everything they could find into three enormous bonfires, which they lit, presumably warming their hands as they stood around enjoying the conflagration. The building had been virtually gutted, although the stained-glass window of St Mark wearing dashing purple slippers had not been fatally damaged. It was next to the Lady Chapel, and in it St Mark was writing in a large book, though he had been distracted (presumably by St Peter in the adjacent window) and had twisted away from his work as if eager to see what was going on. Besides the slippers, he was wearing a sumptuous emerald robe. I had grown very fond of the image.

'How was the South Pole?' asked Father Tom brightly.

It seemed very far off.

The next day my father drove me to the Royal Air Force base at Brize Norton in Oxfordshire.

'Where's the entrance?' he asked as we crawled along outside.

'How should I know?' I snapped. This brief re-entry into the real world had made me disorientated and irritable. Since leaving McMurdo I had felt as if I existed only in suspended animation.

'Sorry, dad,' I said weakly.

After a good deal of hanging around I flew to Ascension Island on a TriStar, the cover of the in-flight magazine in front of me depicting a customer descending by parachute. By mistake, the pilot referred to 'the camera crew' rather than 'the cabin crew' over the loudspeaker; you couldn't help wondering what was on his mind. The air force refuels its TriStars at Ascension en route to the Falkland Islands, and from there a British Antarctic Survey Dash-7 was to convey me back to Antarctica. I discovered that two other people on the plane were heading for Rothera, the main British station on the Antarctic Peninsula. They were both employees of Tilbury Douglas, the construction company contracted to carry out rebuilding works for the British Antarctic Survey as part of its Way Forward Programme. John was a plumber who had never travelled beyond Bournemouth, and George was a sixty-eight-year-old manager who had been brought out of retirement to oversee the job. George had already been south once, and was keen to impart his knowledge on this and any other matter. He emitted noise non-stop, in fact, like the continuous-loop soundtrack at the Antarctic Encounter.

The crinkly coastline of Ascension, laced with white surf, was ringed with a band of streaky green which faded into the china-blue Atlantic. The island was goose-bumped with small peaks. When we landed the braying and overfed senior officers in the front row got off first, met by a mini-squadron of clean-shaven air force personnel marching along the tarmac in a uniform of pale khaki shorts with long socks and Hush Puppies. They looked like extras in a war film set in the Western Desert. A team of firefighters stood to attention in silver-foil outfits as the VIPs sped past, provoking the squaddies bound for the Falklands into a burst of Gary Glitter choruses. The rest of us were herded into a compound, and locked up. It was very hot and sticky despite the soft tropical breeze, and everyone bought cold cans of Becks beer.

'I've never drunk beer in the morning before,' said John. George and I exchanged guilty glances. The squaddies were dispensing beer as if they might never see liquid again. Most of them were from RAF 20 Squadron, responsible for the ground-to-air missile system in the Falklands. An announcement over the loudspeaker informed us that anyone drunk would be offloaded, at which a great cheer went up, Ascension Island (beyond the compound at least) being rather more agreeable than the Falklands.

The compound consisted of a flagged concrete yard containing wooden tables with integrated chairs and parasols, and a pock-marked 1883 cannon. It was surrounded by a wire fence and lined on one side with palm trees. The small hills around the airstrip were littered with military hardware. One of them, higher than the others, stood out because it was green, not brown, and in a startling fit of imagination it had been named Green Mountain. It reminded me of Juan Fernandez, the Pacific island where the original Robinson Crusoe had been abandoned.

Not much had happened to Ascension Island or its famous green turtles since it was garrisoned by the Royal Marines in 1815, initially to prevent the French rescuing Napoleon from St Helena. Certainly nothing happened while we were there. The flight was delayed. The sun bleached the sky, and the squaddies began revealing an extensive range of tattoos. Hour after hour trickled by in this hot cage as further delays were announced over the rasping loudspeaker. George talked about his 'laddies', by which he meant the builders, as if they were at nursery school. The Becks ran out. An announcement that we were being diverted to Rio provoked another cheer. The squaddies were envisaging sultry nights in the bars of Copacabana – but it was more likely to mean a long, stuffy evening on a bucket seat in another faceless airport.

*

As we flew over wide green spaces and the thin ribbons of dusty, untravelled Brazilian roads, I suddenly longed for the freedom of anonymous travel. Brazil seemed a long way from the constraints of the ice. At that moment, I felt as if I were locked into a claustrophobic love affair, and although it was pulling me back to the south, a voice inside whispered urgently, 'Escape while you can!'

At Rio airport George led an assault on the duty-free shops. We bought a bottle of red wine, a slab of goats' cheese and a box of crackers and had a picnic by the top of the escalators. When we reboarded, a flight attendant marched down the aisles spraying us with disinfectant from an aerosol held aloft like a flaming torch in a Viking raiding party.

We landed at Mount Pleasant airport on East Falkland, the sky a low miasma of blues and pinks. A line of people on the end of the strip were holding up placards inscribed with numbers. They were marking the pilot out of ten for his landing. In the terminal a pair of soldiers stood on the carousel and held up an array of missiles we might like to avoid stepping on; there were, they said, over a hundred minefields lurking in the tussock.

A bus conveyed us across the island to Port Stanley, and I asked the driver about the runway placards. 'That's what we're reduced to down here,' he said, 'to pass the time.'

George was depressed by the news that we were staying at FIPASS, a government-owned pontoon dock, rather than the fabled Upland Goose on Stanley's main street. I asked the driver how long it would take to get there. 'It depends on the traffic,' he said, although we had not yet encountered a single vehicle. It was very dark, but, when we reached civilisation two pairs of whale jawbones were illuminated outside the cathedral like wishbones. We went on, until we passed again into the gloom. 'Welcome to Alcatraz!' the driver said as he deposited us in driving rain at the bottom of a flight of metal stairs.

The Falklands Intermediate Port and Storage System, FIPASS, consists of a series of oil-rig barges built in Middlesborough and shipped in by the Ministry of Defence after the conflict. The Falkland Islands government purchased it from the Ministry of Defence in 1988. It was a perfectly acceptable place in which to stay, although there was a turd in the toilet bowl and a sex novel under my bunk. When I asked for a lightbulb, the nightwatchman handed it over with a sinister remark about how nice it was to look after a lady for a change.

*

With George around, I could abnegate all responsibility for my life, as he planned it out for me in minute detail. It was very agreeable. In the morning we located my kitbag, which had been languishing all season in the bowels of FIPASS. It contained all my British-issue cold-weather gear, which I had tried on months before, on a sweltering day in Cambridge, and which had been sent down by ship at the beginning of the season. Myriam picked us up in the British Antarctic Survey Land Rover (every other vehicle was a Land Rover in the Falklands). She was the BAS representative, a saintly figure who deciphered scrawled faxes from the ice requesting goods for which she was obliged to scour the streets of Stanley. She showed me some of these request sheets. For some reason, there was a run on olives. I wondered what this could mean.

We strolled around Stanley for an hour, George in the lead, past the corrugated iron roofs and exuberant flowerbeds of Jubilee Villas and a vast new school that would have been filled with at least half a million pupils in the U.K. The roof of a small house in the trellis of quiet streets on the hill was painted with a Union Jack.

'Look at that!' said George triumphantly, pointing to a sign indicating Thatcher Street. 'That's the spirit.'

The landscape beyond the town was reminiscent of Tierra del Fuego. It was obvious, geographically, though I hadn't made the connection before, as inside my head the two belonged to different worlds. But there they were, the same purple mists, saffron steppe and cadmium yellow slopes, the trail of lumpy steamer ducks breaking the surface of the water and the striped underwings of upland geese flapping against a bruised southern sky.

CHAPTER TWELVE

One of the Boys

Being set on the idea
Of getting to Atlantis
You have discovered of course
Only the Ship of Fools is
Making the voyage this year,
As gales of abnormal force
Are predicted, and that you
Must therefore be ready to
Behave absurdly enough
To pass for one of The Boys,
At least appearing to love
Hard liquor, horseplay and noise.

W. H. Auden, from *Atlantis*

DEPOSITED BY the peerless Myriam at a diminutive airstrip outside Port Stanley, George, John and I presented our passports to a saturnine individual in a small, bare room while another man flossed his teeth. Nobody was interested in our luggage – they didn't even look at it, let alone set a sniffer dog loose among us.

'Can we get on?' George asked the tooth-flosser.

'If you like,' said the man.

The four-engine Dash-7 plane was luxurious after the Hercules that had conveyed me to McMurdo. It was carrying very little cargo, and there were only eight seats, so I was able to walk freely around the cabin rather than remaining wedged into a red-webbing seat. We could have played a game of football, and there was even a toilet.

The pilot waved me up to the jumpseat for take-off. As he revved the engines at the end of the runway all the long, tired hours in sweaty planes, all the delays and frustrations and wasted days melted into the long strip of wobbling tarmac. I was going back.

Stanley looked like Toytown from the air, neat and circumscribed and little, with primary colour roofs, small animals in green fields and a harbourful of Dufy-bright sails. The pilots chatted as we cleared the isolated farms on outlying islands, and it was odd to hear English accents over the headset. The pair of them cracked jokes about farting. It was a clue to what was in store.

The British Antarctic Survey originated in a secret wartime naval operation code-named Tabarin and launched in 1943 to ward off German cruisers in the South Atlantic. I watched an old film of Tabarin once. The doctor of the all-male team was a gynaecologist. The operation transferred to the Colonial Office in 1945 under the name Falkland Islands Dependency Survey, and in 1967 it transmogrified into a research institute within the Natural Environment Research Council. Before being permanently headquartered in Cambridge, the British Antarctic Survey (BAS, as it became known) was hived out all over the country, administration and logistics dwelling under the auspices of the Overseas Development Agency in London. Mike Richardson, a BAS base commander long before his days overseeing the South Atlantic at the Foreign Office, was put through his medical examinations during this period by a handlebar-moustached retired army colonel.

'Have you got syphilis?' barked the man, pen poised above the voluminous forms.

'No,' stammered Mike.

'Why not?' snapped the colonel.

The peninsula, the wonky finger sticking out of the top left-hand corner of the continent, has always been the most contentious part of Antarctica. In 1948 Argentina, Chile and Britain sent warships south, and in the fifties an American Antarctican wrote that the territorial argy-bargy between the three nations on the peninsula 'was so amusing to an onlooker it rivalled the machinations of a Gilbert and Sullivan operetta'. During this period the explorer Wally Herbert said 'protest notes were exchanged like cards in a game of snap.' When the Chileans announced in 1983 that at the bottom of an inlet off the northern tip of the peninsula, they had discovered two projectile heads like those used by indigenous peoples of Chile in the sixteenth century, the British and Argentinians voiced suspicions that the objects had been planted there to reinforce Chilean territorial claims.

Britain had been making sporadic claims in the region for many years.[1] In 1820 Edward Bransfield claimed portions of the continent for Britain, and in 1908 and 1917 Letters Patent were issued to the same end. In 1920, when British Antarctic policy had begun to assume a coherent shape, the Under-Secretary of State at the British Colonial Office formally proposed that Britain should take over the whole continent for the Empire. Neither he nor anyone else knew what it was that they would be acquiring, even to the nearest million square miles; but they knew they wanted it.

During the Falklands War in 1982 members of the House of Lords voiced the concern that the conflict might spread to British Antarctic Territory. As a result, and after years of resource-paring, in 1983–4 BAS funding rose by more than sixty per cent. The relationship between science and politics in Antarctica has always been ambiguous. Scientists might well dislike political intervention, but the Falklands experience shows that they have had reason to be thankful for it.

It took four-and-a-half hours to reach the peninsula. The crew had purchased our lunch from the Stanley bakery, and we tucked into apple turnovers and slabs of malt loaf. Before long, icebergs appeared in the Southern Ocean, rimmed at the waterline with lurid lime green. I was feeling vaguely apprehensive, as I didn't really have a clue what was in store. I had been invited to spend two months with the small British team at Rothera and to travel with some of them on the peninsula. It was reputed to be a tightly knit community, and I wondered how they were going to take to an outsider. At the end of January, the season was already beginning to wind down – science parties would be coming in from the field while support staff on base prepared for winter. An ice-

---

[1] British people often wonder why the U.K. didn't claim any territory explored by Scott, notably around Ross Island. The answer is almost certainly that it was too far away for any British mission to have any hope of establishing a presence. The peninsula is far more accessible.

strengthened ship was due to arrive at Rothera at the end of March to resupply the station and take the summer stragglers – who included me – back up to the Falklands. By then, the polar night would be upon us.

When the peninsula appeared it was fenced with high mountains, and the ocean lapped on a narrow strip of rocky shore beneath them. I had never seen Antarctica so thawed. Rothera Station was ten degrees further north than Ross Island, and on my inflatable globe the peninsula almost seemed to touch South America – whereas Ross Island was perilously close to the air valve, inches from anywhere to the north. At McMurdo the mean temperature in January is minus three degrees Celsius, whereas at Rothera it is a sweaty two degrees above zero. At the Pole, the January mean is minus twenty-eight. It can reach minus fifty at McMurdo in the winter, but the lowest temperature ever recorded at Rothera is minus thirty-nine.

The sun, shining weakly through the clouds, was hovering in the light grey sky some way above the western horizon. Here the nights were already dark, the sun setting before ten o'clock and rising at six, much as it does in a northern summer.

Nobody showed any sign of putting on their cold-weather clothes, and when we landed George was still wearing his tie. After we got off the aircraft, he gripped me by the shoulder.

'The laddies and I have separate billets from the BAS men,' he said. 'But don't worry. I'll come over to see you soon.' With that, he vanished.

I loitered on the apron, waiting once again for whatever was going to happen next. I had not expected banners welcoming me to Rothera but I had assumed that the base commander would send someone out to meet me, if only to avoid having to deal with the removal of my frozen corpse from the airstrip. Eventually I spotted a sno-cat trundling around the edge of the apron. I flagged it down, and smiled weakly at the Beard at the wheel.

'Any chance of a lift to the main building?' I asked.

He nodded, and I climbed up, slinging my bag into the space behind the seats. The Beard was silent. I wondered if he often passed hitch-hikers.

We lurched to a standstill in front of a long, pale green building. It had two storeys, and was separated from the runway by an expanse of gravel and ice. Open water was visible a few hundred yards from each end, and behind the base a ridge of gentle hills, only partially ice-clad, afforded some protection against the wind. The Beard looked at me expectantly. 'Thanks,' I said, dragging the bag down after me. There was only one entrance to the building, so I went through it.

Finding myself in a cramped lobby, I engaged in more loitering and took off my parka. Men were coming and going along the corridors, engaged in a variety of activities but united by the fact that they all ignored me. Short of erecting a sign outside the base saying 'GO AWAY', they couldn't have made it clearer that I was unwelcome. Eventually a balding but youngish radio operator called Stu took me upstairs for a cup of tea. Everyone was crowding round a table of new mail in an institutional canteen-style dining room. Stu consulted a wall-chart and found the number of my pitroom. I was relieved to see my name written up there, for it meant at least they knew I was coming and were not about to send me back, though in reality they could not have done so as there was no means of getting back.

The pitroom was like my room at Scott Base – small, windowless and comfortable – except that there were two sets of bunks rather than one and it was painted in repulsive shades of brown and orange. Each bunk had curtains round it, which meant you could create a separate little box for yourself and hide in it. My morale faltered when I realised from the absence of belongings that I was to be alone in this room, for it meant I was the only woman on base. This late in the season there was no hope of any new ones arriving. Outside the door, someone belched like the volcanic lake in Cameroon which emitted gases so poisonous that hundreds died. I sat on my bunk and burst into tears.

Later, Stu reappeared. 'Do you need anything?' he asked.

'No, I'm fine,' I lied. 'But thanks – thanks for asking.'

'On Saturday nights we have a bit of a special dinner – tablecloths and lots of courses, that sort of thing. We get kind of dressed up.' He thought for a moment. 'Why not come and meet everyone at the bar at seven-thirty?'

'Great,' I said, the tone of my voice indicating that I did not believe it to be great at all. 'Thanks.'

'No worries,' said Stu cheerily. 'See you later.'

'Getting kind of dressed up' was a challenging concept. At half-past seven I made the best of a clean shirt and a half-clean pair of jeans, and sallied forth. There were about thirty-five people in the bar when I got there, and they were all talking loudly or guffawing with laughter. About eight of them were wearing ties. I introduced myself to a man in a sports jacket that was too small for him, but he immediately turned his back on me. Through careful observation, in the manner of a secret service agent, I gathered that purchasing a drink involved entering a tick in a column next to one's name on a special chart which was being tossed around chummily from hand to hand. I looked over a shoulder at this chart.

'I don't expect your name will be there,' said the Beard who had given me a lift. But it was.

The meal was delicious. I sat next to a field assistant.

'What exactly does a field assistant do?' I asked him.

'Babysit the scientists,' he said.

It was difficult to make yourself heard over the permanent dull roar of badinage that characterised social events at Rothera. They practised a kind of chain-joking. A brief food fight broke out during the cheese course. Here were British men doing what they did best – reverting to childhood and behaving like gits. I had become an expert on this type of behaviour at university, having been sheltered from it at my old-fashioned girls' school. (Growing up in an ordinary working-class environment, I had also been sheltered from the horrors of the class jungle. I didn't realise people came off separate shelves until I went to Oxford.) At the end of my second week as a student, a formal dinner was held for freshmen in my college. When the first bread roll whizzed through the air, I thought it was a ball that had escaped from the cricket pitch next door. I was just wondering how they could be playing cricket in the dark when a wrapped pat of butter glanced off my tutor's shoulder and plopped into my brown windsor soup.

*

The next morning, before anyone else got up, I had a look round the base. Labs, the radio room, the doctor's surgery, the boot room . . . Antarctic bases were starting to look awfully familiar. Rothera was about the same size as Scott Base and Terra Nova Bay, and it was about one twentieth of the size of McMurdo. The building was still, and silent, like a museum after closing time. I ran the palm of my hand over a smooth white wall. Then I heard a woman laughing faintly. I stood very still, trying to detect where this promising sound came from. Slowly, I padded along a narrow corridor until I was standing outside an unmarked door. A woman was talking very softly. I held an ear to the door. There was something . . . familiar about the voice. Several minutes passed. Suddenly, an orchestra struck up. I pushed the door open quietly. There was the night watchman, slumbering peacefully in an armchair, and on the video screen in front of him Julie Andrews was leaping down an Austrian mountainside followed by a row of rosy-cheeked von Trapp children. He had fallen asleep watching *The Sound of Music.*

Later, I sat in the sunshine on the steps of the main building drinking tea with Ben, a tall, lean marathon runner from Sheffield who was working at Rothera as a general base assistant. I had met him at the conference in Cambridge, and as soon as he spotted me stalking the Rothera corridors, he had welcomed me enthusiastically. I was pathetically grateful. Ben was pushing sixty and had first come to the ice as a dog-handler in 1961. He was a vegetarian, drove a Citroen two c.v. without a seatbelt and got up at 5.30 to meditate. He was revered by the others, who were all a good deal younger than he, as he had worked many seasons in the south during the golden age. I got the impression that he had come back to say goodbye.

Others were racing snowmobiles up an icy hill opposite the base. This hill was the gateway to the rest of the island. A route was flagged to the top, where it turned right along a tortuous traverse below Reptile Ridge, a 250-metre serrated edge extending north-west from Rothera.

'It's their base now,' Ben said suddenly.

'You're not gone yet, old boy,' said a small man who had thrown a portion of apple tart across the room at dinner the previous night. 'And talking of going, we're supposed to be taking the boats out.'

Ben jumped up.

'Come on, Sara,' he said. 'I'm sure there's room for you.'

We took the tea things upstairs, struggled into red immersion suits in the boot room and walked down to the wharf. The small man was busily winching two fifteen-foot Humber inflatables with twenty-five-horsepower engines into the water. We climbed down a metal ladder attached to the wall of the jetty. It was a cloudless day, and the mountainsides around one side of the bay were gilded with sunlight. The apple-tart thrower smiled at me. The bergs were spotted with seals and penguins, and Wilson's petrels skimmed the wake behind the other Humber, the white bar on their tails twirling gracefully over the ruffled water as if they were dancing on the hem of a slip. After a three-month ornithological diet of skuas they looked miraculously tiny. A man in the bows was making notes on a small green pad. He was a terrestrial biologist working in the Life Sciences division of BAS.

'Death Sciences, more like,' said the apple-tart thrower as this was explained to me. 'They bloody kill everything!' The notetaker had spent the summer poking around under rocks in the ice-free areas around Rothera. He was looking for insects.

'I haven't noticed any insects,' I said.

'You need a microscope,' he replied apologetically. 'They're mainly mites and springtails.'

'What happens to them in the winter?' I asked. 'Presumably they freeze.'

'No, they don't. They accumulate anti-freeze. It's a substance close to glycerol, very similar to the stuff you put in your car. It means the water in their cells doesn't freeze.'

Life Sciences, as well as a number of other scientific divisions within BAS, is highly regarded in the international Antarctic community for the quality and value of its research. Besides investigating terrestrial, freshwater and marine ecosystems in and around Antarctica, BAS also funds ground-breaking geophysical work and a range of upper atmospheric sciences. BAS people beat NASA, the American Antarctic programme, and everyone else in the field into a cocked hat when they announced that there was a hole in the ozone layer.

We stopped at a blue-eyed shag colony and scrambled up a rock to see the dark-eyed chicks, almost as tall as their parents but cocoa-brown and fluffy. The adults were white and black with long, smooth necks and eyes like blue marbles. Antarctica was throbbing with life, here on the banana belt. It seemed a long way from the biological haiku of the plateau.

Having crossed the Antarctic equivalent of the Atlantic, I had to make certain linguistic adjustments. I knew already about flashlights becoming torches and sleds mysteriously metamorphosing into sledges. In addition, in the 'British sector', Scott tents were pyramid tents, Coleman lanterns were tilley lamps, Tuckers were sno-cats, thermarests were karrimats, bunny boots were RBLTs (this stood for rubber-bottom leather-top), dorms were pitrooms and the galley was the kitchen and dining room. Weather was defined by two words: manky, which meant bad, and dingle, which was good. In-between weather apparently never occurred.[1]

Thinking nostalgically of the office bestowed on me at McMurdo, I parked my laptop and notebooks in a corner of the sledge store. Soon I discovered that someone slept on the floor of this room, presumably in order to escape the pitrooms, which were known as deprivation chambers. In the mornings I was obliged to skulk outside, establishing whether this individual had risen.

I learnt how to drive Hondas, the four-wheel drive mini-tractors, and John Deeres, little green pick-ups which were a permanent feature of the landscape around Rothera, beetling across the gravel. I had a snowmobile refresher course and went to Radio School to learn how to set up a high-frequency antenna and squelch a VHF. I went to Meteorological School where the weatherman, Steve, taught me how to tell the difference between cirrus and stratocumulus, a Shutdown School to learn how to turn the engines off if a pilot keeled over in his plane, and a Medical School in which I learnt of the beneficial effects of athlete's foot powder on crotch rot and was taught how to perform a tracheotomy with a Swiss Army knife.

Twice a week everyone gathered in the dining room for a 'Situation Report' at which the base commander announced news and impending events. This was followed by communal viewing of a video. The video was chosen on a rota system. Most people had seen all the videos on station several times, and their favourite trick was to pick a really bad film when it was their turn and then walk out after five minutes.

One day, after one of these videos, I tried to socialise in the bar. It was in a large room with a low ceiling, an institutional brown carpet and walls lined with the obligatory team photographs of hairy winterers clutching dogs and looking as if they played bass

---

[1] Antarctica might be the last frontier, but it has been occupied by man long enough to begin developing its own language. A sparky Australian researcher is currently compiling the world's first dictionary of Antarctic English. The book is listed as an official project by the Australian Antarctic Division.

guitar for a superannuated heavy metal band. The drinking area was festooned with postcards of women's bottoms. There was a music system, a collection of vinyl records, a pool table and a dartboard. In the winter they held radio darts contests with other bases. After a couple of years of competition someone went to Bird Island and discovered that the small scientific station there, its occupants always keen participants, had never had a dartboard on the premises.

A man approaching the end of a two-and-a-half year tour of duty as a member of base support staff announced that he had remembered a good joke.

'Why do women have periods?' it went.

Nobody knew the answer.

'Because they deserve it!' the man burst out, no longer able to keep this side-splitting information to himself. Everyone laughed.

It was as if I had entered a time capsule and been hurtled back to an age in which Neanderthal man was prowling around on the look-out for mammoths. Later that evening, safely removed from the bar, which I had come to think of as occupied territory, a Byronic youth apprehended me next to the tea urn.

'I hope you weren't too offended by that joke,' he said.

I couldn't think of anything to say.

'It does seem to mean a lot to them – I mean, keeping it male,' the man went on. 'I came down here from Grimsby on the BAS ship. Three women got on at Signy base, and it electrified the atmosphere on board. It sparked the major debate of the whole trip – even some of the young guys were arguing passionately against women down here. By the way, I'm Lucas.' We shook hands, took our tea and sat down at a formica table. Lucas was working for BAS as a summer-only field assistant, and felt 'at one remove' from the community at Rothera.

'Why on earth do they feel so strongly about it?' I asked.

He hesitated. 'They don't want the complication of a female in such a pristine place,' he said eventually. 'It's visceral.'

I didn't need to be told that. I felt it every day.

'Were the Americans like it too?' he asked.

'Er, no.'

'I suppose you have to remember that the majority of support staff here sign on for a two-and-a-half year tour of duty. It's a long time to live on an Antarctic base. Attitudes get entrenched.'

'The support staff seem very young here,' I said. 'Much younger than they are in other programmes.'

'Well, they are. Twenty isn't an uncommon age. You can't get a man to leave a wife and kids for two-and-a-half years.'

'They seem to find it hard to cope with outsiders . . .'

'There aren't any outsiders except you! They've never had a writer here before.'

It was as if I had moved into a family home and tried to pretend I was a relative. It wasn't fair to blame them for it. There was a highly developed sense of ownership among the British. The incumbents owned the base, figuratively, just as in their heads they owned 'their' bit of the continent. Besides the fact that most support staff were deployed for such a long period, the scientists were all employed by BAS. They worked in the same building in Cambridge, saw each other on the ice year after year, and were imbued with the same culture. Other Antarctic programmes worked with scientists from a wide variety of universities and external institutions, but BAS people were all members of the same club. There was an exclusivity about Rothera. It was in part a function of size, at least when compared with its larger American counterpart, which had gone as far as institutionalising writers and artists. To a greater extent, however, it was a function of historical continuity. BAS had been in the Antarctic longer than any other programme. The cultural differences between Britain and America in Antarctica had revealed themselves to me before I got further south than Cambridge or Virginia. At the orientation conferences the gloom of Girton College and cosy nights in the cellar bar were centuries away from the antiseptic vastness of the Xerox Document University. While BAS tried hard to introduce modern methodology to the training programme, with the result that at Girton we dutifully sat in small groups in front of flipcharts in sessions called Lifestyle, it symbolised a nod in the direction of progress, and when we had to use the flipchart to write a list of potential sources of conflict on base, Sexual Harassment was followed by Not Enough Sexual Harassment, and Farting was noted.

To me, the notion of shutting people out betrayed everything Antarctica represented. The women who had breached the BAS defences had fought hard, and minor battles had been won. The institutional subscription to *Mayfair* magazine was no longer provided by the benign employer and left on Rothera's coffee tables. There were many wars still to be fought, however. Men had always wanted to keep Antarctica for themselves, and since the Norwegian Caroline Mikkelsen became the first woman to set foot on the continent on 20 February 1935, the cause had advanced with the speed of a vegetable garden. Only the American programme has taken the matter seriously, and yet, in 1995, still only 61 of the 244 winterers at McMurdo were female.

Sir Vivien Fuchs wrote in his book *Of Ice and Men*, published in 1982, 'Problems will arise should it ever happen that women are admitted to base complement', and when I sat drinking tea with him at his house in Cambridge on a muggy Monday afternoon before I left England he suggested helpfully that the answer was to put women in all-female camps. In September 1966, an article in the American *Antarctic* magazine ran a headline '*Women t Worries*', and Admiral Reedy said breezily to a reporter from the same journal two years later that Antarctica would remain 'the womanless white continent of peace'. Rear-Admiral George Dufek, an early commander of U.S. operations on the ice, summed it up when he said, 'I think the presence of women would wreck the illusion of the frontiersman – the illusion of being a hero.'

The Soviets brought the first female non-wife south in 1957, and two years later the Australian programme followed suit. One of the first Australian women selected wrote later, 'We were invaders in a man's realm and we were regarded with suspicion.' The Americans sent the first four women south as programme participants in 1969, inciting the memorable headline, '*Powder Puff Explorers Invade the South Pole*'. When the first two females finally wintered at McMurdo in 1974 the programme managers weren't taking any chances – one was a nun, and the other 'mature', which meant (they hoped) past the age at which she could inflame the passions even of desperate men.

The American Harry Darlington took his wife south in 1946 when he was chief pilot and third-in-command of Finn Ronne's expedition to Stonington Island. He had met Jennie when she fed his husky a bone, and the dog went on to be their only wedding guest. When it was suggested that Ronne and Darlington should take their wives to Stonington, seven members of the expedition signed a petition protesting that it would 'jeopardise our physical condition and mental balance'. Poor lambs. Even Harry wasn't wild about the idea. 'It's no place for a woman,' he said. But in the end Jennie had to go, since Ronne insisted on taking Jackie, and the dissenters reckoned two were better than one. So they went. One man commented, 'The Admiral [Byrd] took along Guernseys. One had a calf. We might do better.'

Jennie had never been further south than Florida, and she was twenty-two when the ship set sail. She packed nail polish, but it froze. 'To him Antarctica symbolised a haven,' Jennie wrote of her husband, 'a place of high ideals and that inner peace men find only in an all-male atmosphere in primitive surroundings.' She was accepted in the end, and she learnt to drive the dogs, but probably only because – some good exploring notwithstanding – the expedition turned into a disaster. Relations with the British team camped nearby were strained. (An Englishman who had been in the field for several months and was unaware of Jennie's presence mistook her for a mirage and ran away.) The social fabric of the American team disintegrated into violence, and Harry was relieved of his responsibilities while forced to remain on the ice. Jennie and Jackie watched the men quarrelling, fighting, flouting safety measures, sinking into despair and allowing their personalities to take precedence over the aims of the expedition, and still, in *Man and the Conquest of the Pole*, published in 1964, P. E. Victor wrote of the Ronne saga, 'The expedition ran into all the difficulties ordinarily caused by the presence of women in such circumstances.' Even this was not quite as imaginative as the efforts of Abraham Cowley, who was caught in a storm in the Southern Ocean in the *Batchelor's Delight* in the 1680s. He concluded in his journal that *talking* about women had caused the storm.

The only other book written by a woman in the early years includes whale recipes and detailed instructions on how to knit bootees for penguins in order to protect polished floors. In the fifties Nan Brown spent two-and-a-half years on South Georgia with her husband, who was a radio operator. The Norwegians took her whaling, and she brought out her knitting on deck. She called her book *Antarctic Housewife*. Nan and Jennie Darlington were both pregnant when they left the ice (nothing else to do but procreate and knit), but the first child born in the vicinity of the continent was supposedly to a waitress aboard a Russian whaler in 1948, and she called the poor infant Antarctic. The Argentinians began bringing spouses south in 1977 to reinforce their territorial claim, and in 1978 one of them obligingly gave birth – though she was flown south seven months pregnant. By 1984 the Chileans were at it too, and they even established a school.

Private expeditions have been even more of a male preserve. The abiding characteristic of many of them seems to be hostility between members – you only have to read what Reinhold Messner wrote about Arved Fuchs, what Will Steger wrote about Geoff Somers, and what Fiennes and Stroud wrote about one another. The American Women's Antarctic Expedition to the South Pole in 1992–3 was refreshingly different. One member wrote afterwards, 'We each had our hard times and received the caring support of the other three . . . We found that although we got annoyed by some idiosyncrasies, we still valued and needed each individual and the qualities she had to offer the group.'

I am not, of course, suggesting that men are incapable of this kind of loving support (God forbid). It's exactly what Apsley Cherry-Garrard describes in *The Worst Journey in the World*. But it does seem to have disappeared from their repertoire of emotions. I found it unfathomable that, only eighty years after the expedition Cherry describes, things had come to such a pretty pass.

Scott wrote movingly about the value of friendship from the last tent. It was in a letter to J. M. Barrie. 'I never met a man in my life', wrote the captain, 'whom I admired and loved more than you, but I never could show you how much your friendship meant to me – for you had much to give and I had nothing.' How many men must have gone to the grave 'never being able to show', and how much they could learn from Scott's story.

Scott had been wooed by Barrie, creator of the eternally youthful Peter Pan, after returning from his first expedition. Barrie would have loved to have gone south. 'I want to know what it is really like to be alive,' he had written to Scott. After the tragedy had unfolded on the polar plateau, he identified Scott with Peter. For years he carried Scott's letter around with him, whipping it out at any opportunity. He said, 'When I think of Scott I remember the strange alpine story of the youth who fell down a glacier and was lost, and of how a scientific companion, one of several who accompanied him, all young, computed that his body would again appear at a certain place and date many years afterwards. When that time came round some of the survivors returned to the glacier to see if the prediction would be fulfilled, all old men now; and the body reappeared as young as on the day he left them. So Scott and his comrades emerge out of the white immensities, always young.'

Scott's son, in later life a distinguished naturalist and conservationist, was named after Barrie's immortal Peter. Barrie was his godfather, and when the boy was five, he took him to see the vastly successful *Peter Pan*. After the performance, Barrie asked him what he had liked best. Peter thought hard. 'What I liked best', he concluded, 'was tearing up the programme and dropping the bits on people's heads.'

*

At sixty-seven degrees south and sixty-eight degrees west, Rothera Point sits at the entrance of Ryder Bay, in the south east of Adelaide Island and about one third of the way down the Antarctic Peninsula. Adelaide Island was discovered and charted by John Biscoe as he weaved in and out of the archipelago alongside the peninsula. On St Valentine's Day 1832, he named it after Queen Adelaide of Sax-Meiningen, queen consort of William IV. The point was surveyed in the 1950s and named after John Michael Rothera, a surveyor for what later became the British Antarctic Survey. It was the haunt of Weddells and the occasional fur seal, as well as a proliferation of Adelies and dominican gulls. The rocks were covered in a type of branchy lichen from a group that exists in the Scottish highlands. Puffs of surf slapped the shore, and in the bay the bergs resembled a scene cut from a marble quarry. The maritime climate gave the continent a different dimension after the fastness of the Ross Ice Shelf.

As I grew familiar with the station, and felt the weight of history behind it, I became aware that something was missing. I couldn't put my finger on it until in the dining room one day I found myself staring at a five-foot wide framed photograph of a working dog team captioned 'In memory of the old dogs'. The ghosts of the dogs roamed everywhere at Rothera. On the duty-rota board in the dining room, next to the crowded columns headed Night Watch or some other domestic duty, the plastic letters of the Dog Feed column were jumbled in a heap at the bottom of the board. The Dog of the Day hook was still next to the front door, field rations were still called Manfood to distinguish them from

Dogfood, and framed photographs of bearded giants gazing ador-
ingly at small fluffy bundles lurked in the most unlikely places.

In 1991 the Antarctic Treaty nations declared that under the
terms of the Environmental Protocol to the Treaty the huskies
were to be 'phased out' of Antarctica by April Fool's Day 1994.
The breeding programme at Rothera was stopped immediately.
BAS had kept dogs continually since 1945, though they had not
been used in support of scientific work since 1975. With the
arrival of reliable snowmobile travel, the dogs became ever more
obsolete and were retained primarily for recreational purposes. In
the Rothera archives I found a telex from the Foreign Office,
dated 1963, suggesting that breeding should cease since mechanical
transport was increasing, and it was scrawled with indignant comments from men on base pointing out that one plane was
grounded and the motorised toboggans were stranded while the
Spartans, Giants and Moomins were lazing comfortably on their
spans outside the door. Besides mechanisation, another argument
for the removal of the dogs was the suggestion that they passed on
canine distemper to seals, and, more plausibly, that the seal chop
necessitated by their voracious appetites was now 'inappropriate
to the environmental aims of scientific organisations within the
Antarctic'.

I asked Ben about the dogs one day while we were washing up.

'You can't bond with a snowmobile,' he said. 'The huskies kept
up our morale. The Antarctic would have been far lonelier without them. Our dogs kept us sane, no doubt about it.'

'Do you miss them?' I asked.

'Oh yes. You can form relationships with the dogs like you do
with two-legged travelling companions. They were my friends. I
used to have the same team for two years, and you got to know
them so well – I could anticipate when trouble was going to start
from a little mannerism, say, or a low growl. I could even tell
which one had broken wind.' He turned away from the sink and
wiped his hands.

'I'll never forget going down to say goodbye to them at the end
of my tour, just before I got on the ship. Ask any dog-handler if
he'd like to take his team with him at that moment, and he
wouldn't think twice, I can tell you.' He thought about this for a
moment, and continued, 'The dogs formed a link with the past,
too. They gave the base a bit of historical continuity. That's all

gone now. In a couple of years there won't even be anyone here who remembers the huskies.'

John Sweeny, who was half Ben's age, was the last dog-handler at BAS. He was the Irishman whom I had met at breakfast on the first day of the conference and who had run along the river with me in Cambridge.

'How was the trip, John?' someone had asked him over the cornflakes at Girton College.

'Fine,' John replied.

'Where have you been?' I enquired.

'On a skiing holiday,' he said.

I imagined that this holiday had taken place in Sauze d'Oux or Chamonix. Later I found out that he had skied all the way across Greenland, pulling his sledge behind him.

BAS decided that it would be fitting to use dogs in their traditional role of science support to mark their departure from Rothera. As a result, John and another handler had taken two teams on a final seven-week survey around the Milky Way and Uranus Glaciers, and on a shallow-core drilling traverse of central Alexander Island. It was the last dog journey ever in Antarctica. I read John's report of the trip. It ended with a quotation from Helmer Hanssen, Amundsen's dog-handler. 'Dogs like that, which share man's hard times and strenuous work, cannot be looked upon merely as animals. They are supporters and friends. There is no such thing as making a pet out of a sledge dog; these animals are worth much more than that.'

The transport programme to get them out was called Operation Tabarin in commemoration of the expedition which brought dogs from Greenland to Hope Bay in 1943. John and the dogs travelled, via Brize Norton, to Newry in Maine, and then the younger ones went north to the Inuit village of Inukjuak on Hudson's Bay where they formed a working team. 'It was a bittersweet experience,' John said as we jogged along the river. 'I didn't realise until I got up there that the dogs weren't going back.'

One day, while walking around the point with one of the pilots, he stopped in front of a slumbering Weddell seal. 'You know they used to shoot those guys around here, to feed the dogs,' he said. 'I saw it. The romance of the huskies is very misleading. More seals were killed than dogs were fed. The seal chop — that was when they sliced them up — was brutal and disgusting, and the smell on the dog spans was foul because the high fat content of their diet had a poor effect on their digestion.'

'Don't you miss having them around?' I asked.

'No, I don't! They used to kill each other and snap at us!'

*

At eleven in the morning and four in the afternoon the men gathered in the dining room for the *smoko* ritual. Al, the cook, would appear with trays of hot sausages, crispy bacon and fresh rolls, or, in the afternoon, his legendary flapjack. He was an ace cook, and so was Dave, the wintering cook. They always made me welcome in the light and airy kitchen, and I used to go in there whenever I could think of an excuse. A cleaver on the wall was inscribed with the words *Queue Here For Haircuts*. Al and Dave were both from the north of England, and Al had been cooking for BAS since the sixties. Six months after I returned from the ice he was awarded the Polar Medal, and he took me with him to Buckingham Palace. A hundred other people were being decorated at the same time, from doughty Bermudan dowagers to Tory Members of Parliament and frail old ladies rewarded for 'services in Paraguay'. The best dressed man was a chieftain in a black and gold robe, though the flunky announced that he came from Liverpool. Apart from the chieftain, the only man who hadn't hired top hat and tails was a director of Oxfam who looked as if he'd got his suit from the back of one of his shops. The Queen had mugged up and commented to Al that cooking was a very important job.

*

It was dark by nine o'clock now. Field assistants returned from two months on the ice with their beakers, and they clattered around the base sorting out their equipment. Ground sheets, hoisted up to dry, bestowed upon their storerooms the alluring air of a Bedouin encampment. One of the field assistants was a rangy geography teacher called Neil with a Liverpudlian accent and hair that flopped into his eyes. He used the analogy of a rollercoaster to describe his Antarctic experience. 'It can be great here,' he said. 'But it's not really living.'

I had just finished reading Thomas Keneally's Antarctic murder mystery *Victim of the Aurora*, published in 1977. It was narrated by an old man who was once the artist of a five-man team of explorers closely resembling Scott's group. A journalist is murdered on the ice. 'To me', says the narrator, 'the world was simple and the lying hadn't begun when I joined the expedition . . . Ever since [the murder and its aftermath] the world has been fuelled and governed by lies. That is my concise history of the twentieth century.' In addition, a refugee found hiding in an ice cave becomes a symbol of the human condition. 'But you can live, weeping and cursing,' says this character. 'Oh yeah, it's possible,' and commenting on the fact that he can't quite stand up in his shelter, he adds, 'I suppose that I'm characteristic of mankind.' The narrator returns to the Antarctic as an old man, and is flown back to the Pole, which makes him feel sick. 'I suppose I may have been suffering the shock of reaching the Pole, that trigonometrical siren of the Edwardian age, to find it an ice plain without character, staffed by disconsolate young soldiers who would rather be in Vietnam. In other words, the Pole was no longer a mythical place.'

Like me, Keneally visited the Antarctic as a guest of the American programme. 'The basic futility of Antarctic exploration', he wrote after he had returned, 'was . . . brought home to me as I saw the nullity of the place, the meaninglessness of most of the geographic data for which men like Scott gave their lives. The Pole itself was a prodigious nothingness, a geographic void. But the wealth of impressions and memories that arose from my Ant arctic odyssey will always enrich my writing.'

George reappeared, the loquacious chief builder who had accompanied me south from Brize Norton. He came storming in to our building one day and invited me to his birthday dinner on Saturday evening. I was touched. He was going to be sixty-nine.

'Are they looking after you all right here?' he asked, adding conspiratorially, 'if not, come on over, I'll see what I can do.' Quite what he would have been able to do was a baffling question. Later, he showed me round the builders' quarters. 'I think it's all right for intellectuals to share four to a room,' he said, flinging open the door of a pitroom and speaking as if he had spent years acquiring this knowledge, 'but for my laddies, two is preferable.'

A blizzard descended on George's birthday, and the outside of the windows appeared to be hung with sheets of muslin. In the evening I fought my way over to the party. They had put tablecloths and candles on the tables, George and his sidekick were wearing ties, and a notice on the blackboard said 'Guest Star – 9.30: Stripper. 10.30: Haircuts'. George dispensed sweet sherry, and if anyone swore, he made them apologise to me. John the plumber, who was a vegetarian, told me that on his first day he had been presented with a box of sixty-four microwaveable veggiburgers. Later, I heard rousing choruses of 'Alouette' in the lounge area behind me, and people began appearing in thermal longjohns with boxer shorts on top. These they referred to obliquely as their 'drinking outfits'. When I turned round later, George had his trousers round his ankles.

'I'm the oldest man in Antarctica,' he shouted, which was almost certainly true.

CHAPTER THIRTEEN

Fossil Bluff and the Ski Hi Nunataks

> The Clowds near the horizon were of a perfect Snow Whiteness and were difficult to be distinguished from the Ice hills whose lofty summits reached the Clowds. The outer or Northern edge of this immence Ice field was compose[d] of loose or broken ice so close packed together that nothing could enter it; about a mile in began the field ice, in one compact solid boddy and seemed to increase in height as you traced it to the South; In this field we counted Ninety Seven Ice Hills or Mountains, many of them vastly large . . .
>
> From Captain Cook's journal, January 1774

FOSSIL BLUFF lies about 230 miles from Rothera on the east coast of Alexander Island. A group of men from the British Graham Land Expedition were the first to set foot there; they surveyed it roughly in 1936 and found Jurassic fossils, so they called it Fossil Camp. Lancelot Fleming, a member of the expedition who later became Bishop of Norwich, made a cine film which, fifty years later, was put on video with a narration by another member, the redoubtable Duncan Carse. Carse had gone on to be a successful actor, playing Dick Barton in the 1940s BBC radio series. He has a mellifluous voice made for a piece of film which perfectly captures the lost innocence of a golden age. After the expedition he spent some time alone in South Georgia. In a film about that he said, 'I enjoyed a peace of mind there I've experienced nowhere else. It was an island where I belonged.' He tried to retrace Shackleton's route over the mountains, and had what he described to me as 'an experience on the astral plane'. In his South

Georgia diary he wrote of low cloud hanging in pearly streamers 'like wraiths of the imagination. But through them and above, the unattainable heights of the Allardyce Range fired the skyline with stupendous beacons of icy luminosity . . . no one had ever seen them before: a thousand years might pass before they showed themselves again.'

The British Graham Land Expedition, led by John Rymill, was a private venture and, like all the best expeditions since Columbus, it was chronically short of cash. They were even obliged to straighten out packing-cases to retrieve nails. They had £3,000 with which to buy a ship and ended up with the *Penola*, a 130-tonne three-masted Brittany fishing schooner which they were able to equip with a de Havilland Fox Moth light aircraft.

Nobody knew much about Graham Land in those days. John Biscoe had named it after Sir James Robert George Graham, First Lord of the Admiralty and later Home Secretary, and it was annexed in 1908 as part of the Falkland Islands Dependency. Fleming's film shows the *Penola* leaving London's St Catherine's dock in 1934 to explore this *terra incognita*. She was away for three years.

They were dogged by bad luck at the beginning but, as Carse put it, 'It came good at the end.' The expedition made numerous discoveries and surveyed great tracts of unknown territory. At the conclusion of the film Carse declares triumphantly: 'Graham Land was the Antarctic Peninsula' (it had been thought that it was part of an archipelago), much as Columbus must have declared that there was land west of Iberia. Carse said, 'We were the expedition that links the Heroic Age – Scott, Shackleton, Amundsen and Mawson – with BAS of today. We lived and worked on the watershed between too little regard for personal welfare and too great a reliance on impersonal technology. We were the fortunate ones who practised Antarctic exploration at its all-time best.'

Though it achieved more knowledge per pound spent than any other Antarctic expedition, the British Graham Land team never received the recognition it deserved. Colin Bertram, one of the surviving members, told me: 'People realised that the war was imminent, and they didn't have time to think about us.' Nobody died, which meant the media wasn't interested, and the expedition had nothing to do with the South Pole, always the sexiest part of Antarctica.

After I returned from the ice I took a train through the New

Forest in the south of England on the hottest day of the year and looked through cracked albums of sharp black-and-white photographs of the expedition with Alfred Stephenson (known as Steve) who said he remembered taking every one – and he had gone south only twenty years after Scott. In the pre-departure pictures, the men were lined up in baggy trousers, hair slicked-back from pasty morning-after faces. On the deck of the *Penola*, they were taking tea and laughing into the camera as if they were on a college trip. I pointed out a picture of men making dog harnesses, and Steve reeled off the names of the dogs. Barring Amundsen's, it was the most dog-orientated expedition ever. They had to shoot the last eighty of their working dogs because they were unable to feed them on the long voyage home. 'I still mourn them,' Bertram said sixty years later.

Fleming filmed a man making a canoe out of a barrel and paddling it furiously through the pack ice. He also recorded puppy training on the snowfields, all hands on a storm-washed deck, and three fabulous skiers slaloming down pristine slopes. They were all tall and handsome and looked as wholesome as Greek gods. They were making history, and having the times of their lives. Above all, there was an innocence about them; something untainted. In John Rymill's book *Southern Lights*, they all seem to be indescribably happy all the time. When they were leaving Antarctica, Rymill wrote of 'a feeling of loss as though a friend had died'. 'To think', the book ends, 'that when we return to England one of the first questions we shall be asked – probably by a well-fed businessman whose God is his bank book – will be "Why did you go there?" '

Alexander Island was roughly mapped as far back as 1821 by members of Bellingshausen's Russian Antarctic Expedition, who named it after Tsar Alexander I, their patron. A British team surveyed the Fossil Camp site in 1948 and renamed it Fossil Bluff, and BAS scientists have been working on Alexander Island ever since. The focus of their investigations was primarily the relationship between glacier climate and atmospheric climate. In the middle of February I asked if I could hitch a ride to the small Bluff camp on a fuel flight. Nobody raised any objection, which was a relief, as I was becoming increasingly desperate to get off base – for two weeks I had been hanging around there without much to do. I had no idea how long I would be able to stay at the

Bluff, but I couldn't have cared less about that. Someone would presumably tell me when I had to leave.

Alexander Island is separated from continental Palmer Land by George VI Sound, which, when I flew over it, was streaked with blue melt pools. We landed on the edge of the island next to a line of black drums. A couple of men hooded in fluorescent orange ventile were waiting to refuel the aircraft, and after we had waved the pilot on his way south I rode the mile to the Bluff itself in a sledge. The hut, now occupied only in summer, was established in 1961. It had recently acquired a smart wooden veranda on which flapped the obligatory Union Jack – upside down, as usual.

We went in to the smell of burning jam tarts and a lively row over who had forgotten to take them out of the oven. A man with a beard like Rasputin's was defending himself on the basis that he had been discussing an important matter on the radio. Steve Rumble, an electrician and winter base commander who had been on the ice for twenty-seven months, kept his Walkman clamped to his head and remained supine on his bunk. Hans Cutter, a German geodesist inevitably known as Herr Cutter, sat at the table looking baffled at the sudden inflamed talk of tarts, especially as it had coincided with my arrival. The fourth temporary resident at the Bluff, Ian, was standing in the middle of the hut in his apron, grasping the tray of smouldering ex-tarts. He was the outgoing doctor at Rothera, and an endearingly eccentric character with firm opinions and a wild glint in his eye. I had met him on base before he left for the Bluff – he was one of the few who came up to shake hands when I arrived. Although he spoke Home Counties English, I think he was Scottish, as I had seen photographs of him skiing in a kilt.

The population of the Bluff was transitory. The hut was used as a staging-post for science parties on their way further south, a holiday cottage and a place to send people if they were getting in the way on base. Ben, the veteran dog-handler from Sheffield, had flown in with me, and shortly after we arrived a science party of two turned up after seventy-two days on the Uranus, a glacier which had provided many hundreds of punning jokes for generations of Rothera Beards. Graham was a tall glaciology postgraduate from Belfast with ginger hair. He was studying how light was reflected in the snow pack. This affected heat absorption, and yielded data which could be used to assess the rate of global warming. His much shorter field assistant was a chunky mountaineer from south London called Duncan. They both said they weren't sure if they could sleep between walls after seventy-two nights in a tent. Having eaten field rations for so long, they were astonished to find real mushrooms in the spaghetti sauce. They held pieces up on forks, just to look at them. In the evening we drank wine the winterers had made from raisins and sultanas. It tasted of cooking sherry, but they had decanted it into Chateau Lafite bottles.

The hut, which for years had been known as Bluebell Cottage, was about fifteen feet by twenty-five, with a small partitioned sink area and an arched wooden ceiling. Built in at one end were two sets of bunks with metal legs and no ladders. There was a wooden table, a dresser strewn with magazines and books, the latter including *The Bluffer's Guide to Seduction* and *The Beauty of Cars*, and a noticeboard upon which someone had pinned a register of fuel drums, a black-and-white photograph of a killer whale, a clutch of cartoons and a Moral Fibre Meter, the latter inaugurated in honour of a pilot who issued regular tirades against the flaccidity of modern youth. One corner was filled with communications equipment, and this area was known as the radio shack. A few pictures of women had been ripped from magazines and stuck to the wall, and pots and pans dangled from beams. The room was dominated by a drip-oil Aga upon which an antediluvian kettle sat in permanent residence, growling menacingly. Off the entrance, a slender room called Arkwright's was jumbled with tools and bags and cases of beer, and on the other side of the hut, in a room crammed with snowshoes, crampons, ropes, karrimats, a soda syphon, nuts and bolts and an old wooden sign saying 'No Dumping', there was a portable toilet.

I slept in the food store, a blue wooden hut on the slope behind Bluebell Cottage. A small window at one end cast an orange rhomboid on the opposite wall in the early morning. At night – by mid-February as long as an autumnal northern night – I had to read by torchlight. The room was stacked with ziplocks of split peas, boxes of suet, shiny metal cubes of sugar packed in July 1985, a large cardboard box containing khaki foil packs of the ubiquitous 'Biscuits, Brown' eaten by British Antarcticans since the dawn of time, and a surplus of sardines. On the floor boxes of shampoo had collapsed on to crates of leaking tile cleaner. The door wouldn't shut from the inside, so I was obliged to tie myself in.

I emptied my p-bag on to the floor. This object was shaped like a golf caddy and contained an airbed, two karrimats, a sheepskin underblanket, a bivvy bag and a sleeping bag with two liners. As I inflated my airbed between the shelves I couldn't help thinking guiltily of what Wilfred Thesiger said to Eric Newby and Hugh Carless when he saw them inflating their airbeds in Nuristan in 1956. It is the last line of Newby's *A Short Walk in the Hindu Kush*. 'God, you must be a couple of pansies,' said Thesiger.

Bluebell Cottage was the only hut on an island the size of Wales (the size of England if you counted the ice shelves attached to it) and it had hardly changed since 1961. I knew that for I had seen photographs of Beards hunched in the radio shack or grinning over a saucepan. Drune, the mountain directly behind the hut, and Pyramid, the ziggurat next to it, were usually striated with snow. It was always more attractive around the hut when it snowed; a light covering over the scree and moraine broke up the brown. On the other side of King George VI Sound the Batterbee Mountains and Ryder Glacier changed colour as the light faded and glowed like old stained glass in the great cathedrals around the time of evensong.

At the Bluff, Ian taught me to chart the speed and direction of the wind, the cloud type and extent of cover, the height of the cloud base and the air pressure at sea level. He was a good teacher, and seemed pleased to have something to do. He had come to the end of his year's tour of duty as a doctor, and his replacement was already installed at Rothera. Everyone at Bluebell Cottage had finished whatever it was they had been doing in Antarctica. They were waiting to go home, and it was more agreeable to sit it out at the Bluff than at Rothera – not least due to the absence of a base commander.

My newly acquired skills meant I could take my turn at weather observations and relay the data back to Rothera over the radio. Often we had to do this hourly, if aircraft were trying to come in. They often brought more avtur, the aviation fuel used by BAS, as the Bluff functioned as a service station for planes transporting scientists further south. It was a fuel-intensive business, as the Otters bringing drums of fuel had to refill their own tanks before returning to Rothera.

Ian taught me how to test the forty-five-gallon drums of avtur for water contamination, and how to fill up the tanks when a plane arrived. In addition, we occupied ourselves for a couple of hours each day at the drum dump, a pit into which trash had been deposited in a less environmentally aware age. The work involved digging debris out of the ice and piling it into empty fuel drums. When these drums were full, the Otters ferried them back to Rothera.

While I was working on the dump one day with Graham, the tall Belfast glaciologist, he said irritably, 'No wonder they call them the good old days. They chucked all their bloody rubbish straight down where they stood.'

Graham had a strong northern Irish accent, for which he came under constant fire from the others, but no account of teasing could provoke him. One day at the dump he decided to requisition the unclaimed portion of Antarctica for Ulster.

'Storming,' he said as he contemplated this idea. He was affable, lively and spontaneous, and kept a tin whistle in his pocket. Duncan, the field assistant from South London who had spent seventy-two days on the Uranus with Graham and his whistle, was more reserved and less cheerful. I noticed that he made a quick exit from Bluebell Cottage whenever Graham's hand approached the pocket containing his whistle.

I stayed at the Bluff for two weeks, and each day walked along a thin path across the scree at the foot of Drune towards the Eros Glacier. It ran alongside a frozen inlet, and beyond the windscoop on the opposite side the glacier fell to a ledge over a pearly blue cavern. On the way back I used to lie on the scree and contemplate the Eros, and watch the rose pink glow of sunset die over the Batterbees on the other side of the streaky Sound.

As further evidence of Scottishness, Ian had his bagpipes sent over on a passing Otter. He needed constant stimulation, and displayed none of the pubbish characteristics of the other BAS men. I got the impression that he had not particularly enjoyed the winter as a result. He stood on the veranda playing 'Amazing Grace'. It was not a great success, due to cold drones.

'Let me have a go,' said Graham, who was game for anything. Ian handed the pipes over, and Graham expended a great deal of energy producing no sound at all.

'Why don't I blow,' said Ben, who, as a marathon runner, had a reliable pair of lungs, 'and you hold the bagpipes and press the buttons?'

After a good deal of jostling on the veranda, a single reedy note wheezed out of the pipes. It had a dying fall.

'Where's all the breath *going*?' said Ben.

Graham gave up, and fetched his tin whistle. Perhaps it was the first time bagpipes and a tin whistle have ever been heard together in Antarctica.

'And I hope the last,' said Duncan when I mentioned this.

The manfood boxes that had sustained Graham and Duncan in the field were packed in 1986. Everything was years past its sell-by date in Antarctica. When it was all over and I got home, I was shocked to see sell-by dates in the future, as if it worked the other way round, and that meant you weren't supposed to eat the goods. But it didn't seem to matter – we were never ill. Some things were less appetising than they might have been. Upon contact with heat the tinned spaghetti disintegrated, as it had been thawed and refrozen so many times. In one field camp I saw a tub of Parmesan cheese bearing the printed label *Matured ten months*. Underneath, someone had written, FROZEN TEN YEARS.

Still, care parcels arrived sometimes from Al, the medal-winning Rothera cook, and one day a joint of beef was tossed out of a refuelling Otter. Ian cooked it, with Yorkshire pudding and all the trimmings. He was an excellent cook. Besides two loaves a day, he churned out pies and scones, and one morning he produced Danish pastries. After we had eaten the beef, he was bored, so he cut the obliging Graham's hair.

'We could play Trivial Pursuit after this,' said Graham brightly.

Nobody said anything. We were bored with Trivial Pursuit. Like everything else at the Bluff, the game in the hut was an early model, and it was an American version to boot, the orange questions asking us who joined the National Hockey League in 1983. Ian would shout wild guesses to these arcane questions, which irritated Rasputin, when we managed to coax him out of the radio shack. He favoured a more intellectual approach to the game.

Rasputin was a highly skilled surveyor on secondment from the Ordnance Survey, the government mapping department. He had been in the south for five weeks, taking photographs of Antarctica in order to go back to Cambridge and produce detailed maps of small areas. In the hut he held forth on the importance of maps in society with missionary zeal, and talked eloquently about the cultural absence of what he referred to as 'map awareness'. After I had been at the Bluff for a week I realised that I had never seen him with a camera in his hand.

'Where is your camera?' I asked him, expecting him to whip it out of his pocket.

'It's mounted in the back of a Twin Otter,' he said huffily. 'It weighs more than 200 pounds, you know – it's not a bloody Box Brownie.'

Three days later, Rasputin went back to Rothera on an Otter, as he was supposed to be taking the next flight to the Falklands. While we sat on the veranda waiting for the plane, he looked south and sighed.

'Look at that,' he said ruefully. 'Nothing between us and the Pole except 1,250 miles of empty ice. So much to map – so little time.'

I moved into the old generator shed where he had been sleeping. It was a lean-to on the side of the cottage with a tiny wooden door. Like Alice, I had to crouch down to get through it. The shed had a kind of wooden shelf which served as a bed, with a sliding hatch next to it, so I used to lie with the hatch open and look out over the Sound and Georgian Cliffs, listening to the bergs calve and the ice crack. It was as if the landscape were alive, just as Coleridge described – though he had never seen anything like it:

> The ice was here, the ice was there,
> The ice was all around:
> It cracked and growled, and roared and howled,
> Like noises in a swound!

Coleridge conceived *The Rime of the Ancient Mariner* as he walked over the green hills of the south west of England between 1797 and 1798 and watched the moon rise over the sea. He had never been abroad; he saw the ice with his inner eye. Many writers have tried to transform a voyage to Antarctica into a spiritual journey, but it was Coleridge who made me believe the analogy worked. The Mariner travels beyond the boundaries of knowable knowledge, on to the wide, wide sea of the spirit, and into the wondrous cold, the isolation of the human condition – 'And never a saint took pity on/My soul in agony'. My own Antarctic journey offered a glimpse of the bounties beyond knowable knowledge, not the torments; but I had made the trip to cold, dark desperation before. That terrible experience of misery and depression was not part of my Antarctic journey, though I carried the memory of it with me, and it made the peace I grasped on the ice more profound.

When it snowed, refuelling was such a thoroughly unpleasant business that a rigorously democratic roster was established. The brown slopes of the moraine were then like leaves stained with dye, and the light covering of powder revealed the different texture of each one. One snowy day, the plane brought mail. A quixotic friend of mine sent me an old brass whistle, and as the boys had picked up the phrase 'It's a testosterone thing' from me, my gift immediately became the testosterone whistle, and I was instructed to blow it when the level got too high.

Although the temperature rarely fell below minus three, a system brought high winds and persistent snowfall, and we were trapped in the hut. Ben entertained us with stories of the old days, mostly involving dogs.

'All the dogs just disappeared in front of my eyes – zip! zip! zip!' he said at the end of a long and colourful story about a thousand-mile sledging journey. 'I crawled to the edge of the crevasse, looked down into the gloom, and there they were, swinging in their harnesses, with Dot, the leader, hanging forty feet down on the end of the trace!'

'What happened?' we all said at once.

'My partner lowered me down into the crevasse, and I un-clipped the dogs from the trace one by one and hoisted them all out. I had been leading, so it was technically my fault – but the dogs never held it against me.'

After two days of total cloud cover, plus rain and snow, incarceration began to induce cabin fever. We decided to found a cult and broadcast Churchillian speeches over the Sound. In a fit of domesticity I asked whether anyone minded if I washed the shelves down, and Steve said, 'It's your hut as much as anybody else's.' The men at the Bluff had made me feel part of the team, something that no one at Rothera had even attempted.

After four days the weather cleared, and we walked up to the penitentes, a snowfield of sculpted ice cones named after their resemblance to monks in prayer. Their smooth, biomorphic shapes and the simplicity of their curves and swellings and tapering gradients reminded me of Barbara Hepworth sculptures. They conveyed the same sense of the eternal, too; or, at least, of serenity. It was a Cornish landscape which inspired Hepworth. I looked out over the Sound, groping in vain for signs of the Cornwall of my childhood.

Agreeable though life was at the Bluff, after two weeks I was beginning to wish I could see a different peninsular landscape. It seemed too far to come to sit in the same place for two months. I asked the Rothera base commander over the radio if I could hitch a lift on a plane refuelling at the Bluff on its way to a field camp further south. Three days later, I stumbled into the hut from my tiny room as usual to find that the boys were taking it in turns to hit a tuning fork against a bunk leg and then press it on their teeth.

'By the way,' Ian remembered after I had made coffee. 'You were mentioned on the early morning sched. You're going to Ski Hi this afternoon.'

*

The Sky Hi nunataks were 220 miles from the Bluff, north east of the Merrick Mountains on the West Antarctic ice sheet. They were too far south to be described as on the peninsula at all – so I was back in what I had come to think of as the proper Antarctica. These rocky extrusions, ablated of snow, disappeared as soon as low cloud descended over the ice sheet. They were first surveyed by Americans in the early sixties and named after a camp which later changed its name to Eights Station. Now a small team of BAS scientists and technicians were studying that portion of ice sheet with aerial radar equipment and, as a result, a rudimentary camp had been established not far from the nunataks. It consisted of no more than a couple of fuel lines, half a dozen pyramid tents and a weatherhaven.

When we landed, a furious wind was whipping over the ice sheet and it was very cold. The tops of the tents were snowy, like mountain peaks. Vasco was there. He was a small, striking field assistant with flaming eyes and a big heart. The nickname – after Vasco da Gama – had been bestowed upon him when he sailed south, as he had spent the entire voyage from Grimsby on the bridge with the first officer, learning to use a sextant.

'Welcome to hell on earth,' he said. Neil, the rangy Liverpudlian geography teacher, was there too, and he took me to the weather-haven and made me a cup of tea. It was an arched tent, twelve feet long and six feet wide, with board flooring and a permanently lit tilley lamp hanging from the ceiling. An array of dripping gloves and hats also dangled from an overhead network of string.

'It gets a bit crowded in here,' Neil said. 'You'll have to fight for a space in the evenings.'

'How many people are here?' I asked, warming my hands over one of the two primuses.

'Ten, with you,' he replied, totting them up on his fingers. 'Two scientists who've just arrived from a more remote camp and are waiting to go back to Rothera, the five guys on the radar survey team, and Vasco and I. We aren't really sure what we're doing here.'

'I think we're supposed to be packing up the camp,' said Vasco, who had followed us in. He was shovelling snow into the small pond in the middle of the floor. When the snow had absorbed all the water, he shovelled it out again.

The radio was on a jerry can and one end of the weatherhaven was entirely occupied by half-empty tins and jars, their contents granite-hard, dribbling packets of soup, plastic mugs and a red plastic sack in which everyone took it in turns to collect ice.

'Don't you ever turn these primuses off?' I asked, as there was no saucepan sitting on them.

'We leave them on to heat the air,' said Neil. 'It's seventeen or eighteen below most days – sometimes much colder. You'll notice the difference between this and the Bluff. You're further south, and the ice sheet is far more exposed than the peninsula.'

I was sharing the furthest pyramid tent with Keith, an electronics engineer on the radar project. Although an American Scott tent and a British pyramid tent are, to all intents and purposes, the same, the entrance to a pyramid is two feet off the ground, making entry and exit harder and reflecting the higher levels of snow accumulation in the 'British sector' on the peninsula. When I looked at my photographs later I realised that the Scott tents used by the Americans are less steeply angled, for the same reason. Most amazing of all, I had begun to find these details interesting.

I laid my sleep kit down one side of the tent. Our territory was divided by a pot box, a food box and a geophysics box, and on top of these stood a primus, a tilley lamp, a radio, a compact disc Walkman, a James Clavell novel and a tube of Extra Strong mints. An open tin of peaches with feathers stuck to the lid was wedged between Keith's airbed and the primus, as well as a tin half full of Dutch camping butter (1988) and numerous discarded wrappers of Cadbury's Milk Chocolate. It was clear that the acquisition of a tent-mate was not the best thing that had ever happened to Keith. On the first night, he stayed in the weatherhaven until everyone else had retired to their tents, delaying the moment at which he was obliged to join me.

'Hello,' I said as I heard him fighting his way through the tent flaps.

'Hello,' he replied, in a kind of disappointed way, as if he had nourished hopes that I might have dematerialised. I had hatched a cunning plan, however. I could see from the tent that Keith was a gadget man. He had installed – for example – a digital thermometer which took the temperature inside and outside of the tent at the same time. The only way to deal with a gadget man is to feign interest in his equipment.

'This is useful,' I lied, pointing at the double display on the thermometer. 'How does it work, exactly?'

Keith cleared his throat. I had won.

The reason Keith had enjoyed a tent to himself before my arrival soon became clear. He could have snored for England. I didn't mind. Being able to sleep anywhere at any time and in any circumstances was part of the job description, as far as I was concerned. When Keith was awake I enjoyed his company, once he thawed out a bit. And he made me tea in the morning.

'Here's breakfast,' he used to say, handing me half a bar of Cadbury's. If it was windy, we had to shout at one another. On the second day I was granted earphone rights to the cd player, and I dipped in and out of Keith's extensive and catholic collection. Getting dressed was hellish though, and made harder by the gloating presence of the thermometer, which informed us irrefutably that outside it was minus twenty-five. I began plotting its destruction. On really bad days, when the plane carrying the radar equipment couldn't fly, some people never left their tent, except to go to the toilet, and even this was an ordeal as it involved sliding down an ice chute into an underground ice chamber and climbing on to an empty fuel drum.

While trapped inside for days, everyone ran out of books and started reading the backs of food cartons. People said that in the field they had learnt how to mix up the porridge oats in Dutch and Swahili. There was a long established tradition of this. Gunnar Anderssen, marooned at Hope Bay in 1902, wrote that his party had no books, and to delight the eye with the printed word they got out their tins of condensed milk and read the labels. On the whole, we couldn't really enjoy anything much at Ski Hi, or even do any serious thinking. Existing, as opposed to freezing, seemed to take up all our energy.

We rarely took off our windies, the fluorescent orange ventile over-the-head windcheaters and enormous trousers worn by Scott and every subsequent Briton in Antarctica. They suited what was often referred to in the weatherhaven as 'the Antarctic experience'. The boys used the adjective 'gnarly' all the time: it meant living what they perceived to be the 'authentic' way in Antarctica, eschewing the comforts of base for the derring-do they associated with the old days. Almost all the men became coarser and more consciously macho in the field. It was as if they had reverted to a basic level of mental existence as well as a physical one. Fancying yourself as a bit of a polar hero is harmless enough, but so much cultural baggage came along with it. They were committed to a grim type of schoolboy humour. When a field assistant shat in his overalls by mistake, he recounted what had happened over the radio and it became the story of the day on base; terribly funny, everyone agreed. If someone left a camera around, you could be sure it would be used for a few shots of someone else with a cigar up his bum, to edify the owner's mother when the film was sent home to be developed. When the air unit left for the season they scrawled a final message on the operations board: 'Shaggin' in the U.K.' A man who had recently left the ice after two-and-a-half years sent down a photograph of himself *in flagrante*. Before the ship arrived to take us out, a list went up asking if anyone required vegetarian food on board: someone wrote '*Fuck Off*' next to his name. And so it went on. As Jennie Darlington wrote in the fifties, 'It was like living in a male locker room.'

Why such a brittle mask? I wondered. The British attitude had evolved from a culture in which no one grew up. In their emotional lives, the officers of Scott's day and the generation which followed lived in a prep school world in which boys died heroically in each other's arms while the whole school sobbed. How many times had I heard the latterday men of the Antarctic expressing regrets for the demise of the days when boys could be boys and girls weren't there? Alastair Fothergill, the man who had spent a lot of time in the south producing his award-winning *Life in the Freezer* television series, was very perceptive on this subject. 'The Antarctic brings out national characteristics, it really does. The British attitude – though it's changing – is still rooted in a very outdated vision of the explorer.' As I sat opposite him in his overheated office at the BBC Natural History Unit in Bristol, Fothergill had continued, 'It's inevitably a very male place. For a long time it was a playground. It's about keeping people out, and that's a male thing. I get a bit sick when they moan about the tourists.'

The irony was that, despite the collective fantasy of macho polar endeavour, both Vasco and Neil, among the few who viewed it with an objective eye, said that they found camping in Scotland tougher than in Antarctica. It rained more in Scotland, the tents were smaller, the grass was damper, there were midges, you had to look further for water and, hell – food and fuel were unlimited on the ice. As for Scott himself, I felt sure he would have been on my side. That was a further irony, given that the majority of my companions identified with him. As an early biographer wrote, 'In some ways, Scott's sensibility was more like a woman's than a man's.'

*

I got into the habit of 'doing the weather'. This involved marching out on to the ice sheet and having a good look around. When the pilots wanted hourlies, it was tempting to poke your head out of the weatherhaven for ten seconds and hazard a few guesses, working on the assumption that nothing much had changed since last time. I felt feeble even thinking about doing this until I saw everyone else at it. It even had a name: Giving Tent Weather.

As for the inner weather, once again I was struggling to cope with the pressures of being an outsider. The refreshing interlude at the Bluff notwithstanding, the background hostility I was experiencing on the peninsula was grinding me down, and, more seriously, it was getting in the way of my response to the continent. It wasn't quite the dark night of the soul at Ski Hi – but it was damned crepuscular.

They were desperate for co-pilots on the radar project. Everyone else had done the job many times and said it was boring. It was obviously my turn. I set my alarm for 5.30, now a time of bleak half-light, and stumbled over to the aircraft, where the technician was warming up the hard disk of his laptop with a hairdrier.

'All you have to do', said the pilot as he cleaned his teeth in the cockpit, 'is keep looking at that dial there' – he pointed – 'and tell me when the needle goes beyond that figure there.' He stabbed with his finger. 'And don't talk to me apart from that, as I have to concentrate.' I could see why this was not a popular job.

It was a sunny morning, and when I dared glance up from the dial, I noticed that around the nunataks the patterns in the snow were as regular as a carpet. Further south, the blue glacier ice was glassy and cusped. The pilot glanced darkly at me looking out, and I sank back into my seat, eyes glued to the dial. At least I was warm, once we got going. I ended up doing this job several times – being comfortable gave it a purpose, and anyway, there was nothing else to do. I was cold all the time at Ski Hi. Sometimes, in the tent or the weatherhaven, I would think myself back to a warm place, just to try to deceive the cold for a few moments. I used to imagine swimming in the Aegean Sea and diving through pellucid green waves to the ridged and sandy bottom. It is difficult now to remember why I kept doing this for it never worked.

*

I was at Ski Hi for a week, and during this time the weatherhaven became increasingly derelict. Everyone was expecting to be gone in a few days, so there wasn't much point in clearing it up. We all crowded in for the evenings, and took it in turns to cook. One day I found Vasco stirring a pan of tomato soup.

'There's this field assistant and his beaker holed up in a tent for days in a blizzard, right?' he began, addressing no one in particular. 'The beaker goes out regularly to piss, but never the field assistant. Eventually the beaker says, "Look, how do you do this? It's incredible", and the field assistant replies, "Easy. Every time you go out, I piss under your airbed." '

Apart from these bursts of pyrotechnic wit, conversation meandered through the same familiar topics (the arrival of the ship, the condition of the Dash-7 plane, the mental health of BAS management and where they were all going to travel when they left the ice), eventually reaching the end only to start again at the beginning. At about that time we heard on the radio that a piece of ice the size of a minor English county had broken off the Larsen Ice Shelf and was heading purposefully for the Falklands. This newly-created iceberg inevitably propelled the press into a feeding frenzy of catastrophe stories about London and New York being flooded by the tide of melted glacier water pouring off Antarctica. The formation of a berg, however – even a particularly huge one – is part of the natural cycle of renewal, and not therefore necessarily indicative of imminent global disaster. It is the gradual disintegration of the ice shelves year on year which is a new phenomenon, and one which is gripping glaciologists. Since 1990, for instance, the ice which formerly occupied Prince Gustav Channel and connected James Ross Island to the Antarctic Peninsula has crumbled away, and not long before that the Wordie Ice Shelf on the west coast broke up. The regional climate on the peninsula, always the warmest part of Antarctica, has heated up by 2.5 degrees Celsius since the 1940s, and this has weakened the ice shelves. In fifty years, more than 3,000 square miles of them have disappeared without being renewed.

Even the gradual disintegration of the ice shelves won't necessarily raise sea levels. According to the Archimedes Principle, floating ice displaces its own mass of water. If, however, the crumbling of the ice shelves causes the ice sheet lying over Antarctica to discharge more ice, then sea levels will rise. Even in that situation, the extra discharge would have to take place off large areas of the coast, not just the peninsula, before the rest of the planet were to be significantly affected.

Although the new berg was enormous, it was an infant compared with a 3,000-square-mile predecessor named Trolltunga which snapped off Antarctica in 1967 at about twelve o'clock on the map. The record holder measured over 12,000 square miles, inevitably leading to comparisons with Belgium, a country which seems to function almost exclusively as a measuring device for natural disasters.

Neil rushed into the weatherhaven one evening and flung himself on to a crate, hair flopping into his eyes. He had been reading *Anna Karenina*.

'I just can't stand the way Tolstoy is always absolutely completely right about everything! He's so incredible! He knows everything! Every nuance is the right one! Every insight makes me think Yes! It *is* like that!'

We all thought about this for a while.

'Ah yes, Neil, but was he happy?' asked somebody, stirring the ice in a pan on the primus.

'No,' said Neil, 'he was all fucked up.'

'But he had a great beard,' said somebody else, 'and that's what counts.'

*

Back at Rothera, the field assistants were hunched gloomily over formica tables in the labs or the sledge store, writing the reviled end-of-season reports before the ship arrived in three weeks. At least once an hour someone would come to find me on the spurious grounds of a spelling enquiry – either that or they would engage themselves in any other displacement activity which came to hand. I occupied myself agreeably enough, and it was thrilling to be warm again. On Shrove Tuesday, a week after I returned from Ski Hi, I tossed seventy-five pancakes. I had also been assigned the taxing job of skua monitoring. In Cambridge they were collecting data on skua distribution in order to tackle the aeronautical problem of birdstrikes, and I had to stroll around the point intermittently, counting the birds.

March was an odd time. Summer had ended, yet winter hadn't begun. One day the base commander announced the name of his winter replacement, drawn from the ranks of the fifteen winterers. Bits of paper were posted to the doors of the emptying labs staking out room claims. Twenty or so people were going out on the Dash, and eighteen of us were waiting three weeks for the ship. Men who had been on the ice for two-and-a-half years began discussing what they were going to do first, in Stanley and in the U.K. There was talk of trees, and fruit, and pubs, and handing over money and getting something back.

The weather veered between savage snowstorms and sunshine, crisp air and clear skies. Time dripped away slowly in the bad weather, and the field assistants prowled around like caged animals.

I worked my way through a pile of Antarctic films stored in dented tins in the tiny windowless archive. Life took on an agreeably even rhythm, bleached of highs and lows. The days grew shorter.

The easy equilibrium was hijacked one day by the arrival of mail. I was sitting in the library, with one eye on a pair of Adelies outside the window, when someone tossed a pile of letters secured by an elastic band on to the desk in front of me. I forgot about the penguins and began ripping envelopes open. The first one, forwarded from my home, unleashed a wave of regret. It contained a stiff, embossed invitation to my publisher's Christmas party two months previously. The Jonathan Cape bash was acknowledged to be the best on the literary circuit – drunken, stygian, overheated, late and a hotbed of incestuous gossip. The previous year it had been the scene of disgracefully bad behaviour, perpetrated not least by the Patron of my expedition and me. It was all very well to relish the absence of clutter and the spiritual opportunities of the Antarctic wilderness, but I missed the debris of urban lowlife. The invitation threw me off balance, and I spent the remains of the day kicking up snow disconsolately around the point and glaring murderously at the seals.

In the second week of March, Ben, Vasco and Steve Rumble were going on a recreational three-day trip to Lagoon Island. It was an end-of-season treat.

'Why don't you come?' said Ben.

'Won't I be taking someone else's place?' I asked. I had become absurdly over-sensitised to my superfluity.

'Of course not. Nobody else wants to come. I've asked the other two, and they'd be pleased if you joined us. Go on.'

We fitted crampons, stole bread from the kitchen and filled a manfood box with supplies, struggled into red inflation suits, winched two Humber inflatables into the bay and nudged our way through the pancake ice. It was a perfect day, without a cloud in the sky.

Lagoon was the northernmost of the Leonie islands, in Ryder Bay. It was charted in 1936, and formed a lagoon with the island on its west side. When we arrived, it was five degrees above zero and the sun was beating down. Vasco, the dark, flaming-eyed field assistant named after Vasco da Gama, put on a pair of shorts and took off his t-shirt. I was especially aware of the date – 10 March – as it was a friend's birthday. The previous year we had driven up to the Peak District for the weekend to celebrate at a twee hotel nestling in a dale. An unexpectedly harsh frost had fallen on Saturday night, and when we woke on Sunday the temperature outside was minus five Celsius – the perfect excuse to stay in bed all morning. I made a note to write to my friend to tell him that on the same day a year on it was ten degrees warmer in Antarctica than it had been in the north of England.

Steve set about hoisting the flag. He was the former winter base commander and electrician whom I had met at the Bluff. Ben went off to doze behind a rock, and I joined Vasco to do nothing on the veranda. The wind soon began whipping up small white horses on the lagoon, and Vasco lit the paraffin heaters in the hut and went to sleep inside. I was so cold that I put my inflation suit back on and walked up to a large area of shingle above the tide line. There were many of these raised beaches on the island, formed when the glaciers retreated after the last ice age.

We were struck on the head by skuas dozens of times each day on Lagoon Island. They came at us with open beaks and extended talons. The hut diary was bristling with anti-skua advice and designs for combat gear, but nothing worked except holding a broom aloft and waving it vigorously as you walked. The hut had been built several years previously, purely as a holiday cottage. It was twenty feet square, on stilts, and the walls and ceiling had been painted canary yellow. Besides an unplumbed sink, it had two primus stoves, four wooden bunk beds, three windows and, in the middle, a formica table. The shelves around the sink were jumbled with rusty tins of peaches and jars of separated mayonnaise. Two tilley lamps hung from the ceiling, as well as a coil of wire and a collection of fraying teacloths. A single shelf was stacked with a dozen novels and a chess set.

The evenings were drawing in, and we were obliged to light the tilleys at eight o'clock. After that, on the first night we drank rum and ate scones from a plastic bag shoved into our arms as we left base by Al, the cook, who never forgot field-party care parcels. Nobody had anything particular to do. Steve was at the end of a two-and-a-half year tour of duty, and inside his head he hadn't really been in Antarctica for some months. At the Bluff he had spent most of the time lying on his bunk with his Walkman clamped to his ears, but at Lagoon, in a smaller group, he opened up. He was far less concerned with being gnarly than most of the men at Rothera, and for that reason he wasn't very popular. This alone would have been enough to endear him to me, but he had also gone out of his way to be friendly. As he was unpacking the contents of his bag on to his bunk at Lagoon, he held out a folded t-shirt.

'I thought you'd like this,' he said. 'I bought two when the consignment arrived from Cambridge last year and, well, you'll appreciate it.' I unfolded the gift. It had been produced to commemorate the departure of the huskies.

After the sun had finally struggled over the horizon on our first morning at Lagoon we sat on the veranda for breakfast, an event made memorable by the fact that I had mistaken egg powder for milk powder and put it in everyone's tea. There had been much discussion about climbing a mountain, and we had brought plastic boots and a frightening array of harnesses. Like all field assistants, Vasco was a passionate rock and mountain climber and raced up a peak at the drop of a hat. I couldn't tell one end of a harness from another, and I had never worn plastic boots before, but I hadn't dared to raise any objections. God smiled on me that day, as He sent a thick cloud down over the mountains.

'We'll have to go for a walk instead,' said Vasco over breakfast as he scanned the horizon.

'What a shame,' I said.

We took the boats to Anchorage Island, another of the Leonies. It was reported by members of the French 1908–10 Antarctic Expedition as possibly providing anchorage for a small ship, and charted by the British Graham Land Expedition in February 1936. As we climbed, the lichens on the shingle beaches got thicker. Above them we spied a vein of brassy yellow pyrite, fool's gold.

'Look at this,' said Ben when we got to the top. 'I've found a splinter of whale bone.' He strode ahead, fiddling around looking for treasure. He was in his element off base. In the sixties, when he was driving dogs, he had spent almost all his time in the field. He accepted that BAS wanted him on base now because of his advanced age – but it wasn't the same.

I awoke the next day to a sound like sizzling bacon, the noise made by ice melting in a pan on a primus. In the months after Antarctica I often heard it in the boneless moments between sleep and consciousness; then memories ached like an old wound. Sunshine was pouring through the window. Steve brought tea to our bunks, and some of the ice must have been brackish, as it was salty. I made up a jug of milk for our breakfast cereal, and that was salty too. I wasn't having much luck with breakfasts. But it didn't matter. Nothing mattered. We basked on our veranda, and a flock of Antarctic terns flew by, their high-pitched chirp exotically foreign after the coarse squawk of the skuas. Later we took out the boats and followed a minke whale around the bergs, sailing through Daliesque arches and poking the Humbers' noses into cold blue grottoes. The sun was low, and the honeyed air was so still that the growlers and bergy bits[1] were barely moving. It was a golden evening. A day like that made everything worthwhile.

*

When we got back to Rothera the planes were parked on the apron, spruced up for their long ferry flights to Cambridge like cars on a showroom forecourt. The four Otters looked helpless without their skis, crouching behind the Dash.

The next day the seven pilots and five air mechanics trooped in and out of the station, discussing routes in loud voices. In the evening Al produced a four-course dinner, the air unit supplied champagne, a number of people made speeches, bread rolls whizzed through the air and we all got drunk. I was on housekeeping duty the following morning, and when I started the dining room looked like the site of a very small civil war in which neither side had emerged victorious. A pair of training shoes had been stowed in the fridge, and congealed baked beans clung like glue to the sandwich maker. We saw the planes off at eight o'clock. It was gusting forty knots, and very cold. Great swathes of snow were sweeping across the ramp like smoke, tumbling over the ice cliffs opposite the point and dissolving into a gunmetal grey sea. The sun was peeking over the bergs in the bay as one by one the pilots zipped themselves into their flying suits and took off for Stanley, first stop on the long haul home.

The sense of shut-down was especially powerful then. We felt as if the birds had migrated. People lingered longer at the tables after dinner, and at night the bar might be empty except for two or three men playing Scrabble. People talked to me more easily, and seemed to find it less of a gruelling experience than they had

---

[1] Fragments of floating ice. Also used to refer to lumps in the custard.

done during the first weeks of my tenure. Our favourite topic of conversation was Relief. It was what they called the week when the ship anchored at the wharf and disgorged a year's supplies.

'I hope that one stays,' one of the winterers said as we pressed our foreheads against a window one morning and watched a particularly fine iceberg in the bay. They were waiting for the landscape to settle for the winter, and they wanted their favourite bergs to be marooned, like them. As for the rest of us, at particular moments, when the evening light fell at a certain angle on the pack, people who had been talking for months about going home would say that they were going to miss the ice.

*

On Sunday 19 March at eight o'clock in the morning we were sprawled out in the dining room, clutching mugs of coffee, when we heard the low elephant grief of a ship's horn. RRS *Bransfield* had appeared beyond the furthest berg. We all went down to the wharf, of course. Some of us were boarding the ship for the day, as it was taking a clean-up team to Horseshoe Island before Relief. The base there had scarcely been touched since the fifties, and as a short-term measure it had been decided to remove the rubbish and make the huts good against the depredations of time and weather.

The captain sent over a boat with a scow lashed to its side, and we filled nets with rolls of roofing felt and towed them down into the scow. Then we climbed down from the wharf into the boat and motored to the rope ladder dangling over the side of the ship.

We sailed on a calm, steely sea, past snowy petrels dancing in the bands of light on the horizon and solitary penguins on tabular bergs. A chippie from the building team was standing next to me on deck. He was a diminutive creature with powerful shoulders, a gallery of tattoos and a rasping Glaswegian accent, and when he was drunk he always ended up in a fight (though not with me). A rainbow had arched over Horseshoe. The chippie said it was amazing how the sunshine changed everything.

'I'm a bit of an agnostic,' he said, 'a doubting Thomas. But this – it makes you think there is a God.'

Horseshoe Island was shoe-horned between Bourgeois Fjord and Square Bay, off the Fallieres Coast. A station was established there in 1955 and occupied continuously until it was evacuated on 21 August 1960, since when it has been used occasionally by field parties. It was imaginatively known as Base Y. In his book *Of Ice and Men*, Sir Vivien Fuchs recounts a radio hoax at Horseshoe in 1955. They used to indulge in radio pranks every five minutes in those days, but this one was particularly well orchestrated. Two of the men tuned the bunkroom receiver so that their colleagues thought they had picked up a Falklands radio station, whereas in fact they were listening to material broadcast from the room next door. Naturally all the music played was drawn from the meagre selection on base, so to allay suspicion one of the perpetrators performed on the bagpipes and mouth organ (it was gratifying to learn that at the Bluff we had unwittingly been adhering to tradition). Even after they had broadcast a news story announcing that Marilyn Monroe was to lead an expedition up Everest, one man still hadn't tumbled to it. 'The final broadcast', Fuchs wrote, 'took place the day before everyone except this man was to leave on a sledging trip, he being left behind as caretaker. The "news" received that evening reported a revolution in Argentina where fighting had broken out between the Army and Navy. It included a warning that likely conflicts which would follow at Argentine Antarctic stations could well lead to the losers seeking political asylum at the nearest British bases, and called on everyone to keep calm and use their heads.'

Before I left England, Sir Vivien had invited me to his home in Cambridge to talk about his Antarctic adventures. A pair of porcelain penguins were guarding the fireplace, and Sir Vivien was wearing a blue plaid BAS-style flannel shirt. He was in his eighties and still handsome, with clear, china-blue eyes and an efflorescence of nut-brown eyebrows, and when his face creased into a smile he was irresistible.

As a young man his tutor at Cambridge was James Wordie, Scott's chief of scientific staff. Fuchs spent many seasons in the Antarctic, and in 1950 the Falkland Islands Dependencies Scientific Bureau was founded under his direction. During the 1955–8 Commonwealth Trans-Antarctic Expedition, which he led, with Sir Edmund Hillary in command of the New Zealand support party, Fuchs crossed the continent for the first time, using dogs and tractors. Together they wrote a book about it, and in spite of the sno-cats and the radio telephone and the electric sewing machine they seemed to mark the end of an unbroken line which Scott started when he sailed down the Thames aboard *Discovery*.

At one lapidary moment in the Fuchs–Hillary account the authors are invited aboard a visiting ship, and the captain sends a smaller vessel over to fetch them. Faced with a twenty-foot ladder up to the deck, a sailor asks Hillary if he can manage the climb.

Fuchs was committed to the memory of the dogs. 'I remember very well,' he said, 'back at Stonington in the forties a chap got annoyed and said, "Well, I'm going outside to have a word with the dogs." Then he'd come back in and the whole argument had disappeared. I spent years driving dogs and then I became a tractor man, perforce; though I don't think a dog man ever becomes a real tractor man.'

When I returned from the ice a magazine ran a competition requesting readers to submit their all-time favourite newspaper headlines. Several people with long memories had sent in 'DR FUCHS OFF TO SOUTH ICE', but only one had saved the cutting from the same newspaper which recorded a subsequent visit Sir Vivien had made. The sub-editor, following the hallowed principle that if it works once it can work a second time, had settled on 'DR FUCHS OFF AGAIN'.

*

Relief began on Monday morning. We had been divided into four teams, and mine spent the morning in navy boilersuits and hard hats unloading boxes on the 'tween deck. In the afternoon, we put the goods away on base. Everyone's eyes lit up when they saw crates of oranges. During the afternoon we sat on the step in the sunshine, waiting for fresh loads and taking it in turns to fetch pots of tea and plates of flapjacks.

Mealtimes were changed to bring us in sync with the ship. We had tea at five, then returned to our duties for a further two hours. It was my birthday on the second day of Relief, and after this last shift I was drinking tea in the dining room when Al emerged from the kitchen carrying a pink-and-white cake designed to look like a book and iced with the words *Into The Unknown: Happy Birthday Sara*, with my name down the spine and a bookmark protruding from the top.

For the last two days we unloaded fuel drums while the winterers took it in turns to visit the ship's dentist, returning looking pained and asking Al for soup. The grease ice[1] around the wharf was thickening every day: in Antarctica the freeze and thaw of the sea replaced the rise and fall of sap. When the sun emerged, the dull matt grey water lit up like a face breaking into a smile.

I was appointed nightwatchman for my last three days at Rothera. It was a duty shared among all the support staff, to prevent the base from burning down, among other things. On the first night I was suffering from excruciating period pains, and at dinner someone had told me that my face looked like a bowl of porridge.

'It's because I have severe menstrual cramps,' I announced loudly.

Silence descended, and I immediately felt better. I didn't want to be an honorary man, and I was fed up with carrying used tampons around in a plastic bag in my pocket, trying to find somewhere to abandon them. It was tempting to play people at their own game and stow these bags under their pillows.

Nightwatch began with a midnight patrol. I was convinced that I was going to be responsible for the total destruction of base, and then everyone would be able to announce triumphantly that both writers and women were superfluous to requirements in Antarctica, and that the combination of the two was nothing short of deadly. At half-past twelve I found myself wedged between two small huts, shining my torch into the dial of the ice-core freezer. I was especially terrified of melting the ice cores. I had heard many stories about it happening, producing what they called the most expensive ice cubes in the history of the world. This dial read ten below. 'Shouldn't it be twenty?' I thought. 'Or am I being paranoid?' A wrong decision would either mean having my head bitten off for unnecessarily waking a slumbering electrician, or melting hundreds of thousands of pounds worth of ice cores. I went to wake the hapless electrician. I was very pleased that I did, as the freezer was off, but it made me frightened about what might happen next.

In the hangar I told myself cheerily that Antarctica was the world's last refuge from fear, but the dangers lurking in the shadows of a high, empty, unlit concrete building had been inculcated too effectively into my psyche. Every two hours I checked

[1] Film that forms before the sea ice freezes

the generator and the reverse-osmosis plant, and at three o'clock I climbed the hill behind base to take a weather observation. At five-thirty I turned on the coffee urn and the pastry ovens and began the waking-up routine. This involved creeping into pitrooms and shaking slumbering male bodies by the tautly-muscled shoulder. It should have been a highlight, but somehow it never lived up to expectations.

I got to know the base better during those quiet, dark nights. Rothera was a warren of nooks and hidden corners. I found places where I hadn't been before, and finally poked my head into the sauna, which I had never dared to visit during the day. It was an old fridge heated by a spiral coil in a cast-iron bucket. A torn copy of *Motorcycling World* lay on the floor.

On my last night, the one before the ship left, three people partied all night, so I had company on watch. At six in the morning we drove down to the ship in the enormous Delta truck, its lights flashing, and fell out of the high cab on to the wharf. It seemed a good way to end.

*

I found my cabin, and slept through the journey to Horseshoe, where we collected the clean-up team. In three days the grease ice had thickened into pancake. When we got back to Rothera the crew threw a party on board for the winterers. At five o'clock the captain gave the word, the horn sounded and after a flurry of awkward embraces the fifteen winterers, who wouldn't see another soul for seven months, walked down the gangplank. As they shrank, reeling and striding around the wharf, they set off pink flares and yellow rockets, and we waved until they disappeared.

Winter. It was as if a door had closed.

CHAPTER FOURTEEN

Afloat in the Southern Ocean

Lo! now the direful monster, whose skin clings
To his strong bones, strides o'er the groaning rocks:
He withers all in silence, and his hand
Unclothes the earth, and freezes up frail life.

William Blake, 'To Winter'

I ONCE MET a former captain of the Antarctic support ship HMS *Endurance*. He had a great love of the south.

'I took a ship where no ship had been before,' he said, 'and that was a thrill. In the mid-eighties I felt that we were pushing back the boundaries of man's knowledge. It was good sailoring down there.' Like Scott, he had been obliged by the Navy Act to conduct a church service on board each Sunday, and described reading the lesson on deck in the wintry sunshine while Antarctic terns flew around the prow.

The Royal Research Ship *Bransfield* was old and decrepit, but we had 'good sailoring' on her, too. The journey to the Falklands took a week. There were three decks: one for the officers and senior BAS personnel, one for other BAS people and one for the crew. Each had its own mess. Ours – the middle one – was furnished with chipped blue formica tables seating twelve, each equipped with a row of sauce bottles standing to attention in slots.

I was sharing a cabin with an amiable cargo supervisor from BAS HQ. She had been invited upstairs to eat in the wardroom, but I had not, which made her feel very embarrassed, but I couldn't have cared less. The cabin had a long leatherette couch along the porthole wall. The walls were mint green and the carpet and bunk curtains were orange, a colour scheme designed to make you puke should the roll of the sea fail.

The builders were with us, which made the trip more entertaining and the lounge friendlier. One day a pair of them pretended to the others that everyone was obliged to participate in iceberg patrol and handed out hard hats emblazoned with the words BERG ALERT and broom handles to shove away stray islands of ice. Two chippies fell for it, and dutifully stood on the lower deck wearing the Berg Alert hats, smoking and occasionally glancing around to see if any giant icebergs were bearing down on the ship. When they spotted the others taking photographs of them, the game was up.

The BAS men who were leaving Rothera after two-and-a-half years sniggered into their beer as they imagined the winterers back on base. It was traditional to sabotage winterers upon departure, and on this occasion a trout had been stowed in the ventilation system, a gallon of green food colouring poured into the water tanks and small cubes of stilton cheese balanced on the lattice ceiling of the bar. The winterers had tried to effect proleptic revenge, knowing something horrible lay ahead, and half a mackerel was found in a bunk shortly after we sailed, provoking much discussion about the possible location of the other half, which was, in fact, never found. I discovered a portion of trifle in my left boot.

The Southern Ocean was very still as we sailed up the peninsula. When a penguin broke the surface, the ripples spread into enormous concentric circles until they died far away in the silver-blue water. On one side of the ship serrated mountain ranges sliced through the water, the sheerest faces, ablated of snow, shading the landscape with patches of charcoal engraved with a fine white lattice. The clouds massed into dark purply tornadoes that stormed through the fuzzy peach light of the sky, or sometimes they remained expressionless for days, hanging down to the narrow band of light on one side of the horizon. Icebergs came to seem as normal to us as trees on the side of a road.

We had to pick up ten men from Faraday, a small BAS station on Galindez Island. They were at the end of their tour of duty, and were going home. When we got there, on a Saturday afternoon, most of us went ashore.

The bar at Faraday, a magnificent piece of polished woodwork, was famous in Antarctic history. Two builders had been employed to construct a hardwood extension to the pier, but instead spent the whole winter toiling over this fine bar. The wharf was never finished, and the men were dismissed, though they are remembered daily with pride and gratitude. The current incumbents had alighted on the idea of brewing beer in fire extinguishers, and when we arrived they were busily squirting it out of the syphons.

We remained at Faraday for twenty-four hours, and I was able to roam freely around the station and its few outposts. In a small library tucked away off the famous bar I found a shoebox of replies to a collective advertisement the base commander had placed in a dating magazine back in England ('Dear boys, Hope you're not too cold down there . . .'). Photographs stuffed between the books revealed the recent Faraday Buddhist Night, when the residents shaved their heads, put on their windies and sat crosslegged and barefoot. A blurred picture of Viking Night showed them careering through the snow in horned helmets brandishing torches.

The station was opened as a geophysical observatory in 1954, and called Base F; it was renamed in 1977 after Michael Faraday, the nineteenth-century English chemist and physicist who discovered electro-magnetic induction and introduced the basic principle of the electric motor and dynamo. Along the way he probably believed more wrong theories than any man alive then or now, a gratifying testament to the perseverance of the human spirit. Geophysics had remained the main thrust of the science at Faraday, though it was an important meteorological station and collected weather data from British, American and German bases. This information eventually found its way into the World Meteorological Organisation database, and who knows what happened to it then. There was no airstrip at Faraday. It was a very cosy base, and less institutional than Rothera; but it was about to cease operating as a British station and be handed over to the Ukrainians, who badly wanted a base of their own. They renamed it Vernadsky. It seemed like the end of an era.

The Faraday joiner, who had shown me a coffin he had made, unilaterally decided that I should visit Winter Island and propelled me down the wharf and into a small and precarious boat with a four-horsepower Seagull engine. The slipway at Faraday was positioned directly below the sewage pipe, which meant that one was obliged to dodge flying turds while getting in one's boat. We motored past a wooden signpost saying 'Crown Land' against which a crabeater seal was manifesting signs of disrespect. The hut on Winter Island was opened in 1947 as a wintering station for three meteorologists and a general assistant. Called Wordie House, it was maintained for seven years until Coronation House, now Faraday, was opened, and has been closed ever since, except for the year when a team making for Adelaide Island got caught out by bad ice and bivouacked in Wordie House.

Inside, it was like a set for a fifties film, dotted with blocks of Marmite and tiny tins of gramophone needles 'each good for eight records'. The shelf of books included *Instructions on How to Play the Bagpipes*, novels by John Buchan, girlie annuals displaying women in swimsuits which looked as if they had been designed for army combat – and, harking back to the old days, Tennyson. One room was dominated by a massive typewriter of the kind that would be presided over in the film by a straight-backed woman wearing horn-rimmed spectacles and ropes of fake pearls. The thick cotton trousers folded over the back of a chair were exactly the same as those sported by the *Bransfield*'s third engineer, a Geordie who had come with us.

'You know you're getting old,' he said, slurping tea out of a blue-rimmed tin mug, 'when your keks are in a museum.'

That night, in eighty-knot winds and horizontal rain, two bergs converged on the *Bransfield*. When the golden rods of our searchlight beams tunnelled through the darkness and alighted on the bergs, we saw that the ice was scratched with the red ship's paint. The *Bransfield* dragged her anchor, and at one point – black smoke pouring from the funnel and soaked crewmen wrestling with ropes in pools of light on the foredeck – we were only twenty yards off the rocks.

*

The sun shone during our passage through the Lemaire Channel, and most of us spent the day on the monkey deck. Unclimbed mountains wobbled in the polished surface of the water, and pods of whales fluked among the bergs. We passed the deserted red buildings of an Argentinian base and its Chilean neighbour, the latter sporting a particularly large flag. I thought of my first visit to Antarctica, when I saw it through South American eyes. The Chileans at Marsh were wonderful hosts; they wanted to share it.

Everyone addressed me immediately in the familiar '*tu*' form, which they hadn't done in real Chile until the ice was broken. Antarctica didn't seem a problem to them. It wasn't so much that they had made their little bit of King George Island home, but that it was home. 'The water in the bay', they would say, 'has lapped on our shore.' They had a school, a hospital and a bank on base, they brought their wives and children down with them, and they broadcast Radio Sovereign FM from the weather station. On Friday evenings Radio Sovereign ran a quiz show. The questions were about Antarctica, and all the bases on the island took part, although first they had to find someone who could speak Spanish. While I was there a Chinese contingent arrived to collect their prize, which – I suspected to their chagrin – was a specially baked cake.

Because it was only a three-hour flight from the tip of South America and not permanently ice-covered, King George Island, squatting in the archipelago named the South Shetlands by Scottish sealers, was a popular site for bases. The Russians were there, as were the Poles, the Uruguayans, the Brazilians and the Argentinians as well as the Chileans and the Chinese. I had eaten syrupy balls of undercooked dough at Great Wall, drunk vodka at Bellingshausen and been given a piggy-back across a deep stream by a Brazilian lieutenant commander. Each country transports its culture to the bottom of the world when it sets up in Antarctica – the good and the bad. In Bellingshausen the piles of rubbish, the acres of crusty mud, the puffy-faced men with silver teeth, the ghostly outlines of the metal letters CCCP which had been clumsily jemmied off doors, the abandoned machinery of failed scientific projects, the single inadequate Lada – well, they were Russian all right.

Chile and Argentina base their Antarctic claims on medieval bulls and decrees inherited from Spain, and they have clung to these claims like children to comfort blankets. One of the few things the two nations have ever agreed upon was to take a common line against Britain – twice in the 1940s – by reinforcing the concept of a South America Antarctic (though later they squabbled even about that). General Pinochet flew down to King George Island in 1977 and declared that it was merely a continuation of Chilean territory. Six families were despatched there in 1984 to institute a 'permanent' settlement. On the other side of the Andes the entire Cabinet took off from Buenos Aires and landed on the ice to prove how very Argentinian that part of Antarctica was.

Other South American republics have also cast their eyes south. The Peruvians named their base Machu Picchu. Much of the scientific data produced by the smaller nations was valuable, but some of it was privately questioned by the larger, richer countries. All programmes are required to submit descriptions of their science projects to an international Antarctic science body, ostensibly so that research can be shared. The Uruguayans once sent in details of an experiment which involved playing loud music to penguins to see how they reacted.

Geopolitics dwelt in the north; on the ice there was only one enemy – the cold. I remember stopping next to a stream between Marsh and Bellingshausen with my Chilean minder and a Russian biologist.

'We are very proud of this river between us,' said the Russian in Spanish.

'What's it called?' I asked.

'Volga,' said the Russian immediately.

'Mapocho,' said the minder simultaneously, and they both screamed with laughter.

'*En Antartida*,' the minder had said later, '*No hay fronteras*' – there are no borders. On the continent it was still as it had been in the forties when Chilean and Argentinian warships arrived at the British base on Stonington Island and the captains delivered official protests about British presence in their territorial waters and followed them up with invitations to dinner and picture shows. 'Beyond the Polar Circle', said the great French Antarctican Jean Charcot, 'there are no Frenchmen, no Germans, no English, no Danes; there are only people of the Pole, real men.'

*

The birds were especially abundant when the whales were churning up krill, and we argued when we tried to identify them. Of petrels alone we recorded morphs, Antarctics, giants, pintados (the zebras of the southern ocean), snowies and Wilson's. Ben was the most authoritative spotter.

'There!' he said one day, pointing to a bird wheeling around the ship. 'White-chinned petrel.'

'I can't see a white chin,' someone piped up. 'Looks totally brown to me.'

'You'd have to be holding the bird in your hand to see the white chin,' Ben said. 'But it's there.'

While it was light, Ben was always out on deck.

'Well,' he said, when I remarked on this, 'I'll never see all this again.' It was as if he wanted to drink in the landscape and store it up, like water in a camel's hump, and live off it in the seasons still to come, sitting out his retirement in Sheffield.

What thrilled us most were not birds but whales. We saw humpbacks and minkes and bottlenoses, and one morning a large pod of killers came fluking past our ship.

Whalers played an important part in the discovery of Antarctica, especially after they had bled the Arctic dry. A group of Dundonians set out in 1892, their thoughts fixed on the riches waiting for them in the Southern Ocean. They were sharp in turning their attention to southern waters: the Falklands sector of the Antarctic is the richest whaling ground in the world. But in technique, the Scots had already been beaten by their Norwegian rivals. Their equipment was outmoded and they were looking for the wrong kind of whale: they wanted bone for umbrellas and corsets, but the market wanted oil, not least for munitions.

Before setting out from home I had walked along a salty spit in Dundee to see W. G. Burn-Murdoch's paintings of this expedition in Broughty Castle, a deserted museum with a spiral staircase curling between mildewed floors. The second floor featured a programme from the Royal Terror Theatre on the *Discovery*, advertising the Dishcover Minstrel Troupe. Whaling died out in Dundee before the Great War, and the *Terra Nova* was the last whaler ever built by Dundonians. But in Antarctica the trade took off in the first two decades of the twentieth century after the Norwegian Carl Larsen founded Grytviken on South Georgia and floating whale factories were developed. The industry reached its peak in southern waters in the 1930s. Despite the mystique – an early participant called it 'the greatest chase which nature yieldeth' – to which a number of writers succumbed, whaling was one of the hardest trades, and it employed the hardest drinkers. It was not unknown for men to break the ship's compass to quaff its alcohol. In the twenties a crewman wrote, 'There were two kinds of days, bad days and worse, and each lasted twenty-four hours.'

Business dropped off dramatically during the Second World War when synthetic glycerin was developed and most of the fleet sunk by German raiders. After a few dying spurts, the last whaling station on South Georgia closed in 1965.

In the late nineteenth century deep-sea trawling took off in the north of Britain in the wake of whaling. My grandfather knew a trawlerman from Grimsby whose eight sons had all become trawler skippers. I remember hearing this man talk about 'the wondrous freedom of trawling, when time didn't exist'. I was a child then, and he made it sound like the most magical occupation in the world – I wrote in a schoolbook that when I grew up I wanted to be a trawlerman. Now it reminded me of what the old Antarctic explorers wrote in their diaries. None of them could submit to the nine-to-five.

Lying on my bunk as we ploughed up the side of the peninsula, I read the last of the books I had brought south. Fearful that I was going to finish it before the journey ended, I went through it very slowly. It was a volume of Edward Wilson's diaries, and in it I discovered that Scotland had another connection with Antarctica. Scott and Wilson had planned their last journey south on the rose-covered veranda of a bungalow near the mouth of one of the lovely glens of the Angus. Originally a shepherd's stone cottage, it was bought in 1902 by a London publisher called Reginald Smith, and he converted it into a tiny shooting lodge. Wilson and Scott went to see Smith in London in 1905 to ask him to publish Scott's *Voyage of the Discovery*, which he did. They all became friends, and when Wilson was commissioned to write a report on grouse disease by the Department of Agriculture, Smith lent him the bungalow. Wilson spent months there, and wrote in his diaries about long walks when he saw snipes and corncrakes, curlews and peewits, tawny owls and golden plover and greenfinches feeding on dandelion seed. Scott used to visit, and once, when they went stalking, he let a deer pass unharmed 'because it was so pretty'.

The glen was called Glen Prosen, and in 1917 Smith's widow commissioned a monument to Scott and Wilson and their dead companions. By the time I got there the bungalow had become a bed-and-breakfast, so I slept in a back room, like them, and watched the lights of Kirriemuir twinkling from the balcony beyond the row of birches and the two plane trees where the shepherd had tethered his cow. The monument was fashioned out of red sandstone, and the inscription read, 'For the journey is done and the summit attained and the barriers fall.'

*

Circuit training took place in a cargo hold. The teacher shouted 'Come on lads,' adding as an afterthought, 'Come on Sara.' The smell of diesel put me off, besides which it was very noisy, and the hold looked like a Heath Robinson design for a Victorian canning factory. People were becoming bored. The bar, in which we read and re-read a six-month-old copy of *Hello!* magazine, was always unevenly dotted with men, like churchgoers at a poorly attended matins. In the mess, meals were despatched in less than half an hour, though the menus were models of imaginative ingenuity. They were typed up each day, as in an old-fashioned hotel on the coast, and featured items such as Cold Cuts, which was a euphemism for Spam. Cheese and Biscuits followed Dessert on the menu as regularly as petrels followed feeding whales, but never once did they make an appearance. Grilled Fresh Herring was announced one day, marking quite an event in maritime history; presumably the cook had let a line down over the side.

At night, when the water darkened, we became particularly desperate. At the end of March the nights are long in the Southern Ocean. The videos screened were so appalling that the best attended was *Snow White and the Seven Dwarfs*. Al, the medal-winning cook from the north of England, threw a drinks party in his cabin. It was a characteristically generous gesture. Gin was scarce on the *Bransfield*.

'In the old days, at Stonington.' Ben told us, perched on the edge of Al's bunk and gripping his mug of gin as the ship did a little roll, 'we had so much gin that we used it to clean the windows.' We had several more room parties after that, and people began finding vodka and tonics in their tooth mugs in the morning. Later, someone had the idea of sundowners on deck, and we gathered round half-frozen wineboxes in our balaclavas and parkas. Sometimes we hadn't seen the sun all day, though if we were lucky it found a porthole in the clouds just before it disappeared, and the vertical faces of the bergs shone briefly with a virulent salmon light.

Then suddenly, when I woke up one morning and drew back the curtain, it was all gone. I ran up to the monkey deck and looked around. It was a clear and sunny day, the water was grey but sparkling and the blank horizon stretched for 360 degrees around us, flat and featureless. It was all over. I watched a sooty albatross hovering over the stern. It was just as the explorers back at home had told me it would be – as if I had come back from another planet. A terrible grief flooded over my heart as if someone I loved very much had died.

On 1 April we arrived at East Cove in the Falklands, and woke up to see gently modulating hills, rays of sunshine piercing the clouds like a Blake painting and miles of dun-coloured grass. The *Bransfield* moored alongside a pontoon to refuel and a notice went up in the mess advising us that shore leave was not granted, and that in order to avoid being shot we should remain on board. A cormorant perched on a container on deck. The sun was shining on the port as we finally approached. Stanley still looked like Toytown – neat little coloured boxes with bright roofs nestling among dark green bushy foliage, with the cemetery at one end. Shackleton wrote in 1916 of Stanley: 'The street of that port is about a mile and a half long. It has the slaughterhouse at one end and the graveyard at the other. The chief distraction is to walk from the slaughterhouse to the graveyard. For a change one may walk from the graveyard to the slaughterhouse.' Beyond it the camp[1] stretched out flat, to the south. We languished on the monkey deck, and the people who had been on the ice for thirty months looked hunted.

A small boat ploughed to and fro as we waited. Our mail came up, and we fed on it obscenely in the bar while the builders shouted football results. Jeremy, the Patron of my expedition, wanted to know more about Incinolet toilets, details of which had been included in my last letter. He was troubled by the distinction between solids and liquids, and was anxious to know what one did about diarrhoea. I privately vowed never to send a child of mine to public school.

In the evening we went ashore, and Steve, the man who had given me the doggy t-shirt at Lagoon, and who had not lived in a cash economy for two-and-a-half years, forgot to take any money. We visited all the pubs. The Globe had whitewashed walls and a brick-red corrugated-iron roof. It was a hotel once,

[1] The countryside beyond Stanley is known to Falklanders as 'the camp'.

patronised by seamen glad to be on land, as we were, a spit-and-sawdust place with a pool table and Nazareth playing on the jukebox. At the end of the evening everyone went off to Deano's, but I couldn't face it. I liked going home on to a ship.

Cargo began the next morning, and I spent the day in Stanley. From open windows bursts of the Forces radio station took me halfway home. I walked up to the museum along Ross Road West, beyond the memorial to the Battle of the Falklands in 1914, when Sturdee routed von Spee, and past skeletal hulls poking out of the grey water like icebergs. The Falklands attracted shipwrecks like a siren, and their presence rooted the islands in their past. The mizzen mast from HMS *Great Britain* was lying on the shore. The ship limped into the Falklands in 1886, having been driven back from Cape Horn, and remained afloat for fifty years, when it was beached at Sparrow Cove. In 1970 the vessel was salvaged and returned to Bristol, where Brunel had designed it. I can remember walking in a crocodile from school to watch it coming triumphantly home up the Avon.

At that end of town the odd horse and sheep grazed in quiet gardens and washing flapped energetically from drooping lines, diminutive fragments of colour in the vast southern sky. The museum was in Britannia House, a wooden chalet with heart-carved shutters and a jumble of rusty canons in the garden. Inside, they had an 1895 symphonium. It was a coin-operated jukebox from the Globe Hotel in a big polished wood case, like a wide grandfather clock, and its vertical silver record was playing the duet 'When we were married' from *The Belle of New York*. While I was standing in front of this object the curator of the museum introduced himself.

'Regard the museum as yours!' he said cheerfully, flinging his arms out to indicate the extent of his domain. Around the corner, a sepia photograph of a man in a rocking chair next to a blazing fire was captioned, 'About eighty years ago there was a time to relax in the Falklands'.

Later, I went swimming. I couldn't wait to swim; I had missed it so much. No one was in the water except a handful of BAS men from the ship, lounging like seals. We were all thrilled to be splashing about. On the way back I tried to buy fruit in the main shop, but they didn't have a single piece.

We spent a few days in the Falklands, waiting for a TriStar and living on the *Bransfield*. I walked through the low shrubs and Yorkshire Fog grass, and when upland geese rose out of the undergrowth and flew away from me and steamer ducks careering over the rocks flapped their redundant wings irritably, I thought once again of solitary days in Tierra del Fuego, a lifetime ago. I went to Yorke Bay; the dunes were wired off with signs saying 'DANGER! MINES', but the rolling sand made me think of hot places. At least there were still penguins. Over towards Gypsy Cove stripy magellanic penguins brayed and peered out of their earth burrows. When I stooped to look in at them, they fidgeted, twisting their heads from side to side. I thought with a pang of the fearlessness of the Adelies and emperors. I was so frightened of it all slipping away from me. I followed a Falklands thrush to the end of the bay, looked down and saw more penguins swimming in the clear green water far below. Then I walked slowly back to my ship as a soft white fog fell, and the other boats were calling to each other like partridges in the evening when the mist lies low on the winter field.

*

The alarm ripped through the ship at five o'clock one gloomy morning, and we ran around with our kitbags and bundled into a coach on the dark and glistening tarmac quay after hasty goodbyes to those who were sailing on to Montevideo. One of them, a man who had ignored me during my entire stay at Rothera, loomed out of the crowd, pressed his hand to mine, drew close to my face and said, 'It's from the Eternity Range.' He disappeared back into the darkness, and I opened my fist. It was a seashell.

It was a long trip to Mount Pleasant airport, and the diminutive Glaswegian chippie fell asleep on my shoulder. The coach was flooded with sunshine, and outside the windows the island looked resplendent. By the evening we were in Ascension, where it was twenty-seven degrees Celsius. After a lengthy delay another long haul took us to the English meadows of Brize Norton. The in-flight magazine still bore a photograph of a happy customer descending by parachute.

I wondered what was going to happen to the still, small voice when I flung myself back into the cacophony of civilisation. I wasn't afraid of permanently losing sight of the certainty and calm I had found – but it was going to have to fight off a lot of competition once I had the nuts and bolts of urban life to worry about.

This flight was supposed to define the end, the termination of a long physical journey and the beginning of a mental one. But nothing ended. It was all one continuous journey which never ended. I thought of a sentence Darwin wrote in his *Beagle* journal: 'Only the other day I looked forward to this airy barrier as a definite point in our journey homewards; but now I find it, all such resting-places for the imagination are like shadows, which a man moving onwards cannot catch.'

After all, the geographical questions may have been answered, but the metaphysical ones remain, and the most foreign territory will always lie within.

PART THREE

We shall not cease from exploration,
And the end of all our exploring
Will be to arrive where we started
And know the place for the first time.

T. S. Eliot, 'Little Gidding'

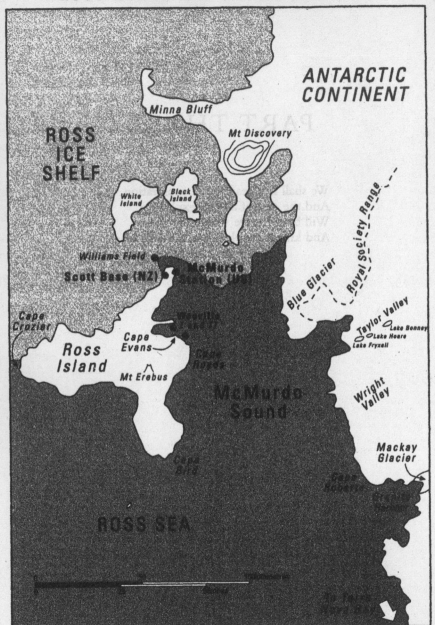

ANTARCTIC
CONTINENT

Minna Bluff

Mt Discovery

ROSS
ICE
SHELF

White
Island

Black
Island

Royal Society Range

Williams Field

Blue Glacier

Scott Base (NZ)

McMurdo
Station (US)

Taylor Valley

Lake Bonney

Lake Hoare

Cape
Crozier

Ross
Island

Cape
Evans

Cape
Royds

Mt Erebus

Lake Fryxell

McMurdo
Sound

Wright
Valley

Cape
Bird

Mackay
Glacier

Cape
Roberts

ROSS SEA

Kilometres

Miles

To Terra
Nova Bay

CHAPTER FIFTEEN

Wooville I: The Erebus Glacier Tongue

There are so few temptations. Mentally, man there is invulner-
able. He is so remote from the human struggle, the economic
uncertainties of existence, from politics and wars, he realises that
they mean just nothing at all.

Louis Bernacchi, veteran Antarctic explorer

I ARRIVED back in London at the beginning of April. All the
plants on my roof terrace were dead, but the spring sun was
shining weakly through the tame northern clouds. As I began to
pick up the threads of my life, the Frank Hurley quotation I
had stuck on the kitchen wall loomed increasingly large in my
imagination. 'After life in the vastness of a vacant continent,' it
said, 'civilisation seemed disappointingly narrow, cramped, super-
ficial and empty.'

It had not been one long idyll, but the unhappy memories had
begun to fade before I even unlocked my front door, and it seemed
to me that I had been cast out of paradise. I felt perpetually
thwarted. Above all, I sensed that I had not yet completed the
journey.

Something was left undone.

The Patron dragged me out to seedy Greek cafes in north
London, and random thoughts on the Scott myth bounced
between us like a beach ball. Jeremy was writing the official biography of Cyril Connolly. The book was also a covert autobiography, though Jeremy rarely admitted it, and I couldn't quite see
why it was necessary as he had published two books about himself

already. So flattered was he when I told him he was to appear in my book that he was trying to smuggle me into Connolly's life. Feeling at last he had something to offer to justify his patronal role, Jeremy glugged another tumbler of retsina and launched into a lengthy peroration on Connolly's response to the Scott myth.

'You see, Connolly writes that when he was seven he shook hands with Scott in Simonstown, South Africa,' he concluded.

The *Terra Nova* had sailed from Britain without its captain. Scott had remained to drum up more funds, and then hurried to South Africa to meet the ship. We both pondered the connections between these two extraordinary men, as different as we were, Patron and protegee. Jeremy was fifty, happily married, irretrievably English and a sedentary anarchist. A darling of London's literary coterie, he had hands like root vegetables and had never been further south than Seaford.

He looked out of the rain-spattered window, ate an olive, and appeared to be on the verge of delivering some small but crucial comment which would enable me to decipher the legend that Scott had become. I waited, wondering what he had done with the olive pit.

'I'm almost certain', he said finally, furrowing his brow and waving the empty retsina bottle at the waiter, 'that Connolly made it all up.'

I talked to my friends on the ice by electronic mail. I lived, vicariously, through the emotional rollercoaster of Airdrop at the Pole, when a C-141 took off from Christchurch, refuelled twice in the air and tossed out boxes the size of upright pianos to twenty-eight people waiting in darkness on the polar plateau in an ambient temperature of minus seventy Celsius. (This, surely, was a testament to what the human spirit can achieve.) The Polies had talked of little else for weeks. When it was over and the parcels had been torn open and the bruised fruit digested, they realised they were only halfway through the winter of perpetual night. One of them wrote about 'a terrible void'.

It started to seem so distant. Nansen had said that when he returned from the Arctic the months on the ice were like 'a far-off dream from another world'. Often, at my desk with the window open on long summer nights, I strained my ears to hear the still, small voice beyond the honking horns, the inebriated shouts and the blasts of music from passing cars. Sometimes I went downstairs, switched on the slide projector standing ready on the dining table where no one ever dined, turned off the lights and watched Mount Erebus appear on the cracked white wall. I would soon let go of my worries about tax bills, broken washing machines, the recalcitrant boyfriend or the vexing queue of newspaper articles waiting to be written. If it was one of the bad days when more pressing anxieties weighed down upon me, and I was haunted by the old familiar ghosts, I could almost always send them away too – though I generally had to persevere with the slides on the cracked wall to do that, and travel beyond the Transantarctics and over the luminous plateau.

In the early days of Antarctic travel, many men got married as soon as they reached home. Both Scott and Byrd noted a stampede to the altar. In the case of Scott's men a double phenomenon occurred – they started marrying each other's relatives, to keep it in the family, as it were. Wright and Griffith Taylor, who now have adjacent valleys named after them, married Priestley's sisters, and Priestley retaliated by marrying one of Debenham's relatives. In desperation I considered this option, but a lack of suitable candidates soon forced me to reject it.

One night, when I couldn't sleep, I went out and lay in the hammock. It was easier to take myself south when it was dark, as by then it was dark there all the time. As I looked up, suddenly I realised what I had to do. I had seen the door close on Antarctica as darkness crept over the peninsula. I had to see it open again. This time I didn't need to travel around when I got back there. I wanted to sit still and take it all in.

Only God knows what made me think I could do it. The American programme alone sends people to Antarctica in August, so I asked them if they would take me. They chewed it over for a while, and rang me up a few times. It was a hot summer in England. Then one Friday night in June, while I was sitting at my desk with the window open, trying to describe the underwater call of the Weddell seal, Guy Guthridge called from the Office of Polar Programs at the National Science Foundation.

'Pack your bags,' he said.

*

On the plane to Christchurch I began to read a book by a clinical psychologist called Glin Bennet. It was called *Beyond Endurance*, and one chapter was about 'the intellectual inertia' of wintering in Antarctica. To demonstrate the way groups can disintegrate, Bennet quoted the story of a meteorologist arriving at an Antarctic base in the fifties, just as winter ended. Nobody came out of the hut to greet him and his party, and they slowly realised that the group had collapsed during the long months of darkness. 'We discovered, in the different rooms', the meteorologist wrote, 'little animal dens where, as base life had broken down and they had become no longer on speaking terms with one another, each man had retired to make himself a little corner in the wreck of his personality.'

Academics had had a field day with the psychology of the Antarctic winter. Papers had been presented to a conference on 'The Human Experience in Antarctica: Applications to Life in Space', and, using winter bases as laboratories for human behaviour, one academic said, 'Lessons learned in the Antarctic and other extreme settings should facilitate interplanetary exploration and the establishment of permanent settlements in space.' The U.S. Navy recognised 'a winter-over syndrome' in which seventy-two per cent of the sample reported severe depression and sixty-five per cent had problems with hostility and anger. A condition called Big Eye had entered the textbooks, a result of insomnia caused by total darkness. References were made to the incident in 1955 when one member of the team sent in to prepare for International Geophysical Year developed such acute schizophrenia that a special room lined with mattresses had to be built next to the infirmary.

The Eskimos could have saved them the trouble of their research – they know all about the depression of the long night. They call it *perlerorneq*, which means 'to feel the weight of life'.

Just as 'the long, dark night of the soul' is a popular literary metaphor for spiritual turmoil, so the polar winter perfectly mirrors the inner darkness which seems to have fallen so often. Frederick Cook, one of the first to overwinter in the pack ice, wrote in his diary in 1898, 'The curtain of blackness which has fallen over the outer world of icy desolation has also descended upon the inner world of our souls ... The night soaks hourly a little more colour from our blood.'

A cart grated past my seat, followed by a cheery stewardess propelling it down the narrow aisle. She laid trays on the fold-down tables above our knees as the sun spilled through the pebble window. I carried on with Cook. 'The grayness of the first days of the night', he wrote, 'has given way to a soul-despairing darkness, broken only at noon by a feeble yellow haze on the northern sky. I can think of nothing more disheartening, more destructive to human energy, than this dense, unbroken blackness of the long polar night.'

I wondered what in the world I was going to find.

*

Camilla, my old friend, flew down from Wellington to join me in Christchurch, and I smuggled her into the clothing-issue session. It was nine months since I had gone through the same routine in the same room, only this time the piles were higher. Winter temperatures required even more layers. I left Christchurch for McMurdo at three in the morning, on the same turbo-prop that had conveyed me there before, and as we cruised over the Southern Ocean the temperature jumped up and down while people jammed their elbows through the red webbing. I enjoyed a peanut butter and jelly sandwich.

The sky was streaked with angry apricot flashes when we landed, and the ice had absorbed a gloomy purple light. A mist was hanging at the feet of the Transantarctics so that the peaks appeared to be suspended between ice and sky. Once again, I felt as if I had come home. That no longer seemed bizarre — it was a comfortable feeling. When I caught sight of myself in someone else's glacier glasses, I saw that I was smiling.

Three days before I arrived, on 20 August, the sun had risen over Ross Island for the first time since 24 April. Already, for a few hours in every twenty-four the residents of McMurdo were enjoying a dusky daylight, though they had not yet seen the sun, as from McMurdo it was obscured behind Mount Erebus. My physiological clock had responded to total light by urging me not to go to bed; I wondered if so much darkness would have the reverse effect.

The flight was one of eight which made the round trip between Christchurch and McMurdo during the third week of August in the annual operation known as Winfly. The function of this complex annual undertaking, timed to take place during the continent's brief cusp between darkness and light, is to resupply the station and bring support staff to the ice to prepare for the forth-coming science season, which begins in October. It also allows a six-week handover period with winterers preparing to leave the ice. Of the 244 winterers in 1995, thirty left during Winfly (one because she was pregnant), and 200 new faces arrived on the ice.

The first person I saw had tied a knot in his beard, but everyone looked healthy enough after their 'weary spell of darkness'. They were fish-belly white, of course, and they all caught colds from us and diarrhoea from the freshies our planes brought them. Most of them weren't sure how they felt. When I sat down to breakfast on the first day, the woman opposite me burst out, 'Wow, it's so good to see new faces!', yet posters appeared in the dorms saying *Coming soon to a room near you: the roommate from hell, Winfly 1995* next to a screaming Munch-like face and a bemused individual standing in a doorway holding a suitcase. I didn't need a poster to tell me I had entered staked-out territory – it was obvious. They had been padding the corridors and battling along the windy walkways for six months without seeing a single new creature.

'I felt the futility of my existence,' the woman at breakfast told me when I asked her how she had found the winter isolation. 'Nothing mattered. And the hopelessness of the world surviving. It lingers still.'

It was like watching a whole community coming out of hiber-nation. I trod very carefully. The experience put me in mind of an extremely ancient uncle in the west country who was appren-ticed as a printer at the age of fourteen. On his first day he had boarded the bus to the factory at six in the morning, clutching a packet of corned-beef sandwiches. All was well until a group of hoary old printers got on the bus a mile or two later. One of them stopped alongside my young uncle and thundered: 'That's my seat, lad.'

I was allocated a bed in a room in the same dark corridor as the Corner Bar, the latter no longer under the supervision of Mike the carpenter, as he had retired to ply his trade in the north during the austral winter. It had been left in the hands of his henchman John, its only regular social gathering Coffee at ten o'clock on a Sunday morning.

'Come along,' said John when he passed me in the gloomy corridor.

Outside the window, daylight lingered like a promise. Six

people were lounging around the low smoked-plexiglass table, which was spread with coffee mugs, plates of muffins and bottles of liquor. The Budweiser clock and target-practice penguin were there. When the six people saw me, they fell silent and stared as if I had been wearing no parka, no jeans, no layers of thermals, no boots nor socks and no underwear. It was as if I had walked in stark naked.

'I guess it was like waking up to find a total stranger in the bedroom,' one of them said later.

The winterers stood alone, as they always had. I envied them. Charles Laseron, Mawson's assistant biologist, put it like this. 'As the first rounding of the Horn is to the sailor, so a winter in the ice is to a polar explorer. It puts the hallmark on his experience. Having successfully emerged from the embryonic stage, he is now fully fledged, and can take his place in the select fraternity.'

Frozen-Sausage Bill was back, his eyes still the colour of cornflower hearts. He was preparing to whip pork products out of boots at safety lectures. Just as the same names cropped up in the history books, so I saw the same faces back on the ice. J. M. Barrie, who only travelled south vicariously, noted from his leather armchair that everyone who went to Antarctica came back vowing that nothing in heaven or earth would tempt them to go near polar regions again – and at the end of six months they were on their knees in front of whoever might be able to get them there.

It was certainly cold, typically about thirty below, and in those first few days the sun didn't rise until shortly before midday, and it set two hours later. When a storm came in, ropes were strung up between the dorms and the galley, so we had something to cling to. But when it was clear, the skies were diaphanous, frosting the Transantarctics in pastel pinks and blues, the slopes of each peak as sharply defined as the faces of a diamond. Each morning was lighter than its predecessor. It seemed as if summer were rushing in at unnaturally high speed, like one of those long exposure natural history films of a flower opening.

*

I was installed once more in the same office in the Crary. I could see the ghostly outline of words I had written on the board the previous summer. My identity this time was manifest in the label W-006; I had been demoted from W-002. The lab was inhabited only by three groups of atmospheric scientists busily making the most of the period of ozone depletion, and some hardy individuals heading for the Dry Valleys. These included John Priscu and his S-025 entourage, en route to their home on Lake Bonney, and the contents of their large lab exploded into the otherwise pristine corridors. Cristina of the flying condoms was back, and so was Ed, the physicist and mountaineer with whom I had hiked to Lake Bonney the previous summer.

'Another pilgrimage!' he shouted down the corridor when he saw me. We sat up late in the lab, once the radioactivity work station, and Ed sipped bourbon from a 250-millilitre glass beaker while two of the graduate students sang karaoke into a Geiger counter.

I continued talking to the Polies by email. Their season hadn't ended yet – winter at the Pole lasted eight and a half months, and planes couldn't go in until the end of October. I received enthusiastic reports about the Three Hundred Club. Admission to this exclusive outfit involved enjoying a sauna at 210 degrees Fahrenheit and then running out of the dome into a temperature of minus 101 wearing only a pair of tennis shoes. Such excitements notwithstanding, the Polies were ready to leave. One of them was still banging on about Airdrop. His job had been to drive a sno-cat out to the drop zone after the pilot radioed an all-clear. 'I tell you,' he wrote, 'some of those packages I brought in were labelled Do Not Freeze. Ninety-five below, you're searching in the dark and they expect the fucking gear to stay unfrozen.'

One day, another WOO appeared. She was an artist; a watercolourist, mainly. Her name was Lucia deLeiris, and she came from Rhode Island. She was very beautiful, with shoulder-length mahogany hair, fine bones and a diffident manner. She had been south before, nine years previously, to paint wildlife on the peninsula. A plan had been conceived to despatch us both out on to the sea ice in our own hut (it would be towed to a site of our choosing) where we could build up a head of creative steam away from the confines of Mactown. We both thought this was a splendid idea.

As we were going to camp on the sea ice, we were given our own tracked vehicle, a Spryte, and inducted into the mysteries of driving it by Marvellous Marvin from the Mechanical Equipment Center. Our tomato-red Spryte, with which we immediately bonded, was numbered 666 and bore the logo ANTISPRYTE. Lucia and I thought this was a hoot. Later, we were not so amused.

We took a day-long sea ice course taught by a lively character called Buck with a handlebar moustache who, when things got pretty seedy and very cold, had the habit of assuming the voice of an ancient redneck and proclaiming with brio, 'Yep. Just doesn't get any better than this.' He taught us how to distinguish a spreading crack from a straight-edged crack, and introduced us to an ice drill, with which we were to become very familiar.

A day was spent scouting for a position for our huts (we were to' be given two, in case one burnt down) in a temperature of minus forty Celsius. At the fuel pits the Antispryte froze in running mode, so we couldn't turn it off. It was so cold that fata morgana[1] shimmered around the distant sea ice. These mirages created a landscape of their own – a berg floated along in the sky, a row of peaks perched on top of another like skittles and a dark mushroom cloud rose gracefully from the horizon.

Having trundled around the frozen Sound for several hours, testing the thickness of the ice with our new drill and sliding down snowhills on our bottoms, we fixed on a spot in the lee of the Erebus Glacier Tongue. It faced the four Dellbridge Islands that mark the rim of an inundated crater which once stood among the volcanic foothills – Big and Little Razorback, Inaccessible Island and Tent Island. The site was about twelve miles from McMurdo. The ice there was six feet thick, and its surface was uniform, as if it had been hoed with one of the long-handled, small-bladed implements used by Italian hill farmers.

Further instruction followed at McMurdo on the status of the airwaves (some of the repeaters were not yet up), maintenance of the drip-oil Preway heaters with which both huts were equipped, and procedures for refuelling them by towing the diesel fuel sledge out to our camp. We dropped isopropyl alcohol into jerry cans to keep our vehicle fuel from freezing, visited Food (this was like going round a supermarket where you didn't have to pay – The Price is Right, they called it), and spent hours at the Berg Field Center, checking out a vast array of gear ranging from crescent wrenches to tin-openers.

The Antispryte conveyed us safely to the fuel pits before quietly

---

[1] Like all mirages, a result of temperature inversion.

breaking down. As the first field party out since the previous summer, we were fortunate to have taken Buck with us for a one-night shakedown to see that everything worked. As it turned out, nothing did. When we got it going again, the Antispryte moved very slowly, with the result that it took two hours to cover the twelve miles to camp. It had no radio, no headlights and no door-handle on the passenger side (a handle is useful for a quick exit when poised on the edge of a crack), and it complained vigorously if jammed into reverse. But it got us there, and Lucia and I whooped as the two red huts hoved into view. They had already been christened Wooville.

The fuel line had cracked on one hut, incapacitating the Preway, so confining us in the other, smaller hut. The temperature took the opportunity to plummet to minus forty-two degrees Celsius. We watched the flashlights dying almost as soon as we turned them on. Having breathed life into the remaining Preway, Buck, whose role was to ensure that Lucia and I were capable of main-taining a camp on our own, sat in front of it to watch us struggling to set up the Coleman stove.

'Fuck this thing,' I said in exasperation. I had set up hundreds of camp stoves in my time, but this one was making a fool of me.

'The metal's cold,' purred Buck from his position by the heater. 'You need to warm up the fuel rod.'

Once this task had been accomplished and we were fortified by hot cocoa, Lucia and I went outside to rig up the antenna. This involved splitting the top of eight bamboo poles to make a resting place for the wire, and then drilling the poles into the ice. At least Buck didn't come out to watch. When the antenna was up, to palpable relief all round the high-frequency radio behaved per-fectly. Then we battened down the hatches and made some soup.

I awoke to find massive snowdrifts inside the hut. McMurdo reported the news that, with windchill, the air was a sprightly minus eighty-one Celsius.

'Yikes!' said Lucia when this information was relayed. It was her favourite expression.

The generator, which we had been obliged to bring if there was to be any hope of starting the Antispryte, had frozen, despite the fact that it had spent the night on the floor of the hut between us. Buck burnt his new hat on the Preway. We thawed the gener-ator, and to squeals of surprise and delight the Antispryte started.

As I nudged it out of its snowdrift, I noticed that the huts kept reappearing through the front window. The others had come out, and they were screwing up their eyes to look at me. Buck approached the vehicle and started mouthing.

'The hydraulics must have gone,' he said when I opened the door. 'You're going round and round in a circle.'

Visibility shrank to thirty feet. All hope of returning was abandoned and, once again, the hatches were battened down.

'Just doesn't get any better than this,' said Buck.

The following morning a tracked vehicle came to our rescue. We returned to McMurdo, and left the Antispryte to gather snow.

*

The fiasco of the shakedown did not deter us, and within twenty-four hours Lucia and I had obtained all the equipment we had forgotten the first time and prevailed upon Ron, the glowering figure who presided over the Mechanical Equipment Center like a malign deity, to part with another of his Sprytes. Why it was, with virtually no scientists on station and enough Sprytes to invade a small country, that he had chosen to give us the one vehicle famed for its unreliability, only he knew.

The Woovillian huts were ten feet apart, but we roped them together. 'People have been lost in whiteouts in less space than that,' Buck had warned. One was a small high-tech affair called a Solarbarn which offered the luxury of a small solar light, and the other was a regular red wooden box hut twenty feet by twelve equipped with a set of built-in bunks. A small dead cockroach lay supine between two panes of plexiglass in one of the Solarbarn windows. Lucia had a sideline in the administration of acupuncture, and when she laid out her needles on the body-sized table bolted to one wall, the red hut quickly became known as the Clinic. We planned to cook in the Solarbarn, so this was named the Dining Wing.

The bathroom facilities consisted of a small metal drum with a lid which lived outside next to the one wall of the Clinic that didn't have a window. It was lined with both plastic and burlap sacks which we removed when full and took back to McMurdo. The contents were frozen, at least. We also established a pee flag by drilling a bamboo pole into the ice fifty yards from the huts. Peeing on the sea ice was allowed, but it was sensible always to do it in the same place, so the ice around our home did not begin to resemble a Jackson Pollock painting.

Now we were alone in our own camp for the first time. Before we set out, Joe in the McMurdo communications hut had dispensed lengthy instruction in radio operation, and we were then obliged to check in with base every day at an appointed time. The call sign of the communications hut was Mac Ops.

'Mac Ops, Mac Ops, this is Whiskey Zero Zero Six, how copy?' I said, loudly and clearly, as instructed. Joe's voice flashed back.

'We're sorry, no one is home at Mac Ops. If you leave your name and number after the beep, we'll get back to you as soon as we can.'

Nothing happened. 'I didn't hear the beep,' I said.

'Beep,' said Joe.

*

The weather was good, at first. We had a fine view of the Transantarctics shredding the horizon across the Sound. The landscape was dominated by Mount Erebus, the volcano named by James Clark Ross when he arrived on 28 January 1841 at what was to become Wooville on 2 September 1995. It reached right down to us, as a tongue extending from one of its glaciers extended as far as Wooville. There, the sea ice had frozen around it. One day, when I was poking around at the base of the tongue, a beam of sunlight on a cluster of ice blocks caught my eye. If it had been at home, the beam would have captured spirals of dust motes, and if it had been in the hills, clouds of midges. The blocks were gleaming in this light like rocks at the edge of the sea made slippery by the rush of a rising tide. In effect, that is what they were.

The temperature leapt capriciously up and down. One day I threw a mug of boiling water into the air, and it froze in midflight. When the mercury hit minus forty, our eyes froze shut if we blinked for too long. After a long session outside we would come in and cling to the Preway like cats. When the wind abated, and we grew hot digging or engaged in other work outside, we licked one corner of discarded items of clothing and pressed them on the iced-up walls of the Clinic, where they instantly froze into position. Despite frequent total cloud cover and limited sunlight, the HF radio continued to run off its solar panel, which we had taped to a window of the Dining Wing.

We made mistakes, but we made them only once. Frozen food brought in a cardboard box was stowed under the front step of the Dining Wing. After the first storm the box had blown right underneath the hut, and we were obliged to lie on our bellies on the ice, prodding with an ice drill to recover our freezer. Forgetting to weigh down the toilet lid with a block of ice resulted in us having to chase it halfway back to McMurdo. The huts were positioned far enough apart to prevent a fire spreading from one to the other – and then we parked the fuel sledge between them. In addition, the sleeping arrangements caused difficulties. On the first night, Lucia slept on the top bunk. I woke up in the early hours to perceive her, through the gloom, climbing down the ladder and dragging her sleeping bag after her.

'What's the matter?' I asked.

'It's like the tropics up there,' she said. 'I'm sleeping on the floor.' The concept of the tropics in our hut was too difficult to contemplate in the middle of the night, so I went back to sleep.

When I woke in the morning, she was already painting.

'I've worked it out,' she said. 'The temperature differential between outside and inside is so acute that above head height the air in the hut is like the Arizona desert.'

'What was it like on the floor?' I asked.

'Glacial,' she said. 'I moved on to the long table after an hour.' Thereafter, I remained on the bottom bunk, where the air remained stable at a pleasant temperature, and Lucia slept on the table.

If there were no jobs to be done at camp, and we needed a break from painting and writing, we would get into the Woomobile – altogether a more successful machine than its infernal predecessor – and drill a few more flags into the ice to mark our route. First, we had to get the small generator going, as the vehicle was always far too cold to start without having a current run through it for an hour. Lifting this object out of the hut and on to the ice was an awkward, two-woman job.

'I bet our arms aren't strong enough to get this started,' I said as we prepared to pull the handle.

'We did it on the dry run at McMurdo, didn't we?' Lucia said.

'Yes, but it started first time then. If it doesn't now, and we have to keep pulling, our arm muscles will get tired.'

'Wow,' she said. 'You think we can't do anything.'

There was an element of truth in this, and it made me flush with shame. Lucia was quieter than I was, and smaller, and although she lived alone and had travelled extensively, she had not spent months hanging about in the wilderness, as I had. Yet I was the one who approached every practical task with the attitude that we almost certainly weren't going to accomplish it.

When the generator fired up, we both did a little dance on the ice.

The drill, which was three feet in length, resembled an over-sized corkscrew, and after many hours of struggle we established our own system for using it effectively. This involved one person standing on the track of the vehicle and leaning down upon the top of the drill, thereby anchoring it in position, while the other grasped the drill handle and turned it furiously, like an egg whisk, spiralling the corkscrew down into the ice. When the pain in the turning arm became intolerable, the driller would change arms, and when that arm ached, we swapped positions. This routine was avoided if anyone was watching.

Drilling to establish the thickness of the ice was more arduous than putting in flags, as it involved going deeper. Even using the new method, it took us more than ten minutes to penetrate three feet of ice, but at least we did it. If ever seawater bubbled up through the drill hole we would get back in the Woomobile, turn round and scuttle off in the opposite direction.

Many cracks radiated from the Erebus Glacier Tongue, and we monitored their progress keenly. A crack is a fissure or fracture in the sea ice produced by the stresses of wind, wave and tidal action. Sea ice cracks generally look like narrow furrows – they were described by a member of the Japanese *Kainan-Maru* expedition in 1911 as 'resembling divisions between rice paddies'. Around Wooville cracks did not shoot out like bolts of lightning, or open up like Sesame, so we did not live in fear of an inadvertent mid-night swim. None the less, we had received plenty of instruction in the subject. 'Profiling' a crack, which meant finding out how deep and wide it was with a drill and whether it was safe to cross, seemed to us a complicated business.

'Now,' I said to Lucia one day as we got out of the Woomobile and stood looking down at a rip in the ice. 'The effective crack width is determined by the required ice thickness for each vehicle.'

'Yikes!' she said. 'What does that mean?'

'Haven't a clue. It's what Buck said.' At this point one of us would usually fetch what was known in camp as 'The Book'. It was a field manual, written by the staff of the Berg Field Center to assist scientists camping on the ice, and at Wooville it had already acquired biblical status.

Besides ensuring that neither we nor the huts fell through a crack into the sea, we both worked. In addition, Lucia practised acupuncture on herself, and sometimes on me. It didn't seem to matter that neither of us was ill or injured – Lucia said the needles were 'a tonic'. I would lie on the long table in the Clinic, looking out at the thermals threaded with mist, the moon hanging beyond the tongue, or the miasma of blues and pinks over the Royal Societies. When we absorbed ourselves in our work for too long, we began to exhibit symptoms of madness, with the result that a 'Weirdometer' went up on the wall of the Clinic with a swivel-dial for each of us indicating the level of madness to which we had risen or fallen on any given day.

About two weeks after we arrived at Wooville, a helicopter put down in front of the Clinic, and the crewman ran over to us.

'Want to come for a ride?' he shouted.

September was a cold month to be flying helicopters. Away from McMurdo, the pilots never shut down, and they left contrails like toothpaste in the clear blue sky over the Sound. Lucia and I grinned at one another in the back as we shuttled around the valleys, resupplying the camps at Hoare and Bonney and ferrying repeater engineers to windy peaks.

'Wow,' said Lucia over the headset, pointing ahead and pulling out her sketchbook. 'Look at that.' We were heading towards an icefall (a frozen waterfall) thousands of feet deep. It swelled over the edge of a mountain and curled like a lip down to the valley floor. Here and there the surface of the creamy curtain burst into erratic frozen plumes and then sank away like a fallow field. This was the pilot's big chance to prove what a steely chap he was, and he flew the helicopter as if he were performing in a circus. We swooped down through the rock configuration called the Laby-rinth and beyond the dolerite extrusions to Bull Pass, a natural gallery of smooth ventifacts like the relics of a lost civilisation.

'What's the name of the icefall?' Lucia asked.

'The VXE-6 Falls,' crackled the pilot. 'We named it after the squadron.'

267

I suppose it was a better name than I've-Got-A-Big-One, but only just.

Flying low on our way back to Wooville, we watched snow-snakes[1] whipping over the frozen Sound. The marooned bergs cast long shadows, and a dark ten-foot band of open water striped the ice. Before we were dropped off, the pilot decided to take us over Erebus, and the landscape took wings. The crew guzzled oxygen, but Lucia and I stared open-mouthed at the fumaroles billowing vapour. When we crossed the crater the pilot said, 'That's the guts of the earth.'

Sometimes, back at Wooville, we crawled into the configuration of ice caves underneath the glacier tongue. The ice had formed arabesques like carvings in the slender windows of an old mosque, and through it the light fell, diffused throughout glimmering blue caverns. Walls burgeoning with delicate crystals glittered around smooth arching tunnels which opened into glossy domes fortified by rows of stalactites. Had it been rock, it would have been a landscape painted by Leonardo, the pinnacles yielding to glimpses of dreamy vistas of ice.

If our landscapes were canvases, they were conceived by a mind raised above the troubles which afflict the human spirit.

Sunlight infused the sky long after the sun itself had disappeared. At first it was completely dark by about four o'clock, and then each evening the day stretched itself a little further. When it finally gave up the struggle the moon would coast over the tongue and the plumes of Erebus appeared more clearly against the night sky, like feathers in a Tyrolean hat. We ate dinner by candlelight, and the shadow of the volcano flickered on our wobbly card table. Sitting in another hut on the same ice, a mile or two from Wooville, Scott wrote out a verse from a Shelley poem in his diary.

> The cold ice slept below,
> Above the cold sky shone,
> And all around
> With a chilling sound
> From caves of ice and fields of snow

---

[1] Incorporeal ribbons of snow blown across the ice and used by pilots to assess wind speed.

Wooville I: The Erebus Glacier Tongue

The breath of night like death did flow
Beneath the sinking moon.

Shelley wrote 'The cold earth', not 'The cold ice'. Scott naturally transposed them; who wouldn't have? A diary entry made by Scott's physicist Louis Bernacchi was more apposite. He wrote, 'There is something particularly mystical and uncanny in the effect of the grey atmosphere of an Antarctic night through whose uncertain medium the cold, white landscape looms as impalpable as the frontiers of a demon world.' Standing in front of such an impalpable vision on 9 September, we saw our first seals, illuminated by a gibbous moon. Four of them lay on the ice between Erebus and the tongue, resembling, from Wooville, mouse droppings on a dinner plate. We heard their wolf-like calls, resonating off the cold blue walls of the tongue.

Until that moment, life had been absent from our landscape. Our isolation was metaphysical as well as geophysical. We had been living in the silence between movements of a symphony. In *Letters to Olga*, Vaclav Havel used the analogy of Antarctic isolation to express the crucifying solitude of prison. To me, in the stillness of the evening, it was like a reprieve. Again, I heard the still, small voice. It came to me more readily this time.

In the mornings the sea ice cracked like bullets. If the weather was good, Lucia went out painting in the Woomobile, not to get away, but so she had a different view and could stay what we liked to call warm in the cab. She would position her palettes and her long raffia roll of brushes on the fender, where eventually they froze. Sometimes I went with her, and watched small replicas of our landscape appear on paper like polaroid photographs. The little metal tubes of gaily coloured paste soon gave up the battle for plasticity, and then she would turn to her pastels. If I made notes, everything was defined by the exotic labels on the tubes she held in her long fingers: a cerulean blue sky dropped to French ultramarine in late afternoon, and the Transantarctics at dusk were tinged with burnt umber or flushed with permanent rose.

One of our favourite spots was the configuration of pressure ridges around the south-west end of Big Razorback. The island looked like a croissant from there, with a folded-down triangle at the top. It was a spot much favoured by seals, too, and Lucia always added them last.

'Why have you put three in, when only two are there?' I asked.

'Well,' she began, 'it's to do with composition. Three's better. I mean, it suits the shape of the pressure ridges behind. Or rather, it balances this island here . . .' I could hear myself answering a puzzled question about why I had deleted a particular adjective and replaced it with another. The fact was, half the time neither of us knew why we did what we did. We just knew it had to be done.

Then a weather system suddenly came in, and Antarctica shut down. Big Razorback disappeared into a faint grey smudge and the winds roared across the Sound, battering the walls of the tongue and tossing walls of snow through the air. I had often observed the continent's Janus characteristic, switching abruptly from seduction to destruction, but there, living in the lee of the Erebus Glacier Tongue, I experienced it most intensely. We saw heaven and hell in twenty-four hours, like the human mind as described by Milton. We would be trapped inside for days, the windows mute white sheets, listening to wind which never relented. As Frank Hurley wrote of the ice at such a time, it 'lost all its charm and beauty, and became featureless, sullen and sinister'. Living there alone without any contact with the outside world except for our brief morning radio schedule with base, we were very sensitive to its vagaries. We came to know what temperature it was even before we looked at the thermometer hanging on the antenna, and we noticed every degree of change. I never could have imagined this happening. Before I had been to Antarctica someone asked me about temperatures, and I replied, not altogether flippantly, that numbers bored me and the only temperatures I recognised were cold and fucking cold. I was amused to read comments in my first Antarctic notebook about 'getting used to temperatures of ten below'; that had come to seem tropical. We tried to guess windspeeds, but we were stabbing in the dark.

'I wish we had a windometer,' said Lucia one day, 'rather than a weirdometer.' Windspeeds of up to 200 mph have been recorded in Antarctica, but when the wind got really serious every anemometer invented broke down on the job. The McMurdo weather department had rows of broken anemometer impellers mounted on plaques. An inscription underneath each plaque read, '*Damaged by wind*', followed by the particulars, such as '*95 knots, 25 October*

1987. The last in the long line said, '*Dropped by Bill Sutcliffe, 23 March 1990. Winds calm.*'

When one system came in we were ensconced for five days, with only a three-hour window in the middle when the storm dropped and we ran around on the ice like small children. By the end we were beginning to study the backs of cereal packets and conduct comparisons on the three different recipes for bran muffins printed on our foodstuffs. We ran out of coffee. I grew tired of writing about ice and wind, so for a change I tried my hand at steamy love sonnets (this experiment was not a success). When I turned around to see what Lucia was up to, I saw that she had begun to paint green glaciers.

'I'm fed up with doing blue ones,' she said defiantly when she noticed me looking.

The next day she made a batch of muffins over the Coleman stove, undeterred by the fact that all three recipes indisputably called for an oven. They were very good, and very flat. That night the wind was so strong that it kept us both awake. If we dropped off, a particularly violent blast would shake the Clinic and jolt us upright, hearts beating, like a volley of artillery fire. Then it might drop quite suddenly into silence, as if it had been turned off. 'At last!' we would murmur, and settle back into the bags. But it was just building up its strength for a fresh attack. If I had heard it at home, I would have expected to see garage roofs flying through the air. It seemed as if the hut would take off over the Sound and that we would wake up looking out on the ventifacts of the Wright Valley.

This did not happen. The door was always frozen shut on those mornings though, and we were obliged to set to with an elongated s-shaped metal tool extracted from one of our tool kits. What its official purpose was, we never knew. We draped a blanket over the door jamb, but the snowdrifts crept past it while we slept. Strange to say, this did not greatly affect the temperature indoors at Wooville – it was always cosy. Sometimes crystals formed on the outside of the window, and when the wind blew really hard, they moved. It was like looking down a kaleidoscope. We watched snow grow up the antenna poles, and as for the Woomobile and the defunct Antispryte, in the moonlight they resembled vehicles abandoned by Fuchs and Hillary on their continental traverse in the 1950s.

When the storm ended, the world seemed new, and the huts shed their extra cladding of ice like the ark dripping water. The snow had been blown from the foothills of Erebus, revealing polished blue ice stuck fast to the rock which, here and there, protruded like an elbow below the treacherously seductive crevasse fields. A thin band of apricot and petrol blue hung over the Transantarctics, and the pallid sun shed a watery light over thousands of miles of ice. The frozen Sound could have been the silent corner of the African savannah where man first stood upright.

The storm seemed to have blanched our interior landscapes too. We sat outside in the evening calm. Often we saw nacreous clouds[1] then, drifting high up in the infinite reaches of the sky – about ten miles up, actually, far higher than the fluffy white clouds at home that send down rain. There might be twenty-five of them, in twenty-five variations of opalescent lemons, rich reds and reedy greens. They were brightest just after sunset, when the glare of the sun had disappeared at ground level but its light still illuminated high clouds. The nacreous ones were small and oval, and they floated along in a line like fat iridescent pearls on an invisible thread. As Gertrude Stein said, 'Paradise – if you can stand it.'

The dignity of the landscape infused our minds like a symphony; I heard another music in those days.

We got to know one another pretty well. Lucia was a perfect companion. In the early days she often looked worried, especially if she was concentrating on the exigencies of sea ice travel or the problem of how to prevent her paints and fingers from freezing. But if something really funny happened she would throw back her head and laugh loudly. Her whole face was transformed when she did this. It was like watching the sun break through the clouds after a storm. I liked her all the time, but I liked her most then, and sometimes I contrived a reason to tell her a funny story, to make her throw back her head and laugh. She was good-natured, good-humoured and equable, and when she was absorbed in a

---

[1] High-altitude, low-temperature formations. Nacreous clouds are the most dramatic manifestation of polar stratospheric clouds, but they are rare in the Arctic; northern polar regions are warmer than Antarctica. Nacreous clouds, typically, are visible in September. Incidentally, the reduction in ozone only occurs when polar stratospheric clouds are present, which partially explains why ozone depletion is significantly lower in the north.

task she twittered quietly to herself like a small bird. I wasn't as good at living alongside another human being as she was. Cherry wrote that in Scott's hut you had to choose whom you sat by at dinner according to whether you wanted to talk, listen, or just sit quietly. We had no such choice. Lucia gave a lot, unwittingly, during those weeks. I always felt that I couldn't give as much as she did.

CHAPTER SIXTEEN

Wooville II: Cape Evans

Beyond this flood a frozen continent
Lies dark and wilde, beat with perpetual storms
Of whirlwind and dire hail, which on firm land
Thaws not, but gathers heap, and ruin seems
Of ancient pile, all else deep snow and ice.

John Milton, from *Paradise Lost*

A HAGGLUNDS tracked vehicle containing six winterers pulled
up at Wooville. They were out checking the ice to the north.
That morning, a rainbow had arched over hundreds of miles of
the Transantarctics.

'Jump in!' said the driver.

The unheated back half of the Hagglunds was coupled to the
front like a railway carriage, and I lay in it on top of a mound of
survival gear and a bundle of flags. It was thirty-five degrees below,
and ice clung to the nuts, the pipes and the leaking jerry cans of
fuel. As the small windows were frosted up I snuggled underneath
a sleeping bag, swaddled like a mummy. When we lurched to a
stop, the radio by which I communicated with the cab, and which
was stowed down my shirt to keep the batteries alive, jabbed its
antenna up my nose.

The back door swung open to reveal a Beard. He began rummaging around in the debris among which I was entombed.

'We've come to a crack,' he said. 'We have to drill the ice inside
it, to see how far down it goes.' With that, he drew out a drill.

I wriggled out from underneath the sleeping bag and slid down from the back of the vehicle. The snow squeaked like styrofoam.

The Beard and another man were hunched over the drill. Neither of them was standing on the tread of a vehicle, as we did when we drilled. The crack was about four inches wide, and the men got the drill three feet down into the ice inside it in about two minutes. Lucia and I exchanged guilty glances.

Having established that the crack was safe, the men extracted the drill and strode over to another crack they had spotted, whereupon they both began sliding the pick of their axes over the top to locate the safe edges. Lucia and I had forgotten that we were supposed to do this.

'Yikes!' she mouthed at me.

A third Beard appeared from the front of the Hagglunds, clutching a clipboard.

'Are you mapping?' I asked.

'Yep. The guys at the Berg Field Center gave us this rough map of what the sea ice is looking like this year – in so far as anyone has seen much of it, which they haven't really, this early in the season. We're marking any new cracks.'

'Hey, look at this!' said Lucia, peering over the Beard's shoulder. 'Wooville's made it on to the map!' I went to look at the man's clipboard. Someone had inscribed *Wooville* on the map next to a tiny black triangle representing our hut, and it was followed, in parentheses, by our radio call sign, which was the Artheads.[1]

*

Ice was everywhere in those days, like sand in the desert, though it was never uncomfortable. I would not have wished to be elsewhere. Shackleton wrote a poem called 'Two Ways', and I tried to remember it so I could stick it on the wall of the Clinic.

> You may love the calm and peaceful days,
> And the glorious tropic nights . . .
> But all the delight of the summer seas,
> And the sun's westing gold
> Are nought to me for I know a sea
> With a glamour and glory untold . . .

---

[1] Later in the season Wooville appeared as 'Artists' Colony' on another map, and a sign was made for the door of the Clinic saying 'The Ant Art Chicks'.

Of course, we never washed while we were in camp. We did have a fair supply of clothes, however. I was reading Nansen's *Farthest North* at the time.

'Listen to this,' I said to Lucia, who was lying on the table and sticking needles into her arms. 'In Franz Josef Land, Nansen and Johansen turned their shirts inside out once a month instead of washing them. We could try that.'

'You always want to do what the old guys did,' she said, 'despite the fact that they had such a miserable time. We can go back to McMurdo and use the washing machines.'

'What about the "dry washing" system then?' I persisted. 'Loads of the polar explorers adopted that.'

'What does it involve?' Lucia asked patiently, wiggling a needle.

'It's quite simple,' I said. 'You put away dirty clothes until the ones you're wearing are even dirtier, then the old ones seem clean, so you can change them round.'

She started laughing, so I decided to keep this gripping subject to myself. I was especially keen on other people's ingenuity. Admiral Byrd used to wash a different third of his body each night, and I had heard an engineer on station explaining how to make a pair of underpants last a month. (Switch them back to front for a week, then turn them inside out and do a week each way round.)

Outside, Wooville had created its own landscape of windscoops and drifts, and inside it looked increasingly like home, scattered with the ratty pages of a typescript, balls of tissues tinted with blue watercolours, and wodges of photocopied diaries. We established inter-hut communications on our VHFs.

'Dinner is about to be served,' Lucia's voice would crackle over the radio. 'All residents of Wooville proceed to the Dining Wing.' After three weeks I solved the intractable camp problem of how to read in bed by positioning the Coleman lantern on our only stool next to the bunks, and each night ended with its sigh as the mantles faded into the gloom.

I had been in many Antarctic camps, but nothing compared with having my own. I developed a more intimate relationship with the continent, living with it at Wooville. Already I looked on Erebus as a friend. We had claimed Antarctica back from the colonisation of science. Wooville was the only non-science camp on the continent, and we had as much right to be there as the beakers.

I have nothing against either science or scientists, but they don't own Antarctica. You might think they do – the entire human occupation of Antarctica is predicated on the theory of science as an unending process of amelioration. Whatever is said about knowledge for its own sake, the only justification for science in any sphere is that it is a tool of improvement – and, as such, it functions as a highly effective shield for concealing the truth about Antarctica. Collective consciousness must believe in the deification of science on the ice, otherwise it would have to admit that the reason for each nation's presence in Antarctica is political, not scientific. Like the emperor's new clothes, everyone knows but nobody says.

*

Every week or so we cleared the snowdrifts from the inside of the Woomobile, fired up the generator to warm the engine and headed back to McMurdo, where we would see Ron's little face spying on us from his tiny window at the top of the Mechanical Equipment Center. He was very paternal about his Sprytes. In town we washed ourselves and our clothes, recharged all the batteries, raided Food, took slices of wheat bread from the galley, unpacked and repacked, and filled up our fuel tank and our water containers. We stayed one night, occasionally stretching it to two. I picked up electronic mail messages from the people I had left behind at Rothera. They told me stories about their snowmobiles breaking down in the darkness of the far reaches of Adelaide Island. Rothera was 2,000 miles away, but it seemed close.

We socialised during these stopovers. Sometimes I had dinner with the Kiwis at Scott Base, where I felt more at home than ever. Their winter had apparently passed without a hitch. 'Only the North Islanders got sick,' someone said.

I had expected Lucia and me to cling together at McMurdo, having grown accustomed to each other's company, but in fact we barely saw one another. In addition, and as if by unspoken agreement, when we set out again for camp neither of us asked what the other had done on station. It was as if an unconscious release valve were in operation.

On one particular occasion we stayed an extra night in McMurdo for the annual Flag Tying Party in the Heavy Shop. The whole population mustered at this event to drink beer, eat pizza and tie flags on to bamboo poles in preparation for the forthcoming science season. The Heavy Shop was a cavernous building dotted with huge pieces of mechanical equipment in various states of repair, and at the party dancing broke out among the pools of engine oil.

The largest machine in the Shop was a D-8 low ground pressure tractor with fifty-four-inch treads. It was inscribed with the word 'Colleen' carefully painted in a Gothic script, and a man in blue overalls was leaning against it. When he saw me looking, he shouted over the strains of Joe Cocker,

'Want to see my Antarctic girl?'

We climbed up over the tracks to pat the padded ceiling in the cab and admire the monster blade.

There were fewer than six other stretch D-8s in the world, and three lived at Willy Field, an outpost of McMurdo about a mile from the station. The next day an Antarctic veteran called Gerald, Colleen's swain, drove me out to meet them.

The enormous canary yellow machines, made by Caterpillar in the fifties, had seen forty years of Antarctic service and were engraved on the hearts of all who had worked upon them. They had walked themselves to the Pole, and they had flown there dismantled (this took four flights). One of them, at Byrd Surface Camp on the West Antarctic ice sheet, was back in use after spending seventeen years buried under the snow. The catwalk platforms, once fixed above the tread, had regrettably been removed by some philistine of the past. Veterans could remember seeing operators sunbathing on the platforms while the machine was moving along.

When we arrived at Willy Field, Gerald leapt out of our truck and up on to the tread of a D-8 in one movement.

'A gasoline engine gets the diesel engine started,' he shouted as he fired it up. 'Which is why it's suitable for these temperatures.' He jumped down, crunching the snow. 'This is Becky, by the way.'

We contemplated the steaming beast.

'They could almost be living creatures,' I said.

Gerald stared at me blankly. Then he blurted out, 'But they are living creatures.'

Fetching a chair from a nearby hut, he positioned it in the cab, next to the driver's seat. We climbed in, I sat on the chair and

278

Gerald began dozing a pile of snow the size of a minor English county.

'I could tell which of these I was driving with a blindfold on,' Gerald shouted as we dozed along, rocking gently to the rhythm of the enormous tracks. Suddenly he yelled, 'You try,' and whipped back the brakes until they screeched like a freight train. We shifted places, and I drove Becky down the skiway. On the way back, in the limpid light of Windless Byte, we stopped.

'You see, Sara,' said Gerald, taking off his glasses, 'I can't paint, or write, or hold a rhythm. I express myself by making perfect flat surfaces on ice.' He came from a German Baptist background and an Amish community, but he had left it and moved to Wyoming with his wife.

'What was leaving like?' I asked. Having spent some time in an Amish community myself, I knew how they felt about members leaving the fold. I admired the Amish very much – that was why I had gone to Lancaster County to live with them – but the way they shunned men and women who could not be as they were was one aspect of their faith that I found hard to swallow.[1]

Gerald thought about this for a while. Then he said, 'It was like going to Antarctica.'

*

A helicopter put down at Wooville at nine o'clock one morning to take Lucia and me over to Lake Hoare in the Taylor Valley. We had been invited by the residents of one of the only other field camps set up this early in the season.[2] We had often chatted to them on the VHF, comparing temperatures and being neighbourly.

The Sound was veined with cracks, and the band of open water I had seen the previous week was gone, submerged by a pressure ridge which meandered over the landscape like the Great Wall of China.

Three beakers and a mechanic were in residence at Lake Hoare.

---

[1] Another was their disapproval of higher education – at times one almost felt of any education.

[2] It was quite likely that for several weeks Lucia and I had been the only people living in a field camp (as opposed to a base) in an area one and a half times that of the United States.

Condom Cristina was living there too but she had temporarily returned to McMurdo. Every helicopter brought condom advertisements for her from her colleagues at Bonney; the story had become enshrined in the legends of the valley. Nobody had put their tents up yet – it was too cold. I slept on the floor of a small lab. It was odd to be in a camp doing science. It seemed unnatural.

I hiked up towards Lake Chad, following the route I had taken to Bonney the previous summer with Ed the mountaineering physicist. The ice was cracking like a whip on tin. Sometimes, out of the corner of my eye, I caught a white bolt of lightning flashing across the chalky blue. Of course, I knew this landscape, but I had never seen the pink glow of dawn over the Canada Glacier, or the panoply of sunset over the Suess, or, in between, sunlight travelling from one peak to the next and never coming down to us on the lake. We lived in a bowl of shadow during those days. One morning the sun appeared for ten minutes in the cleft between the Canada and the mountain next to it, and everyone stopped working to look up. The lake was carpeted with compacted snow, and from the middle, where the Canada came tumbling down in thick folds, the Suess was cradled by mountains like a cup of milky liquid.

On our last night, Lucia went outside after dinner to empty the dishwater into its drum. Suddenly she appeared at the hut window, gesticulating furiously. I rushed out, thinking that perhaps the propane toilet had exploded again. But it wasn't that. She was looking up at the electric gallery of the southern lights. The sky was streaked with faint emerald shadows, splaying out in several directions to the horizon, changing shape, spreading, and bleeding into the blackness. Iridescent coppery beams roamed among the stars like searchlights, and soft ruby flames flickered gently above the glacier, sporadically leaping forward into the middle of the dark sky. Towards the east, a rich and luminous topaz haze rolled lazily back and forwards like a tide. At one moment the whole sky was a rainbow, flaming with radiant mock suns.

'Heavenly music,' I murmured.

*

The following week, John Priscu sent a message inviting me up to Lake Fryxell for a night. When the helicopter dropped me off, the five men in John's team had just arrived from Lake Bonney, their base further up the valley. Ed came bounding out to meet me. They had tossed their sleep kits over the floor of the Jamesway, which was being blasted with hot air by a diesel blower, and were preparing equipment to pull out ice cores which would be taken back to Bonney the next day. They reminded me of a raiding party of Huns descending from the hills for a spot of marauding among the Visigoths.

Each flight of the drill measured three feet, and after the fifth had been screwed on, they usually hit water. Ice drilling had been going on up there at Bonney for a month in temperatures of minus fifty.

'Everything breaks when it's this cold,' Ed said when I joined them on the lake later. 'You flip the lid off a tin with a screwdriver, and the metal shaft snaps.'

They were pursuing not Visigoths but cyanobacteria, unicellular photosynthetic organisms generally considered algae. These bacteria live in sediment in the ice, and the scientists knew they had them when the core contained a tissue-fine dark layer.

'In certain parts of the lake, it's like a rainforest,' Ed said.

When they went inside, it took half an hour for their beards to unfreeze from their balaclavas.

The day I returned to Wooville, 22 September, the sun rose shortly before seven, and it set exactly twelve hours later. We were halfway there.

★

It was suggested that we might like to relocate Wooville, to give us a change of scene, and we decided to take up the offer. After a few rounds of discussion we settled on Cape Evans.

Before the two men arrived from McMurdo in a sno-cat to tow the huts to their new location, Lucia and I broke down our camp so that everything was tightly secured for its undulating passage over the ice. We were to follow behind in the Woomobile. Our pee flag was so firmly frozen in that it had to be sawn off at the base. Despite our best efforts, the Antispryte failed to start, and it had to remain at Wooville, each day heaped with more snow and looking as maladjusted as we knew it to be.

We made the two men tea in the Dining Wing before setting out.

'What's the news on station?' I asked.

'A circus!' replied one of the pair, a man with a beard like a medieval depiction of Noah.

'The planes are gonna be here bringing the summer folk soon, and all hell's gonna break loose. Everyone's getting ready.'

'You must have wintered,' I said. 'You're used to peace and quiet.'

'Yep,' said the man, as tea and flat muffins disappeared into the wilderness of his beard. 'My fifth winter. Say, is that a cockroach in there?'

It wasn't just the station that was changing. Everything was changing off base too. One morning at around that time we saw our first emperors. The velvet backs of their necks were flecked with grey, and they blinked at the pale sun as it struggled through the cloud cover among the translucent bands of coloured light behind Big Razorback.

We loved the new Wooville as much as its predecessor. On one side we overlooked the striped Barne Glacier, its corduroy-fluted, perfectly vertical cliff sharp against the pearly sky, and on the other Scott's hut and Wind Vane Hill. At midday on our first morning I asked Lucia to walk out with me to a berg a short distance from the Barne Glacier. I had just read this entry in Scott's diary again.

Just before lunch the sunshine could be seen gilding the floe, and Ponting and I walked out to the bergs. The nearest one has been overturned and can be easily climbed. From the top we could see the sun clear over the rugged outline of Cape Barne. It was glorious to stand bathed in brilliant sunshine once more. We felt very young, sang and cheered – we were reminded of a bright frosty morning in England – everything sparkled and the air had the same crisp feel. There is little new to be said of the return of the sun in Polar regions, yet it is such a very real and important event that one cannot pass it in silence. It changes the outlook on life of every individual, foul weather is robbed of its terrors; if it is stormy today it will be fine tomorrow or the next day, and each day's delay will mean a brighter outlook when the sky is clear.

We were glad to be back on the sea ice after our brief holiday in the science camps of the valleys. Inspirational as they were, the dry mountainous landscapes did not seem like the real Antarctica.

'It's good to be home,' I said to Lucia as we sat down at the wobbly card table for our first meal at Cape Evans.

'You called it home!' she said, smiling broadly. Then she added, 'I'm afraid I overcooked the beans.'

On clear days, when I walked around the new Wooville or looked out from the long window by my desk, the landscape spoke to me so directly that it no longer seemed to be made of corporeal ice. It had become a kind of cosmic symbol of harmony and of a peaceful freedom beyond poverty, gas bills and unrequited love. 'For Shackleton', physicist Louis Bernacchi noted in his diary on the *Discovery* expedition, 'Antarctica didn't exist. It was the inner world that engrossed him.' At last, I understood what he meant.

We often had storms, and when they came, being drawn by Lucia was an occupational hazard of Woovillian life. The wind was so strong that we were knocked over taking the few steps to our pee flag, and in some areas the relentless gusts scoured the sea ice clean of snow. If Scott's hut disappeared, we knew we were in for a long session. We were obliged to wear our parkas for the ten-foot journey between huts. To vary the routine, we took turns doing the morning radio sched in one another's accents. I'm not sure which was worse – my American accent or her English one – but neither of them ever fooled anyone. If we were isolated for a long time I tried to identify signs of incipient madness. Would we start using Lucia's paints to divide our bodies into thirds, like Byrd? In reality, we had never been saner.

*

On 3 October, Joe from the McMurdo communications hut came to stay with us. A pair of ozone scientists dropped him off in a Spryte. We went outside to greet him.

'Come on in,' said Lucia as she clapped Joe on the back. He had come to seem like a friend, we had spoken to him so often.

'Thanks,' said Joe. It seemed odd to hear his voice coming out of a mouth rather than a metal box.

'Your solar panels are the wrong way around,' he said the minute he got inside the Dining Wing. 'They're pointing into the hut.'

I had been broadcasting our success with the solar panels, especially after I discovered that no one in the valleys had theirs working. How the radio had continued operating with its recharging panels the wrong way round I never knew.

Later that day we drove over the sea ice to Cape Royds, taking a circuitous route to avoid the cracks that by then were fanning out from the bergs and the shore. Joe came along.

'Look!' he said suddenly, pointing up into the sky. Lucia and I squinted into the glare.

'I can't see anything,' I said.

'That black dot,' said Joe. 'It's the first plane of the season, heading for McMurdo from Christchurch.'

We carried on in silence. For Lucia and me, the start of the season marked the beginning of the end. The female seals were getting fatter, and we had been seeing ice blink in the sky – reflections of open water in the lower cloud layer which appeared as a heavy purple black blanket above the bright band of light on the horizon – so we knew what we would find at Cape Royds. As we crested the hill beyond Shackleton's hut, there it was below us. Water.

On our return to Mactown in the second week of October, it was as if we were witnessing a population exchange: in the first six days of the summer season 300 people had changed places. The parties were fun, but it was hard to socialise after the seclusion of Wooville. Besides that, since my last visit south, and to widespread incredulity, I had given up alcohol. For some years I had been living near the edge, and I had decided to make a trip to the unknown territory of the interior. I do not believe it was a coincidence that this change occurred after my long Antarctic journey.

Drinking large quantities of wine had always seemed like part of the big picture – an essential ingredient in the creative process and a harmless method of making the lights brighter, keeping the demons at bay and enjoying temporary respite from the treachery of the Nomadic Thoughts. *It was what people like me did.* Only most people did it rather less excessively than the small group I called 'people like me'. A curious thing had happened by the time I got back from Antarctica. *I didn't need it any more.* I knew that the peace I had experienced in the south would always come back to me, even if I had to sit out more bleak times waiting for it, and that meant I needn't be frightened of what my vagabond thoughts might uncover. The demons hadn't disappeared, but they had shrunk. Many things changed. Living without a glass of wine in my hand was another voyage of discovery. Like all the best journeys, it had its long moments of agony, too. But I couldn't jump ship now. It was too thrilling.

A psychologist had come in to interview the winterers before they disappeared.

'The lore has it that Antarctica fosters insanity,' he said, 'but the facts don't support the theory. The reality is that the opposite shows up. In other words, it shows how valiant and intrepid the human spirit can be in adversity.'

An influx of new people swarmed over the station, and in the galley we had to wait in queues. Those of us who had come in on Winfly said that we now knew how the winterers must have felt when we pitched up. The Winfly experience glued us together – even Ron, the dispenser of the Spryte vehicles, came to seem like an old friend.

At the same time, it was good to see some old friends back at McMurdo. David appeared, the chainsmoking Russian geocryologist with the ink-black hair which hung over his eyes like a sheepdog, and he gave me a pair of earrings made out of mammoth tusk to match the ring. The Kiwi pilots who had taken me to Terra Nova Bay were back, and we had a great reunion. A fish biologist brought the news that Britta had asked Hans to marry her. The Corner Bar revved up. Housing had tried to close it down, but of course, they had not succeeded.

One day I heard a familiar Chicago accent booming along a corridor in the Crary. It was Nann, the porcelain engineer from the Pole, her hair still looking as if it had been arranged by a blowtorch.

'So you came back!' I said as we embraced.

'Couldn't stand another minute with that sucker,' she said, and I knew she meant her husband.

It was a relief, nonetheless, to get back to Wooville. Various science parties were heading out into the field, which meant that the airwaves were busier, and as a result my accent was no longer the source of apparently limitless hilarity. Soon after our return to Cape Evans, we heard that Wooville was to be disrupted by the arrival of a diving project. I made a 'No Diving' sign and strapped it to the '*Welcome To Wooville*' post we had erected. I had also purloined the plastic penguin with the target on its chest from the Corner Bar, and this we positioned near Wooville, its back to the Sound. We were able to observe visitors climb down from their vehicles, layer up, load film into their cameras and stalk the bird.

I watched an enormous Reed drill, mounted on a tracked vehicle, lurching along the flagged route, and soon Wooville was swarming with people and pitted with diving holes. The divers were studying larval development in *Sterechinus neumayeri* sea urchins, and they were anxious to get under the ice before the algae began to bloom. A hut had been dragged out to cover the main hole, and it was heated, so when the floor hatch was open and the two divers had suited up, we all crowded in. The hole resembled a giant glass of Alka-seltzer. Looking down at the fat white amphipods coiled like ropes on the seabed, Lucia and I were amazed to see what we had been living over for so long.

'What temperature is the water?' I asked one of the divers as he peeled off his dry suit after half an hour under the ice.

'Minus 1.8 degrees Celsius,' he said. The skin around his mouth was numb with cold, and he was talking as if he had just been to the dentist.

'Look,' he went on, waving a bit of old leather. 'I found a shoe from Scott's expedition.'

'If the water temperature is below freezing,' I asked, feeling – and sounding – stupid, 'why doesn't it freeze?'

'The salt lowers the freezing point,' said the diver, towelling his hair. 'The saltier the water, the lower the temperature at which it freezes. That's why you spread salt on highways when it snows – as the salt dissolves, it lowers the temperature at which the water on the road surface freezes.'

A helicopter arrived to whisk the urchins to the aquarium at McMurdo. The shoe went back in someone's pocket.

*

Day after day Erebus appeared without its swaddling clothes. The absence of wind seemed like a miracle after what we had been through. We began taking the card table outside and eating lunch on the ice. Occasionally the silence was broken by the snort of a seal coming through the grease ice which had formed over the dive holes. It was between a gurgle and a squeal, and when the female seals flopped out, they were so fat they could hardly move. By mid-October there were many seals, especially around Big Razorback and Hutton Cliffs. The temperature in those days might swing between ten above and ten below in twelve hours, and from Wooville we began to see mist rising from open water to the north. Hillocks of snow grew on the sea ice overnight as pressure ridges formed. We sensed that something dramatic was happening to the environment. A visiting climatologist put it like this when he sat on a folding chair at the outdoor card table, looking out at the ice blink on the horizon.

'You are currently living through the greatest seasonal event on earth, in terms of mass and energy – the growth and decay of Antarctic sea ice.' Put like that, it was apocalyptic.

When sunlight falls on its fissured cliffs, the Barne Glacier is one of the wonders of the natural world, and we never grew tired of looking at it. Lucia was gazing out at it one day through the window next to the long table. Suddenly she winced.

'I must have some Windex,' she said, narrowing her eyes as if in pain. I began rummaging through the first aid kit in search of an anti-flatulant. But she was only being American. She wanted to clean the window.

An igloo went up in front of the huts, built by a pair of atmospheric scientists who came to stay for a week. They were on holiday, or allegedly taking a break from monitoring the ozone layers in the stratosphere and measuring stratospheric particles that affect ozone depletion by filling balloons with helium and sending them up 100,000 feet. Shortly after they arrived, the pair of them set to and marked out an ambitiously large circle on the ice. This resulted, four days and three nights later, in an astrodome of igloos. As we had only one ice saw, the carving knife was called into service. The entrance was supposed to be facing Scott's hut but, due to an architectural error, it ended up facing the pee flag. The igloo had a carved ice figurehead above the door and a window made out of a disc of ice frozen into shape in the lid of a pan. When it was finished we ate a celebratory meal inside, and then we all slept in it.

*

In the second half of October the seals pupped. The snow on the sea ice was smeared with blood, and we began to see small brown sausages next to the long grey ones. The pups weighed about forty-five pounds at birth. At two days, they discovered they could bite their own tail flippers. Seal milk has the highest fat content of any vertebrate (approaching seventy per cent), and the pups gained five pounds a day. It was like watching dough rise.

On the night of 22 October I slept outside. There was no wind and the temperature was hovering around zero. The sun set shortly after eleven o'clock, and all night I heard seals calling. The eastern slopes of Erebus were violet at first, and then they were bathed in rosy pink alpenglow, and between two and three o'clock, when the sun rose above Wind Vane Hill, they became sunflower yellow.

Immediately before I awoke, I had a vivid dream. I dreamt I was going to die. I was at home, and everyone was there. There was no panic or fear or sadness, and when I opened my eyes I felt peaceful and happy. It had all seemed so real, and I lay supine in the bag, mummified in polypropylene, wondering what I could deduce from it. After a while, Lucia came out of the hut carrying an insulated mug of coffee. When she saw me there without a book or the creased page of typescript awkwardly wedged between the lip of the bag and my face (an irritating problem I never satisfactorily resolved), she looked surprised.

'What are you thinking about?' she asked, imagining, no doubt, that I was hatching a plan and that we were about to go careering off to the ice edge or halfway up Erebus.

'Death,' I said cheerily. 'Thanks for the coffee.' She withdrew swiftly into the hut.

I had been thinking a good deal about issues of life and death. A friend of mine at home had recently become a Buddhist, and the conversations we had in the Japanese restaurant which lay halfway between our flats had kept coming back to me at Wooville. I realised that my fear of losing my faith was based on another, more primeval fear. It was my own death that was haunting me, of course. Faith enabled me to cope with the concept of mortality, but if I lost faith, how would I live with the treacherous knowledge that I was going to die? If anyone asked, I had always said that I wasn't afraid of dying – but I wasn't being entirely honest. I hadn't confronted it. My friend and I had discussed Buddhist teachings on the acknowledgement and acceptance of mortality. It was a long struggle, but it was infinitely more important than everything else. Yet western culture strives to divert these thoughts and mask the concept of mortality so we don't have to confront it. I believe that if it is not confronted, it will slosh around in the subconscious and manifest itself somewhere, unresolved and in disguise. It might do so in an unnaturally heavy reliance on alcohol, for example. I wasn't sure.

I did know that the marginalisation of spirituality in western culture was a shocking indictment of the society in which I lived. In Greece, on the other hand – a country to which I had always been powerfully attracted – an awareness of spirituality was still as indivisible and natural a part of the landscape as the green waters of the Aegean or the wild thyme on the mountainside. I had learnt a good deal from my peregrinations in Greece, but Antarctica had taken me further. When I looked out of the bag at the opalescent swathes of ice and the ribbons of smoke lazily uncurling from the crater of Erebus, issues involving Orthodoxy or the Tibetan blend of Buddhism and vexing questions of personal morality melted like so many weightless ice crystals.

Antarctica was a cultural void, a space in the imagination like the blank pages of Lucia's sketchbooks. It forced me to begin confronting a fear I had barely acknowledged. Despite everything I had gone through to get where I was – the years of preparation and anxiety – it seemed to me then that the external journey meant nothing at all.

*

We had all but relinquished our diurnal clues to the summer, and became desynchronised all over again. I caught sight of something in the distance one morning and realised it was a skua. It was like seeing a tree sprouting out of the ice. But it was the skuas' time – they ate the seal placentas.

I was sitting on a folding chair between Wooville and Scott's hut, looking out at the Barne Glacier. The wind had dropped. I suddenly became aware of a thin black line on the snow near the Barne. It was moving. As I sat there, the line grew bigger and coalesced into the form of twenty-four adolescent emperors who were soon waddling around our huts on their horny heels. Much of the ice was scoured clean, and their breasts reflected yolky yellow in the blue surface.

When the seal pups were about ten days old, it was time for their first swim. In an attempt to lure their progeny, the mothers plunged enthusiastically into the holes, bellowing loudly. As the reluctant pups remained doggedly on the ice, their mothers began to sound increasingly exasperated – but they always won in the end. At about this time we had a cold snap. The ambient temperature reached minus thirty, and with windchill we had minus sixty. The antenna broke in eight places, and I got a metal burn on my hand from a wrench. It was like old times.

All too soon, the terrible day came when a Caterpillar arrived to tow away the Clinic. A group of seal physiologists had returned for another season, and they needed their hut. We moved all our gear into the Dining Wing and, cramped as it was, continued to live there. After a week we steeled ourselves to visit the Sealheads. There were four of them, all men, and the Clinic resembled a refugee camp on the war-torn border of an African country.

'Does it seem different?' they asked as a stack of beer cans toppled over, ripping another animal from the Woo Zoo we had stuck on the wall, beast by beast, throughout our tenure.

'Yes!' we both said, simultaneously.

'How?' one of them asked.

'Well,' I said, 'you're in it.'

*

During most of October the sunsets had consisted of a display of shifting colours which lasted for hours. Each night it lingered a little longer over the Transantarctics, and from the window next to the long table we could see, all night, a flaming band of light in the west. On 25 October, for the first time, the sun stayed with us. I no longer needed the Coleman lantern to be able to read at night, and our candlelit dinners were a distant memory. I watched the female seals shrink until their hip bones showed. The poignant beauty of the last weeks was almost unbearable. I knew that I would never live in such splendour again in my life; not if I had a hundred lives. But it was time to go home. The Solarbarn was a small place in which to live and work, and one night I found a napalm tablet for lighting the Preway nestling up against my toothbrush. I was fed up with having willy slits in my longjohns, pee bottles in my pocket and a VHF antenna up my nose. I wanted Cox's apples, the hammock on my roof and a bathroom without a seal in it. I wanted to hear the Whitmanesque roll call of the shipping forecast before I went to sleep: Cromarty, Forth, Tyne, Dogger, Gale Force Nine, Showers, Good.

CHAPTER SEVENTEEN

Restoration

> Talk of ex-soldiers: give me ex-antarctics, unsoured and with
> their ideals intact. They could sweep the world.
>
> Apsley Cherry-Garrard, from *The Worst Journey in the World*

WE JUMPED over the soft cracks in the snow to reach Scott's hut, and Lucia opened the door with the heavy metal key. It was our last full day at Wooville.

'Remember – ' she began, grinning mischievously.

'I think we've been through that enough times,' I said. I knew she was about to refer to our first visit to the hut, when I had struggled to pull the wooden bar back from the door before unlocking it. To free up my hands, without thinking I had put the key in my mouth, where it had instantly frozen to my lips. Lucia had been obliged to exhale energetically over my face to unstick the key without the loss of too much of the skin on my lips. No lasting damage had been done, but the image of me parading around Wooville with the key to Scott's hut glued to my mouth had kept Lucia amused throughout our tenure at Cape Evans.

As sunlight poured through the door, crusts of snow gleamed on the shovels hanging in the small vestibule. For no real reason, we wandered through to the stables at the back of the hut. They were under the same roof as the living quarters but separated by internal wooden walls. The first of two openings on the left in the small snowbound vestibule led to a storage area and then the stables. In the second opening they had hung a sturdy wooden door which opened on to the living quarters.

The stables consisted of a row of eight horse stalls of conventional design. Each horse's name had been stencilled at the end of its stall.

'Abdul,' Lucia read. 'Is that a common name for an English horse?'

She had an endearing habit of assuming that everything Scott had done, or indeed everything that she observed me doing in our camp, was indicative of activities in which all English people were permanently engaged.

'No,' I said firmly. 'I've never heard of a horse called Abdul before.'

She was standing alongside a window at the end of the stable, concentrating on a lightning sketch of the horse stalls. Next to her I noticed the blubber stove where Oates had cooked up bran mashes for the horses. I narrowed my eyes and imagined Oates there – I had seen him standing exactly where she was, in one of Ponting's photographs. He used to sleep in the stables sometimes, to be near the sick ponies during the night. He was much taller than Lucia, but there was something similar in the chiselled nose and high cheekbones.

I waited till she had put her sketchbook back in her pocket. On our way into the main part of the hut, I stopped in the storage area at the large pile of glistening seal blubber, slabbed like peat and stored by Scott's men for winter fuel, and bent down to touch it.

'It's amazing that it's still tacky,' I said, 'even after the iron freeze of an Antarctic winter.'

'It must have smelt gross when the hut was heated,' Lucia said. 'I don't know how they stood it. Look at those hockey sticks hanging on the wall. I've not noticed them before. That's an idea. We could have had a game of hockey.'

'Do you think two people can play on their own?' I said, fingering the spokes of a crumbling bicycle hooked on the wall of the passageway between the stable and the main part of the hut.

'Sure they can!' she said. 'At Wooville they can, anyway.'

'Yikes,' I said.

Standing in the kitchen in the main part of the hut, I realised how much the place had come to seem like home. We could have shut our eyes and reeled off the contents of the shelves, from the red Dutch cheeses that looked like cannonballs, their metal shells corroded, up to the set of tiny fluted metal pastry moulds.

'You know, I've always wondered', Lucia said, pointing up to a shelf above the officers' bunks, 'why they brought that trilby hat down here.'

'Maybe it was for dressing up – I mean for plays or little cabaret sketches,' I offered. 'They used to dress up a lot.'

'Do English men often dress up in costume, then?' she asked, looking puzzled.

'It's a class thing, I suppose – it was a kind of male upper-class ritual.' I immediately regretted saying this, as Lucia was fascinated by the class system and had often interrogated me on the subject. I had tried to paint her a comprehensible picture, and was irritably aware of my inability to do so. Sure enough, I had reminded her of unfinished business.

'Now,' she said, 'during the night I was thinking of what you said about "tea" meaning two different things according to which class you come from. You said that "tea" means the evening meal in working-class circles, and a mid-afternoon cup of tea and cucumber sandwiches with the crusts off or one of those things you toast – '

'A crumpet,' I interrupted.

'That's it, a mid-afternoon cup of tea, dainty sandwiches and a crumpet in upper-class circles. When I come to see you in England' – visiting one another in our respective countries was now a popular topic – 'if I meet someone on the sidewalk who invites me for tea, how will I know the time to go and what I'll be fed? Will I have to say, "Excuse me, are you upper-class or working-class?" in order to find out?'

'Well no, you can tell by the accent...' I began, wishing I'd never introduced her to the concept.

'Well, I can't, can I? What's your accent?'

'Sort of middle,' I said miserably.

She threw me a vexed look and then, sensing that I couldn't be bothered to talk about it any more, she began getting out her pastels. I realised how much I was going to miss her.

It was too dark in the hut to paint properly, so once she had laid out her tools on Scott's desk, Lucia went outside and shovelled the snow away from the windows. The hut sprang to life like a mosaic sluiced with water. Scott's bunk was tucked in the left-hand corner at the end furthest from the door, shielded by a seven-foot-high wooden partition separating his quarters from those of the officers. The non-commissioned men slept at the other end of the hut, nearest the door. Half a wall of wooden boxes stencilled with brand names extended between the officers and the men; originally this wall stretched right across the hut, broken only by a narrow gap for traffic, but it had been demolished by the members of the Ross Sea party who camped in the hut. Presumably they were desperate to find anything still languishing in the boxes. Now, except for Ponting's darkroom, which was next to Scott's cubby-hole and directly opposite the entrance at the other end, the rest of the living area consisted of one large open space. It was about fifty feet by twenty-five, and narrow bunks were positioned around the edge while the middle was occupied by a long table and, at Scott's end, a black metal coal stove. The corner on the right at the far end, opposite Scott, functioned as a laboratory for the expedition scientists, and in it three or four benches and tables were piled with a plethora of vials and test tubes. The kitchen, still overflowing with supplies, was at the other end, on the right near the door, and here they had installed another stove.

Scott's den was about eight feet by six, and besides the bunk and a few bookshelves on the partition walls it contained only his desk. Two other bunks were also tucked away in there, a few feet from Scott's on the other side of the desk and underneath the medicine shelves. These were occupied by Bill Wilson, the chief scientist, and Lieutenant Teddy Evans, who went home with scurvy and returned in command of the *Terra Nova*. So Scott had never really been alone – at least outwardly.

At the foot of Scott's bunk the light revealed a hot-water bottle we had not seen before. We felt as if we were massaging the hut back to life. It never heated up though. It was colder inside than out, like a reverse greenhouse.

They had been very happy in the hut, as we had been in ours. Who wouldn't have been, in that place? This is what Cherry wrote about its position. He began by saying that he had seen a lot of volcanoes.

But give me Erebus for my friend. Whoever made Erebus knew all the charm of horizontal lines, and the lines of Erebus are for the most part nearer the horizontal than the vertical. And so he is the most restful mountain in the world, and I was glad when I knew that our hut would lie at his feet. And always there floated from his crater the lazy banner of his cloud of steam.

Lucia had decided to paint the freshly illuminated bunk, and positioned her stool so that it faced the hot-water bottle. When I shone my torch into the corner behind her, the beam lit up a small brown glass bottle on a shelf full of medicines. A neat, printed label announced simply '*Poison*', and near the base of the bottle another label read '*Harrods*'.

'Isn't that a store for fancy people?' Lucia asked, following the beam of the torch. Oh God, I thought, here we go again. I nipped sharply into Ponting's darkroom.

'Look at this!' I called. Lucia came in. 'It's a glass negative – it shows a man having his hair cut here in the hut!' The image was fogged, but there, indubitably, was a gnarly old explorer sitting on a stool next to Scott's desk, a pipe protruding from his mouth at a jaunty angle and a pair of scissors held to his already cropped scalp by another man. Both were wearing baggy trousers. I had an idea.

'I could cut your hair,' I said, 'and we could set up an automatic-exposure photograph in here – I mean, to be exactly like them.'

This didn't go down at all well.

'What are you going to cut it with?' she asked. 'That Swiss Army knife you carry around? It's too blunt to cut the muffins.' It seemed only fair that she should let me do it after I had submitted like a lamb to the acupuncture needles. As I was thinking about how I might persuade her, she walked out of the darkroom and into the main part of the hut.

'Do you think they missed Cape Evans when they were back at home?' she called. 'The ones who made it home, I mean.'

'They all said they did.'

'Do you think we will?'

I looked at her standing there, a stick of chalk poised in mid-air, and I realised how rich our lives had been at Wooville. As Frank Hurley wrote, 'We had learned to find fullness and content-ment in a life which had stripped us of all the distinctions, baubles and trappings of civilisation.'

'I'm sure I'll never stop missing it,' I said. 'I'll think of it every day, sitting in my flat, looking out at the traffic. I know nothing will ever be like this again. I'll never feel quite so separated from my anxieties. It's as though God has given me a gift, once in my life, to step off the planet for two months and listen to a different music.'

'Doesn't it make you unbearably sad – I mean, that it's over?'

I had to think about that.

'In a strange way, it doesn't. I sort of feel I'm taking it with me – in my heart, if that doesn't sound naff.'

'What does naff mean?'

'Drippy . . .' That didn't help. 'Mawkishly sentimental.'

She said no more, and I wandered aimlessly around as she painted, imagining them in this place or that, cosied up in their hut.

I wondered why in the world the bunks were so infernally small, and what had induced them to bring down a blue-and-white Chinese porcelain decorative bowl. I remembered, too, reading about a piano they had brought in from the ship (despite the fact that no one could play it) – but this had vanished.

After some time – it might have been ten minutes – Lucia said, 'No, it doesn't.' I knew immediately she was answering my question about whether what I had said sounded naff. We often had conversations which included long pauses. We had learnt the rhythm of one another's thoughts.

She too, I knew, was preoccupied with the notion that it was all over. She called out –

'What was that quotation you were telling me last night, you know, about being restored to a natural state – it was by one of those guys you call Beards?'

Many of our speech idioms had rubbed off – hers on me and mine on her – but I had failed to introduce 'Beards' as a term one could use generically, without qualification.

'It was by Reinhold Messner,' I said. 'The greatest mountaineer alive. When he was down here, slogging across the plateau, he wrote, "It seemed to me as if I were restored to that time and that state when nature alone was God." '

I went down to Scott's quarters to look over her shoulder at the pastel drawing.

'Is it okay?' she asked.

'The megaphone's good,' I said. They had presumably brought this object so they could converse from the ship to the sea ice. It had ended up hanging on a hook above Scott's desk. I had tried to think of a use for it at Wooville, but alas! I was too attached to my VHF.

'There's something wrong with the way this light falls here,' I said, pointing to a corner of the painting. We had grown accustomed to being frank about the other's work – false politeness seemed absurdly out of place at Wooville. It would have been like wearing couturier parkas.

'How about a touch of Naples yellow there?' I said, pointing again. She looked at the sketch, and then at me, wide-eyed.

'I've taught you too much,' she said.

*

Before I could go home, there was one thing I still had to do.

In the hut, a single shaft of light from the midnight sun cut above the mound of snow piled against the window and shone on to the long wooden table, casting distorted shadows against the far wall. It was the table loaded with bottles that Ponting photographed while roistering English voices rang around the hut. Lucia was sleeping peacefully in our own quiet hut, a hundred yards away. The wind reverberated in the small entrance hall like the sound of a train in a tunnel, though the body of the hut was almost silent.

I lay awake for many hours, my head on his pillow, as he, weighed down by his heavy responsibilities, must often have done. How very different the end had been for him. 'Here, then, tonight,' he had written in his diary, 'we have reached the end of our tether.'

The distended shadows shifted along the old wooden walls as the sun wheeled across the sky. I was thinking about my first day in Antarctica and the view from the top of the snowhill as the vulcanologist tap-tapped snow into his specimen tin. I could remember it as if it were yesterday. A great deal had happened since then. I had travelled thousands of miles, lost a lot of body heat, watched hundreds of beards ice up, realised how little I had seen, or knew. It was more of a *terra incognita* than ever. Byrd used the image of a beach and a tide to convey the changing of the seasons in Antarctica: the polar day was the beach, and the night was the tide. I had seen it come in, and I had seen it go out. It had all happened so fast. But I still felt the same about Antarctica.

It was the great thrill of my life — on top of the snowhill, on Scott's bunk, in what was about to become my future. It had allowed me to believe in paradise, and that, surely, is a gift without price.

Then I laid my head on his pillow, and went to sleep.

EPILOGUE

Ulysses

Alfred, Lord Tennyson

It little profits that an idle king,
By this still hearth, among these barren crags,
Matched with an aged wife, I mete and dole
Unequal laws unto a savage race,
That hoard, and sleep, and feed, and know not me.
I cannot rest from travel; I will drink
Life to the lees. All times I have enjoyed
Greatly, have suffered greatly, both with those
That loved me, and alone; on shore, and when
Through scudding drifts the rainy Hyades
Vext the dim sea. I am becoming a name
For always roaming with a hungry heart;
Much have I seen and known, – cities of men
And manners, climates, councils, governments,
Myself not least, but honoured of them all;
And drunk delight of battle with my peers,
Far on the ringing plains of windy Troy.
I am a part of all that I have met;
Yet all experience is an arch wherethrough
Gleams that untravelled world whose margin fades
For ever and for ever when I move.
How dull it is to pause, to make an end,
To rust unburnished, not to shine in use!
As though to breathe were life! Life piled on life
Were all too little, and of one to me
Little remains; but every hour is saved

From that eternal silence, something more,
A bringer of new things; and vile it were
For some three suns to store and hoard myself,
And this grey spirit yearning in desire
To follow knowledge like a sinking star,
Beyond the utmost bound of human thought . . .

    There lies the port; the vessel puffs her sail:
There gloom the dark, broad seas. My mariners,
Souls that have toiled, and wrought, and thought with
    me –
That ever with a frolic welcome took
The thunder and the sunshine, and opposed
Free hearts, free foreheads – you and I are old;
Old age hath yet his honour and his toil.
Death closes all; but something ere the end,
Some work of noble note, may yet be done,
Not unbecoming men that strove with Gods.
The lights begin to twinkle from the rocks:
The long day wanes; the slow moon climbs; the deep
Moans round with many voices. Come, my friends,
'T is not too late to seek a newer world.
Push off, and sitting well in order smite
The sounding furrows; for my purpose holds
To sail beyond the sunset, and the baths
Of all the western stars, until I die.
It may be that the gulfs will wash us down;
It may be we shall touch the Happy Isles,
And see the great Achilles, whom we knew.
Though much is taken, much abides; and though
We are not now that strength which in old days
Moved earth and heaven; that which we are, we are:
One equal temper of heroic hearts,
Made weak by time and fate, but strong in will
To strive, to seek, to find, and not to yield.

Me something sw...

Essential ingredients

Bread (plenty)

Sweetener – sugar is best, if not, use watered–down honey, treacle or syrup. At a pinch, jam (British) or jelly (American). *In extremis*, cocoa or drinking chocolate. Not powdered orange drink, please.

Liquid – preferably some form of milk.

Desirable additional ingredients

Fat – butter, margarine or, if you must, oil

Dried fruit – any kind. If none available, use tinned fruit.

Liquor. There is usually a bottle of something lurking at estab-lished camps – Baileys, more often than not.

Cinnamon

Egg – either liquid (the stuff that comes in cartons) or rehydrated powder. In the highly unlikely event of receiving fresh eggs on a resupply, on no account should these be used in a b & b pudding. They are far too precious.

Utensils

You will need a heatproof vessel. Established camps invariably have some kind of tin or pot among the kitchenware; if not, try ransacking the scientists' equipment. You really do need an oven for this dish. If, however, you are laid up in a tent, Beards love nothing more than experimenting for hours with foil and other items in order to create an oven-on-a-stove.

Method

Slice the bread – any kind will do. (Do not, however, attempt to use Cabin Bread. This is a euphemistic brand name for large, dry crackers. Like eating sawdust.) Apply the fat to the bread in whatever way you can; I know how tricky spreading can be at twenty below, and how difficult it is to butter bread with cooking oil. Just do your best. Grease the pot. Begin layering it with slices of bread and 'butter'. Between layers, add handfuls of fruit, spoonfuls of whatever sweetener you are using, sprinklings of cinnamon, dribblings of egg liquid and milk and splashes of any liquor you have. Do not be tempted to use beer.

Antarctic dried fruit normally requires a lot of soaking – in the case of BAS dates at least ten minutes' hard work with a geology hammer as well. If you are short of fruit, use nuts if you have them, but avoid the salted kind. If you have neither fruit nor nuts you might as well start lobbing anything in as long as it isn't actually savoury. Breakfast cereals work well. Cookies can be used in place of sugar and fruit, but do crumble them up well so that at least they no longer look like cookies. If you are reduced to using the British green foil packs of 'Biscuits, Brown', you might start asking yourself whether it's worth continuing with this project. Tins of rice pudding aren't great in a b & b, but people will still eat it. The Kiwis have good chocolate chips, which go well.

You should end up with the consistency of a dense mushy sandwich. Top off with a final layer of bread and butter and sprinkle something sweet on top. Put pot in the oven for a while. If you have a grill, after removing from the oven sprinkle with extra sugar and grill for another while.

Get on the radio and call everyone in.

SELECT BIBLIOGRAPHY

Excellent Antarctic bibliographies are available. In the United States the Library of Congress publishes *Antarctic Bibliography* for the National Science Foundation. It also produces the monthly *Current Antarctic Literature*. In the U.K. the Scott Polar Research Institute (SPRI) publishes *Polar and Glaciological Abstracts*. Most major books and journals about Antarctica are listed in *The Antarctic* (Clio Press, Oxford 1994) compiled by James Meadows, William Mills and Harry King.

Amundsen, Roald, *The South Pole*, John Murray, London 1912

Bainbridge, Beryl, *The Birthday Boys*, Duckworth, London 1991

Baughmann, T. S., *Before the Heroes Came*, University of Nebraska Press, Lincoln, Nebraska 1994

Beaglehole, J. C. (ed.), *The Journals of Captain James Cook*, Cambridge University Press, Cambridge, 1961

Bellow, Saul, *More Die of Heartbreak*, William Morrow, New York 1987

Beltramino, Juan Carlos M., *The Structure and Dynamics of Antarctic Population*, Vantage Press, New York 1993

Bennet, Glin, *Beyond Endurance*, Secker & Warburg, London 1983

Birkin, Andrew, *J. M. Barrie and the Lost Boys*, Constable, London 1979

Brittanico, Mercurio (Bishop Joseph Hall), *Mundus Alter et Idem*, Frankfurt 1605, new English edition Harvard University Press, Cambridge, Mass. 1937

Byrd, Richard E., *Discovery*, G. P. Putnam's Sons, New York 1935

——, *Alone*, G. P. Putnam's Sons, New York 1938

Cahill, Tim, 'Antarctic Passages', in *Pecked to Death by Ducks*, Random House, New York 1993

Campbell, David, *The Crystal Desert*, Houghton Mifflin, New York 1992

Select Bibliography

Cherry-Garrard, Apsley, *The Worst Journey in the World*, Chatto and Windus, London 1922

Cook, F. A. *Through the First Antarctic Night*, William Heinemann, London 1900

Darlington, Jennie, *My Antarctic Honeymoon*, Doubleday, New York 1956

Debenham, Back, June (ed.), *The Quiet Land: The Diaries of Frank Debenham*, Bluntisham Books, Harlston 1992

Dodge, Ernest S., *The Polar Rosses*, Faber & Faber, London 1973

Eliot, T. S., *The Waste Land*, Faber & Faber, London 1925

——, *Four Quartets*, Faber & Faber, London 1944

Girouard, Mark, *The Return to Camelot*, Yale University Press, London 1991

Hattersley-Smith, G., *The History of Place-Names in the British Antarctic Territory*, British Antarctic Survey, Cambridge 1991

Headland, Robert, *Chronological List of Antarctic Expeditions*, Cambridge University Press, Cambridge 1989

Holt, Kåre, *The Race*, Michael Joseph, London 1974

Huntford, Roland, *Scott and Amundsen*, Hodder & Stoughton, London 1979

——, *Shackleton*, Hodder & Stoughton, London 1985

Hurley, Frank, *Argonauts of the South*, G. P. Putnam's Sons, New York 1925

Jacka, Frank & Eleanor (eds), *Mawson's Antarctic Diaries*, Adelaide University Press, Adelaide 1988

Joyce, Ernest, *The South Polar Trail*, Duckworth, London 1929

Keneally, Thomas, *Victim of the Aurora*, William Collins, London & Sydney 1977

King, H. G. R. (ed.), *The Wicked Mate: the Antarctic Diary of Victor Campbell*, Bluntisham Books, Norfolk 1988

Kushner, Tony, *Angels in America*, Nick Hern Books, London 1992

Lansing, Alfred, *Endurance*, Hodder & Stoughton, London 1959

Lashly, William, *Under Scott's Command*, Victor Gollancz, London 1969

Le Guin, Ursula K., 'Sur', in *The New Yorker*, 1 February 1982

Lessing, Doris, Afterword to *The Making of the Representative for Planet 8*, Jonathan Cape, London 1982

Lopez, Barry, *Arctic Dreams*, Macmillan, New York 1986

Marret, Mario, *Antarctic Venture*, William Kimber, London 1955

Mawson, Douglas, *Home of the Blizzard*, William Heinemann, London 1915

Mear, Roger and Swan, Robert, *In the Footsteps of Scott*, Jonathan Cape, London 1987

Messner, Reinhold, *Antarctica: Both Heaven and Hell*, Crowood Press, Marlborough 1991

Mickleburgh, Edwin, *Beyond the Frozen Sea*, Bodley Head, London 1990

Nansen, Fridtjof, *Farthest North*, Macmillan, London 1897

Newman, Stanley (ed.), *Shackleton's Lieutenant: The 'Nimrod' Diary of A. L. A. Mackintosh*, Polar Publications, Auckland NZ 1990

Select Bibliography

Paltock, Robert, *The Life and Adventures of Peter Wilkins, a Cornishman, Relating Particularly his Shipwreck near the South Pole*, Berwick, London 1784 (first published anonymously)

Poe, Edgar Allan, *The Narrative of Arthur Gordon Pym of Nantucket*, Harper and Brothers, New York 1838

Pynchon, Thomas, *V*, Jonathan Cape, London 1963

Pyne, Stephen J., *The Ice*, University of Iowa Press, Iowa City 1986

Richards, R. W., *The Ross Sea Shore Party*, Scott Polar Research Institute, Cambridge 1962

Riffenburgh, Beau, *The Myth of the Explorer*, Belhaven Press and Scott Polar Research Institute, London and Cambridge 1993

Rodgers, Eugene, *Beyond the Barrier*, Naval Institute Press, Annapolis 1990

Ross, Sir James Clark, *A Voyage of Discovery and Research in the Southern and Antarctic Regions*, John Murray, London 1847

Rymill, John, *Southern Lights*, The Travel Book Club, London 1938

Scott, Captain Robert F., *The Voyage of the Discovery*, Macmillan, London 1905

——, *Scott's Last Expedition*, Smith, Elder & Co, London 1913

Shackleton, Ernest, *The Heart of the Antarctic*, William Heinemann, London 1909

——, *South*, William Heinemann, London 1919

Simpson-Housley, Paul, *Antarctica: Exploration, Perception and Reality*, Routledge, London 1992

Spufford, Francis, *I May Be Some Time*, Faber & Faber, London 1996

Stoppard, Tom, *Jumpers*, Faber & Faber, London 1972

Stroud, Mike, *Shadows on the Wasteland*, Jonathan Cape, London 1993

Thomson, David, *Scott's Men*, Allen Lane, London 1977

Verne, Jules, *Le Sphinx des glaces*, Paris 1897

Wilson, Edward, *Diary of the 'Discovery' Expedition*, Humanities Press, New York 1967

——, *Diary of the 'Terra Nova' Expedition*, Blandford Press, London 1972

Unpublished Sources

Most of the archive material at the Scott Polar Research Institute in Cambridge is fragile, and tends to be accessible only to researchers.

Blackborow, Perce, Talk given at YMCA Boy's Club, Newport, family archive, undated

Bowers, H. R., diary, 1910–12, SPRI

Cherry-Garrard, Apsley, diaries and notebooks, 1910–13, SPRI

Grisez, Dave, diary 1955–7, private archive

Letters to Mrs Oates, various authors and dates, SPRI

Nankyokuki – Records of Antarctica, Japanese Antarctic Expedition

1911–12, translation in progress: Lara Shibata and Hilary Shibata, care of SPRI

Oates, L. E. G., Letters to his mother, SPRI

Orde-Lees, T. H., diaries, 1915–16, SPRI

Scott, Captain Robert F., *Discovery* diaries, 1901–1902; 1904, SPRI

Shackleton, Ernest, diary of Southern Journey, 1902–3, SPRI

Stuster, Jack, 'The Modern Explorer's Guide to Long Duration Isolation and Confinement', prepared for NASA by Anacapa Sciences, Santa Barbara 1995

The South Polar Times, various issues, SPRI

Spencer-Smith, A., sledging diaries, 1915–16, SPRI

Wild, Frank, sledging diary, 1908–9, SPRI

Worsley, F. A., diary/log, 1916, SPRI